Reasonable Democracy

Reasonable Democracy

Jürgen Habermas and
the Politics of Discourse

Simone Chambers

Cornell University Press

ITHACA AND LONDON

First published 1996 by Cornell University Press.

Library of Congress Cataloging-in-Publication Data

Chambers, Simone.
    Reasonable democracy : Jürgen Habermas and the politics of discourse / Simone Chambers.
        p.   cm.
    Includes bibliographical references and index.
    ISBN 0-8014-2668-5 (alk. paper) (cloth)
    ISBN 0-8014-8330-1 (alk. paper) (paper)
    1. Habermas, Jürgen—Contributions in political science.
    2. Democracy—Social aspects.   3. Discourse analysis.   I. Title
JA76.C479   1996
320'.01—dc20   95-45577

Printed in the United States of America

To the memory of my father,
Egan Chambers,
1921–1994

CONTENTS

IV *Discourse and Politics*

ACKNOWLEDGMENTS

This book is dedicated to the memory of my father not only because I miss him and know that of all the people I have been fortunate enough to have rooting for me, he was my biggest fan. It is dedicated to my father also because what I have to say in these pages, my father already said in a public life committed to justice, rationality, and democracy. Indeed, the public careers of both my parents have taught me more about discursive politics and the power of reasonable argument than all the books I have read. While on the subject of family, I must also mention Susan, Glenn, Geoffrey, Michael, Bill, and Rona. For the unwavering support, love, and encouragement you have given me throughout the writing and rewriting of this book but above all for never failing to argue with me, I thank you all.

While at Columbia University, I was fortunate to have the friendship and intellectual guidance of Robert Amdur, who taught me, among many other things, that common sense is the most important asset in good scholarship. I must also mention Anita Mercier, who has always been willing and able, with love and affection, to help me through my philosophic and my personal muddles. My year in Frankfurt as a graduate student was invaluable in clarifying many of my ideas, and I thank the Social Science and Humanities Research Council of Canada for support and Jürgen Habermas for his generous hospitality. I am grateful to Kenneth Baynes, Seyla Benhabib, Axel Honneth, Hermann Kocyba, Andrea Maihofer, and the other participants in Habermas's colloquium for many hours of intense and exhilarating conversation and helpful suggestions. Special thanks are due to Matthew Gibney for all his help.

Since coming to the University of Colorado I have benefited from the support and goodwill of my colleagues and from generous financial support in the form of two research fellowships. In particular, I thank David Mapel whose confidence in the book kept me going in the darkest hours of the writing process and whose comments and criticisms of innumerable versions kept me philosophically, not to mention grammatically, honest. Horst Mewes has also earned my gratitude by being a good friend and providing intellectual support while I was writing this book. Individual chapters, sections, and arguments have been read and criticized by various people including Vicki Ash, Bill Chambers, Gretta Chambers, David Goldfischer, David Johnston, Charles Larmore, Mark Lichbach, Donald Moon, Brent Pickett, Alain Noël, Charles Taylor, and David Van Mill. I thank them all.

Parts of Chapters 11, 12, and 13 draw on material that appeared as "Talking about Rights: Discourse Ethics and the Protection of Rights," *Journal of Political Philosophy* 1.3 (October 1993), reprinted with permission of Blackwell Publishers; "Feminist Discourse/Practical Discourse," reprinted from *Feminists Read Habermas: Gendering the Subject of Discourse,* edited by Johanna Meehan (1995), with permission of the publisher, Routledge NY; and "Discourse and Democratic Practices," in *The Cambridge Companion to Habermas,* edited by Stephen K. White, Cambridge University Press, 1995, reprinted with the permission of the publisher. The review process at Cornell University Press has been invaluable. I thank the anonymous reviewers whose disagreements with my argument proved just what I needed. I owe a special debt of gratitude to Stephen White for the confidence he expressed in this project from the very beginning and for his helpful suggestions for revision. Roger Haydon has been a very patient and supportive editor, and I thank him along with Teresa Jesionowski and Judith Bailey for their rigorous copyediting.

Finally, I thank my husband, Jeffrey Kopstein, who bravely married me two years ago in full knowledge that my manuscript was unfinished. I could never have finished the book without him, and I still do not know how I got as far as I did before I met him. His love, encouragement, sense of humor, and willingness to enter endless discussions about justice and democracy at any time of day or night has been the best part of the whole process.

S. C.

Boulder, Colorado

Reasonable Democracy

1 *Justice, Rationality, and Democracy*

The central political thesis of this book is simple: the more we employ noncoercive public debate to resolve our deepest collective moral, political, and social disputes, the better. In being simple is this thesis also trivial? After all, few would deny that talking through our differences is better than fighting over them. We tell ourselves that we are civilized. We no longer settle our disputes by bashing each other over the head, or, at least, we no longer think that bashing each other over the head is an acceptable method of dispute resolution within liberal democracies. Nevertheless, the readiness with which most of us would say that dialogue and persuasion are better than force and coercion is not evidence that we are all saying the same thing or have figured out what this seemingly obvious piece of common sense means.

Persuasion versus Coercion

For example, consider the question, Are dialogue and persuasion always better than force and coercion? We might want to answer, and indeed I would wager that a great many people would answer, by saying something like, "Well, in principle, yes, dialogue and persuasion are definitely better than force and coercion, but the sad fact of the matter is that we often need to use force." But what does it mean to say "in principle yes but in fact no"?[1] What principle is being appealed to, and why and when should contingent facts overrule it?

1. Kant explores this very same issue in "On the Common Saying: 'This May Be True in

Which "facts of the matter" dictate the use of force will depend on what sort of principle is appealed to in the first place to defend the idea that, ceteris paribus, dialogue and persuasion are better than force and coercion. For example, one possible and popular answer to the question of why persuasion is better than coercion appeals to a principle of rational self-interest.[2] Dialogue and persuasion are constitutive of peaceful cooperation, and peaceful cooperation creates a secure and stable environment in which to pursue our life plans. The costs of force and coercion are too high. They breed violence, discord, disruption, and conflict, which add up to an uncertain and insecure climate for pursuing whatever it is that we choose to pursue.

But notice that this answer attaches a condition to the superiority of noncoercive talk, for the principle being appealed to here goes something like this: It is better to talk through our differences peacefully when not doing so would result in violence, discord, disruption, or conflict. What about situations in which coercively suppressing an opponent would not result in violence, discord, disruption, or conflict? In situations where one's opponent is powerless, with few or no resources to cause disruption, coercive suppression might very well be in one's self-interest, not to mention the most efficient way of resolving the dispute. The desirability of peace over conflict cannot tell us why we should be listening to the grievances of those who do not have the power to disturb our peace. The intuition that talking is better than fighting would be misrepresented if we translated it as talking is better than fighting when fighting would be inconvenient. What exactly is wrong with the rational self-interest line of reasoning I just outlined? One way to describe the misgiving to which it gives rise is to say that it is not really fair that those with the power to disrupt our life plans get a hearing and those without this power do not.

So perhaps we want to say that dialogue and persuasion are better than force and coercion because talking to people, canvassing their opinions, searching for compromise or agreement, and so on are ways of dealing with them fairly, and pushing them around is not. This, of course, does not answer the question. We still want to know why we should be treating people fairly if it is not always in our self-interest to do so. Furthermore, we still need a principle, let us call it a principle of

---

Theory, but It Does Not Apply in Practice,'" in *Kant's Political Writings*, edited by Hans Reiss (Cambridge: Cambridge University Press, 1970), pp. 61–92.

2. See, for example, David Gauthier, *Morals by Agreement* (New York: Oxford University Press, 1986); and Robert Axelrod, *The Evolution of Cooperation* (New York: Basic Books, 1984).

legitimacy, which can tell us when force and coercion are appropriate. We certainly do not want to say that all force and coercion are unfair.

A stronger justification of the superiority of persuasion over coercion might appeal to an idea of respect.[3] Here we might want to say that the reason why we should engage in noncoercive dispute resolution with people who do not have the power to inconvenience us is that we owe it to them. Dealing with people discursively instead of coercively recognizes that we each deserve to be consulted, to be offered an explanation, and to be given the chance to object to actions that affect us. We each deserve these things because above and beyond our particular differences and contingent disputes stands a more fundamental commonality: equal worth.

Conceptions of mutual respect or equal worth are notoriously more difficult to defend than rational self-interest.[4] One of the appealing features of the first explanation was that it rested on a "fairly" incontrovertible premise: People with life plans want to pursue those life plans and therefore do not want things that will hinder that pursuit. But the premise that each individual is deserving of (some level of) respect is not at all obvious. It is not obvious why people are deserving of respect or what it means to confer that respect.

The most famous secular formulation of the principle of respect is found in Kant's account of human dignity: "Now I say that man, and in general every rational being, *exists* as an end in himself, *not merely as a means* for arbitrary use by this or that will."[5] The intuitive idea being expressed here is that people should not treat each other as *things*, that is, as objects to be used for private (or collective) purposes.

Kant maintained that each of us must acknowledge that in some fundamental sense we are free, self-directing agents. An honest (and rational) self-examination confirms that we are put on this earth not merely to serve other people's purposes but to pursue our own freely chosen purposes even if those freely chosen purposes involve serving others. Thus, even the very religious must acknowledge that the dignity of their service to God resides in their having freely chosen it. If rational, we will see ourselves as ends (i.e., as free) and not as means (i.e., as instruments).

3. For an interesting discussion of the relationship between respect and persuasion, see Charles Larmore, *Patterns of Moral Complexity* (Cambridge: Cambridge University Press, 1987), pp. 55–66.

4. Bernard Williams, *Problems of the Self* (Cambridge: Cambridge University Press, 1973), pp. 230–39.

5. Immanuel Kant, *Groundwork of the Metaphysic of Morals*, translated by H. J. Paton (New York: Harper Torchbooks, 1964), p. 94.

From this recognition comes a second: If I am an end by virtue of my rational capacity to direct my life, then all other rational agents are ends by virtue of their rational capacity to direct their lives. Thus, we are all not only free but also equal in this freedom. The conclusion of this line of thought, according to Kant, is the recognition that you must "treat humanity, whether in your own person or in the person of any other, never simply as a means, but always at the same time as an end."[6]

The idea that individuals are not things and should not be used like things has great intuitive appeal for the modern mind. Robert Paul Wolff, echoing a great deal of modern moral theory, describes the passages in *Groundwork of the Metaphysic of Morals* where Kant defends the dignity of each person as "one of the few truly sublime passages in the corpus of Western moral philosophy."[7] Against the Hobbesian notion that worth, including the worth of a person, is simply the price that one is willing to pay, Kant insisted that persons have no price.[8] This idea of dignity then became "the supreme limiting condition of every man's freedom of action."[9] A respect for individuals as ends in themselves, that is, as self-directing rational agents, represents a line we may not cross in the pursuit of our own private goals, wishes, and life plans. And one way to respect individuals as ends is to consult them, to offer them explanations, and to give them a chance to object to actions that affect them.

Despite the great appeal of the idea of human dignity, Kant's defense rests on metaphysical arguments that many today find unpersuasive. It is not clear, for example, that we all do or must see ourselves as ends in the Kantian sense, that is, as radically free and therefore equal. In order to defend the thesis that rational beings are autonomous self-directing agents, Kant relied on the metaphysical doctrine of the two worlds. The idea here is that within the observable world our behavior and actions must be understood as determined and shaped by outside forces. The observable world is structured and understood through causal relations; every effect, including human behavior, must have a cause. The source of autonomy, then, can be found only in a world beyond the observable. Thus, Kant claimed that we are free and equal in a metaphysical sense; only in this mysterious other world, known as the noumenal, are we free and equal. But we live in what has been

6. Ibid., p. 96.
7. Robert Paul Wolff, *The Autonomy of Reason* (Gloucester, Mass.: Peter Smith, 1986), p. 182.
8. Thomas Hobbes, *Leviathan* (Harmondsworth: Penguin, 1968), pp. 151–52.
9. Kant, *Groundwork*, p. 98.

called a postmetaphysical world. Appeal to arguments that wholly transcend our temporal reality are viewed with suspicion. The Kantian idea of the self as noumenal agency existing prior to and in control of its preferences, commitments, wants, needs, and contingent ends has come under a great deal of attack. Once this metaphysical backdrop is gone, it is not clear how we could defend the idea that the capacity for rational self-direction leads to the recognition of an ultimate limit on our actions.

On the one hand, one cannot prove, nor is it a self-evident truth, that the free and equal status of all individuals makes them deserving of respect. On the other hand, without this starting premise it is difficult to explain and justify the content of many of our moral intuitions, in particular, that we should be dealing with people fairly. What we need is a postmetaphysical doctrine of respect and dignity. It is with attempts to develop such a doctrine that this book begins. A fundamental commitment to noncoercive public debate finds its justification in a reformulation of the Kantian insight that individuals are ends in themselves and should be treated as such. To the political thesis that we should be cultivating noncoercive public debate will be added a philosophical thesis: The procedures of such debates can and should be defended as practical expressions of a procedural and deontological moral philosophy inspired by Kant.

PERSUASION AS COERCION?

The defense and clarification of my opening thesis about practical politics will have to start not with politics at all but with moral philosophy. But moral philosophy alone will not be enough to defend the superiority of persuasion over coercion. There are a whole set of different but related issues that are raised by this claim which potentially undermine any defense of my opening thesis.

For example, perhaps it only seems as if dialogue and persuasion are better than force and coercion. Through a poststructuralist lens, this intuition might appear to be built on a false assumption. Dialogue and persuasion are not really better than force and coercion because dialogue and persuasion are a type of force and coercion.[10] We believe that we are civilized because we no longer physically bash each other over the head on a regular basis, but in fact, we have simply found a more

10. For example, in "The Order of Discourse" Foucault says, "We must conceive of discourse as a violence which we do to things, or in any case as a practice we impose upon them." *Untying the Text: A Post-Structuralist Reader*, edited by Robert Young (Boston: Routledge and Kegan Paul, 1981), p. 67.

effective way of bashing each other over the head; we do it with words.[11] Michel Foucault has claimed, for example, that "humanity does not gradually progress from combat to combat until it arrives at universal reciprocity, where the rule of law finally replaces warfare; humanity installs each of its violences in a system of rules and thus proceeds from domination to domination."[12] Whatever rules of public debate we think are fair are really rules that allow some to dominate others—allow some to win the argument and force others to concede. The poststructuralist, as Stephen White has aptly put it, "wants to turn our humanist self-congratulations into self-doubt, to show us that any new discourse is always also another new mode of power."[13]

Although my primary focus in this work is not poststructuralism, there is a skepticism advanced by poststructuralism (but also found in many other intellectual traditions) which must be addressed. Behind the commonsense belief that talking is better than fighting stands a distinction challenged by skeptical critiques of modernity—a distinction between reason and power. This challenge denies that we have a meaningful choice between resolving our disputes reasonably through talk and unreasonably by overpowering, for in fact, reasoning with each other is a form of overpowering. To defend common sense against this type of criticism requires that we show that "common sense" is not a mask that the Enlightenment constructed to put a civilized face on domination but, rather, represents an intuitive grasp of a real distinction. That is, we must show that there is a meaningful difference between talking and fighting, persuasion and coercion, and by extension, reason and power. The problem is, of course, that talking can be a form of fighting, persuasion is sometimes coercive, and appeal to reason may mask an interest in power. Flatly to deny that they can be is to accept an untenable view of language exemplified by Hobbes but captured in the childish taunt "Sticks and stones may break my bones but words can never hurt me." We do things with words in a way that a nominalist such as Hobbes could never grasp. Speech is more than a verbal naming of things; speech is action.[14]

11. Lyotard notes, for example, that "to speak is to fight, in the sense of playing, and speech acts fall within the domain of a general agonistics. . . . I place them [speech acts] within the domain of the *agon* (the joust) rather than that of communication." Jean-François Lyotard, *The Postmodern Condition: A Report on Knowledge*, translated by Geoff Bennington and Brian Massumi (Minneapolis: University of Minnesota Press, 1988), p. 10 n. 34.

12. Michel Foucault, "Nietzsche, Genealogy, History," in *The Foucault Reader*, edited by Paul Rabinow (New York: Pantheon, 1984), p. 85.

13. Stephen White, *Political Theory and Postmodernism* (Cambridge: Cambridge University Press, 1991), p. 17.

14. For speech act theory, see John L. Austin, *How to Do Things with Words* (Oxford:

Through talk we persuade, order, promise, reassure, deceive, teach, discipline, praise, heal, and dispute. These are just a tiny sample of the things we do with words. And of course, we fight with words too. We arm ourselves with words because they are effective weapons when used in a certain way. We can even destroy lives with words. And we can certainly bash each other over the head with words, as, for example, when we use "fighting" words—"those which by their very utterance inflict injury."[15] To maintain that talking is better than fighting we must look at how we use speech—for what purposes and to bring about what ends. Only speech that does not injure can be distinguished from fighting, just as only speech that does not threaten, intimidate, or extort can be distinguished from coercion. Making these sorts of distinctions requires the introduction of language philosophy and an analysis of the things we do with words.

But the potential distortions that may enter into the ways in which we communicate with each other goes much deeper. The problem is not simply what we do with words; it is also what words do to us. We can use words to injure and oppress, but words themselves can also injure and oppress without our intending such violence. There are vocabularies, language games, and discursive practices that, above and beyond the intentions of the speakers, constrain, discipline, control, marginalize, oppress, and dismiss us.[16] Power, coercion, and domination may be embedded in the conventions we employ when talking to each other, the things that are considered important to talk about, and the people who are deemed worth listening to. Seyla Benhabib, for example, notes that any defense of public dialogue involves "identifying the present social relations, power structures, and sociocultural grids of communication and interpretation that limit the identity of the parties to the public dialogue, that set the agenda for what is considered appropriate or inappropriate matters of public debate, and that sanctify the speech of some over the speech of others as being the language of the public."[17]

The task of identifying social relations, power structures, socio-

---

Clarendon Press, 1962); and John R. Searle, *Speech Acts: An Essay in the Philosophy of Language* (Cambridge: Cambridge University Press, 1969).

15. *Chaplinsky v. New Hampshire*, 315 U.S. 571–72 (1942).

16. Jonathan Culler gives a more precise formulation of this idea when he says that "illocutionary force is determined by context rather than by intention." *On Deconstruction: Theory and Criticism after Structuralism* (Ithaca: Cornell University Press, 1982), p. 123.

17. Seyla Benhabib, "Liberal Dialogue versus a Critical Theory of Discursive Legitimation," in *Liberalism and the Moral Life*, edited by Nancy L. Rosenblum (Cambridge: Harvard University Press, 1989), pp. 155–56.

cultural grids of communication and interpretation that distort communication implies that one has an idea of what undistorted communication might look like. Criticism requires a normative backdrop against which we criticize. Criticizing the ways power and domination play themselves out in discourse presupposes a conception of discourse in which there is no power and domination. In other words, to defend the position that there is a meaningful difference between talking and fighting, persuasion and coercion, and by extension, reason and power involves beginning with idealizations. That is, it involves drawing a picture of undominated discourse. Following Jürgen Habermas and Seyla Benhabib, I maintain that the ordinary intuition that talking is better than fighting can be defended through an ideal reconstruction of the presuppositions of communication. These presuppositions can then be linked to a conception of reason which shows that communication, under certain conditions, represents a form of rational persuasion which can be distinguished from coercion.

A linguistically derived coherent distinction between rational persuasion and coercion sheds new light on an old problem in political theory. Rousseau offered one of the most famous and succinct statements of this problem: "Man was born free, and he is everywhere in chains."[18] Politics involves coercion. Everyone who lives within a political community, lives under the yoke of authority. But to live under a yoke or in chains is to live in slavery. How can we be both free, that is, the authors of our own lives, and at the same time governed, that is, limited by coercive laws? Rousseau's proposal was not to smash the chains in which we find ourselves but to transform them. The task was to render those chains legitimate by transforming domination into self-rule. Although Rousseau set the task, it was Kant who pointed to the role rational persuasion can play in such a transformation: "Each individual must be convinced by reason that the coercion which prevails is lawful."[19]

The legitimacy of laws rests on the persuasiveness of the reasons that can be garnered for those laws. Domination is transformed into self-rule when citizens are convinced in a free and equal conversation that the limits placed upon them are not chains but self-imposed limits for good reasons. The introduction of rational persuasion to consent theory adds an important dimension to our understanding of democracy.

18. Jean-Jacques Rousseau, *On the Social Contract*, translated by Maurice Cranston (New York: Penguin, 1968), p. 49.
19. Kant, "On the Common Saying," p. 85.

It is not simple consent that legitimates public institutions; it is reasoned and deliberative, that is, autonomous consent. Noncoercive debate furnishes us with a publicity test through which we can evaluate whether or not "the coercion which prevails is lawful." This publicity test, or principle of legitimacy, can be defended, however, only if we can maintain the commonsense distinction between talking and fighting, persuasion and coercion, and by extension, reason and power.

THE POLITICS OF PERSUASION

Let us say, for the sake of argument, that I am able to show that there are compelling moral reasons to engage in dialogue even when it is not in our immediate self-interest to do so and, further, that I make good the claim that through an analysis of language and its relationship to reason we can distinguish between coercive and noncoercive talk. There is yet another issue to address in defending my opening thesis. This is a pragmatic issue that revolves around the question of whether undistorted communication is a realistic model of democratic legitimacy and dispute resolution. It is not clear that the idealizations that must be presupposed in order to criticize the distorting effects of power and domination can be realized in the real world, or to what extent they can be realized. The question here is how we translate the procedures of an ideal conversation into the real world of politics and dispute resolution.

The most fruitful approach to this question has been to develop a theory of deliberative democracy modeled on the ideal conversation. Deliberative democracy, however, aimed at bringing about a consensual solution to public disputes, faces some pragmatic objections. First, why should we believe that deliberation under conditions of equality and freedom will actually lead to consensus? On what grounds can we predict the convergence of opinion and preference? A second objection is that the procedures of deliberative democracy, particularly when contrasted to negotiation, bargaining, and vote aggregation, appear to require a level of civic, or at least democratic, virtue too demanding for the average citizens of modern liberal democracies. Finally, it can be objected that the procedures of consensual will formation are unruly, inefficient, and outcomes are difficult to measure. A realistic theory of consensually oriented dispute resolution must answer these objections. Thus, in addition to moral philosophy and an analysis of language and rationality, a defense of my opening thesis requires a realistic political theory that can set out the pragmatic contours and requirements of noncoercive debate and describe the place such debate might have within the existing institutional framework of liberal democracies.

An investigation of the role and function of public debate within our existing social and political world will bring up another reason why we should engage in noncoercive public debate. Not only is it the fair thing to do from the point of view of morality, not only is it the rational thing to do from the point of view of democratic legitimacy, but it is also the prudent thing to do from the point of view of political stability. By prudent, I do not mean to invoke the utility maximizer that I put into question in the opening pages of this chapter. Instead, I intend to introduce an argument that concerns cultural reproduction.

Political systems are maintained over time by being anchored in the self-understandings of citizens. For example, it appears to be widely and generally accepted in our culture that we should not enslave each other, that people should not be persecuted for their religious beliefs, and that torture is an unacceptable method of "persuasion." The stability of many of our most fundamental institutions depends on such shared beliefs. Those of us who write about justice and politics usually think that there are pretty good arguments for why we should not enslave, persecute, or torture each other. But the question we often do not ask ourselves is, What is the connection between the arguments available to us and the actual reproduction of these beliefs within a culture? If we believe that there are good reasons not to enslave, persecute, or torture, then it is important that we do not become complacent and think to ourselves: These are settled issues; we do not need to worry about them anymore; we do not even have to talk about them any more.

Complacency opens the door to "drift and inadvertence." These are Hanna Pitkin's words, invoked to describe a collective future that is the accidental and unintended "by-product of private decisions." We allow ourselves as a community to drift down paths that we have not chosen and perhaps do not desire. To avoid these paths, we must talk about and think about our collective future. "Only in public life can we jointly, as a community, exercise the human capacity 'to think what we are doing,' and take charge of the history in which we are all constantly engaged by drift and inadvertence."[20] Noncoercive public debate, in which we talk about our deepest differences as well as our shared com-

20. Hanna Fenichel Pitkin, "Justice: On Relating Private and Public," *Political Theory* (August 1981): 344.

mitments, is one way of taking charge of our history and of avoiding an inadvertent erosion of those shared commitments.

Why, then, is talking better than fighting? Talking is a way of respecting each other as moral agents; talking is a way to reach reasonable and legitimate solutions to our disputes; talking is a way of reproducing and strengthening shared understandings for which there are good reasons. Thus, I hope to show that, when probed and unpacked, this obvious piece of common sense offers up a rich and compelling view of justice, rationality, and democratic politics.

Overview

The defense and explanation of my opening thesis breaks down into three questions: Why are dialogue and persuasion better than force and coercion? What does it mean to persuade rather than coerce? How do we or could we actually go about persuading people rather than coercing them? The answer to the first question requires, among other things, the introduction of a moral philosophy that can give us an account of the idea of fairness that stands behind this intuition. The second question requires that we analyze the relationship between language and rationality. An answer to the final question must rely on a political theory that can set out the pragmatic conditions of rational persuasion and the place of such activity within our existing political world.

The preliminary answer to the question of why we should pursue noncoercive dispute resolution is found in a procedural moral theory that has Kantian roots but departs from Kant in some significant respects. I begin with a general outline of this type of moral argument and proceed to explain how contemporary proceduralist arguments differ from Kant (Chapter 2). The central problem facing these theories is how to be Kantian without Kantian metaphysics. In rejecting metaphysics, proceduralists have turned toward an internal starting point; they begin with an interpretation of common moral understandings. The deontological point of view is defended as a philosophical but nonmetaphysical reconstruction of everyday moral intuitions (Chapter 3). But in placing interpretive reconstructions at the center of deontological moral theory, these theorists challenge long-standing distinctions within Western philosophy, such as description versus formalism, tradition versus reason, contextualism versus universalism. In an effort to break down these dichotomies, I argue, on the one hand, that our culture contains deontological meanings the best interpretation of which is a formal procedure and, on the other, that an interpretive model does not entail giving up ethical universalism (Chapter 4).

From a general discussion of the nature of procedural arguments, I move to a discussion of three of the most prominent and compelling versions of this theory: John Rawls's theory of justice (Chapter 5), Thomas Scanlon's model of reasonable agreement (Chapter 6) and Jürgen Habermas's discourse ethics (Chapter 7).[21] The gist of this comparison is that although I am in agreement with the founding premises of all three arguments, it is the discourse model elaborated by Habermas that is, in the end, the most compelling. Habermas's reconstruction of the moral point of view is deeply embedded in real-world practices. Despite a technical vocabulary that often makes Habermas's work appear far removed from quotidian concerns, it has much stronger roots in ordinary intuitions, everyday practices, and common ways of talking than either Rawls's or Scanlon's. Thus, part of my project is to show that beneath the unfamiliar vocabulary stand rather familiar ideas.

Habermas links moral philosophy to everyday communicative practices. In this way, he is able to answer the second of my guiding questions: What does it mean to persuade rather than coerce? He elaborates the conditions of rational persuasion or, more properly, convincing. Thus, we are given an account of the difference between "talking someone into something" (*überreden*) and convincing them that there are good reasons to do something (*überzeugen*).

That a moral philosophy can be brought into close correspondence with everyday intuitions is a necessary condition for its plausibility and viability. Both Rawls and Scanlon concentrate on this aspect of moral

---

21. There are other prominent figures I could discuss, for example, Ronald Dworkin, Bruce Ackerman, or Karl-Otto Apel. Dworkin does begin his account of liberalism with a conception of respect and can accurately be called a proceduralist, but the procedures he is interested in elaborating are not those used to make ordinary moral judgments but rather those used by judges. In other words, although he starts at the place I think a moral account of liberalism must start, he then takes an alternative route to the one that interests me. See Ronald Dworkin, *Taking Rights Seriously* (Cambridge: Harvard University Press, 1977). Ackerman has been excluded because, although he is a proceduralist and indeed a dialogic proceduralist, his latest formulation has moved away from a deontological understanding of dialogic procedures. In his essay "Why Dialogue?" Ackerman comes very close to the rational self-interest model I have outlined. The procedures of dialogic dispute resolution are defended because they "solve the problem of coexistence." See Bruce Ackerman, "Why Dialogue?" *Journal of Philosophy* 86 (January 1989): 5–22. I do not discuss Apel's work at any length because his moral theory retains a metaphysical foundation. See Karl-Otto Apel, *Towards a Transformation of Philosophy*, translated by Glyn Adey and David Frisby (London: Routledge and Kegan Paul, 1980).

philosophy. Habermas, however, goes much farther. In addition to making the argument that discourse ethics represents an accurate and compelling reconstruction of a modern moral point of view, Habermas also tries to show that modern moral intuitions can be defended on universalist grounds. The three major components of this defense are the idea of a reconstructive science (Chapter 8), a theory of social evolution (Chapter 9), and a universal moral principle (Chapter 10). Habermas's arguments are difficult, controversial, and at important junctures vague. Nevertheless, the project of defending modernity and universalism is an important one, and I offer an interpretation and partial defense of this position.

With the philosophical description and justification of a discourse model of procedural ethics in place, I turn to the application of this theory to real-world problems, that is, to my third guiding question: How do we go about persuading rather than coercing? The first issue to resolve in applying discourse ethics to the real world is how the ideal conditions of discourse can be met in a less than ideal world. As a preliminary answer to this question I discuss some common misunderstandings concerning the role of ideal theory in discourse ethics and the limits of a real discourse in relation to ideal discourse (Chapter 11). From there I develop a concrete picture of the procedures of discourse. I outline a model of deliberative democracy that focuses on the rationalizing of public opinion formation (Chapter 12) and then sketch out some indicators we can use in evaluating whether or not public debates approximate the conditions of discourse (Chapter 13).

The road from philosophy to politics ends with a "case study." Here, I illustrate how abstract moral philosophy can inform both our understanding and our evaluation of real political disputes as well as our participation within these disputes. Appealing to the debate between the English and French communities in Quebec over language legislation and individual rights of expression, I trace out the argumentative dynamic of consensual public opinion formation (Chapter 14).

The opening thesis of this book—the more we employ noncoercive public debate to resolve our deepest collective moral, political, and social disputes, the better—leads me to defend the idea of a discursive political culture. What I hope to show is that a discursive political culture joins the requirements of stability (that people actually believe that institutions are just) with the requirements of morality (that institutions actually are just).

I

PROCEDURALISM WITHOUT METAPHYSICS

2 *What Is Proceduralism?*

Proceduralism in ethics is the view that we determine whether principles are morally valid, right or wrong, by reference to a procedure that can serve as a general test of their validity. The three theorists that I use to exemplify this approach are John Rawls, Thomas Scanlon, and Jürgen Habermas. The procedure Rawls employs is known as the original position. In this position, rational agents are placed under certain fair constraints and asked to choose principles to govern their future interaction. The chosen principles are just to the extent that the procedure for choosing them is just. Thomas Scanlon offers a slightly different test with many of Rawls's constraints lifted, but the basic idea is the same. The choice of principles is morally defensible to the extent that the choice was determined by a morally defensible deliberative procedure. Habermas defends a dialogic procedure known as practical discourse. Here, the test is discursive. Principles are just to the extent that they could be the object of agreement within a practical discourse.

Proceduralism accentuates the distinction between first- and second-order moral principles. "Lying is wrong" is a first-order moral principle that might tell us how to proceed in certain situations, but it is not itself a procedural principle. Procedures represent second-order moral principles. They are once removed from practical activity and do not directly tell us what we ought to do; rather, they tell us how we ought to decide what we ought to do. It is important to note that a procedure is a testing mechanism. It does not itself generate moral principles but validates or invalidates proposed first-order principles.

Often we think of decision procedures in association with institutionalized activity, from parliamentary debate and the legal system to local meetings of the PTA. Sometimes, however, it does seem that we use procedures outside the confines of formal institutions, as, for example, when we employ standard evasive action every time we see the nagging neighbor or reiterate a particular modus operandi that has been successful in the past. But there is a difference between procedures and patterns of behavior. A procedure must be *fixed*; this, in a sense, is the whole point of procedures. I can always decide that it is about time I spoke to my neighbor or that this time, despite similarities with the past, I will deal with the situation in an entirely new way, but changing the rules of parliamentary debate or even the way we conduct our PTA meetings is a different matter. Here the procedure stands as a point of intersubjective agreement about the way to go about doing things. Its fixity and therefore its usefulness depend on its being governed by a generally recognized set of rules.

Procedures in ethics also have this fixed and formal quality. As procedures and not patterns of behavior, they must be fixed in such a way that they cannot be simply altered by one person deciding to do something in a different way. They are formal in the sense that they tell us how to go about doing something, in this case, choosing a principle or maxim of action, prior to events, that is, prior to our knowledge of the moral dilemmas we might face.

The focus, then, of this type of ethical argument is on proceduralizing, that is, expressing in a set of fixed rules, the deliberation process that ought to precede an action. Now, there are several different types of theories that introduce a procedure as a guide to moral deliberation. Further, moral theories that do not make explicit appeal to procedures can often be reformulated quite easily in terms of a set procedure. My use of the term *proceduralism* is not meant to characterize theories which simply employ a procedure, however; it applies to theories that give a special moral status to the procedure. By this I mean that there is something worthwhile about following the procedure itself. I do not mean that the procedure has value *regardless* of the consequences that would come about if it were adhered to but that there is something morally compelling about the procedure above and beyond the consequences that would be brought about by its undertaking.

DEONTOLOGY

One way of talking about the special moral status of a procedure is to say that it has deontological value. The term *deontology* has its etymological roots in the Greek word *deon*, meaning duty or that which is binding. For modern theorists, however, it has come to be most closely associated with duty as it is understood within the Kantian tradition: duty for duty's sake. Deontology involves the study of those duties that dictate right action and are binding in and of themselves. This binding character of duties is often expressed in the Kantian principle that enjoins the priority of the category of right over that of good.[1] Another way to express this principle is to say that the consequences or "good" brought about by an action should not be our only concern in moral matters; rather, we should be constrained by rules and duties that are binding on us prior to and notwithstanding the consequences or "good" brought about by an action.

All the theories I discuss share the view that the ethical procedure should embody an impartial point of view. It is the moral point of view because it is right in and of itself to view certain moral dilemmas from this perspective. Or to use more traditional terminology, it is our duty to be impartial in some situations. It is not difficult to see why impartiality is a deontological value in the Kantian sense I have outlined. Impartiality asks us to find a perspective that stands above competing ideas of the good life and worthwhile ends; in this sense, right has priority over the good. "Priority" and "stand above" are rather vague terms, however, and could mean many things.[2]

To illustrate this point, consider Michael Sandel's critique of deontological liberalism. His definition of deontology accurately captures

1. Immanuel Kant, *The Critique of Practical Reason*, translated by L. W. Beck (Indianapolis: Bobbs-Merrill, 1956), pp. 59–64.

2. Commentaries on the liberal/communitarian debate, for example, are often characterized by the argument that these two camps are not as far from each other as some would think. As Kenneth Baynes notes, "a flair for the rhetorical" often makes these distinctions appear sharper than they are. "On the one hand, most liberals would concede that rights presuppose some notion of the good. . . . On the other hand, many communitarians would surely place liberal rights high on any list of the diversity of goods valued in democratic society." "The Liberal/Communitarian Controversy and Communicative Ethics," in *Universalism vs. Communitarianism: Contemporary Debates in Ethics*, edited by David Rasmussen (Cambridge: MIT Press, 1989), p. 64. See also Charles Taylor, "Cross-Purposes: The Liberal-Communitarian Debate," in *Liberalism and the Moral Life*, edited by Nancy L. Rosenblum (Cambridge: Harvard University Press, 1989), pp. 159–82; and Amy Gutmann, "Communitarian Critics of Liberalism," *Philosophy and Public Affairs* 14 (1985): 308–22.

Kant's understanding of the priority of the right, but it is a mistake to hold, as I believe Sandel does, that all deontological theories reproduce Kant's understanding.

Sandel says that the priority of right over good can be understood in two senses; moral and foundational. The moral sense of priority means that right, usually understood as justice, has a special status among moral values. The basic idea is that whatever ends we wish to pursue, whether individually or collectively, we cannot violate certain basic rules about how we ought to treat each other while pursuing those goals. This view is not peculiar to a procedural understanding of justice, although all proceduralists adhere to it. In fact, it is hard to imagine any liberal theory that would not accept this moral view in one way or another. Sandel associates a second and deeper view of the priority of the right over the good with proceduralism, particularly Rawlsian proceduralism. This deeper or foundational view is derived from Kant's understanding of priority: "On the full deontological view, the primacy of justice describes not only a moral priority but also a privileged form of justification; the right is prior to the good not only in that its claims take precedence, but also in that its principles are independently derived. This means that, unlike other practical injunctions, principles of justice are justified in a way that does not depend on any particular vision of the good."[3]

This is, I believe, an accurate description of the deeper sense in which Kant meant the priority of the right over the good. It must, however, be qualified if it is also to describe the deontological arguments Rawls, Scanlon, or Habermas put forward.[4] First, these theorists no longer offer a metaphysical justification for impartial or fair procedures. What this means is that the concept of right is not going to be defined in quite the same "independent" sense as it was for Kant. Second, they each insist that a moral perspective cannot be fully divorced from its real-world consequences.

Kant began his investigation in *Groundwork of the Metaphysic of Morals* with "common knowledge" and then proceeded to work backward, or analytically, to what he thought to be the only principle that could make sense of this knowledge.[5] His justification in *Groundwork*, how-

3. Michael Sandel, *Liberalism and the Limits of Justice* (Cambridge: Cambridge University Press, 1982), p. 2.

4. Sandel does not deal directly with the work of Habermas or Scanlon, but I believe he would classify both as followers of Kant who adopt this "deeper" sense of deontology.

5. Immanuel Kant, *Groundwork of the Metaphysic of Morals*, translated by H. J. Paton (New York: Harper Torchbooks, 1964), p. 60.

ever, resided in his synthetic argument, where he set out to show that the moral law was a synthetic a priori principle. His transcendental or "independent" derivation of the moral law is largely rejected by Rawls, Scanlon, and Habermas as an unconvincing metaphysical argument. What must now carry most of the justificatory weight is the connection between an ethical theory and the "common knowledge" of ordinary moral agents. I contend that this shift forces theorists working within this tradition away from the analytic/synthetic investigation of ordinary moral intuitions found in the *Groundwork* and toward an interpretive type of understanding of our deepest moral convictions.[6]

If I am right about the interpretive character of contemporary proceduralism, then the meaning of priority of right over good in the foundational sense changes correspondingly. The priority of the right over the good finds one of its major justifications in the contingent fact that the desire to live in a world where justice has priority in the moral sense is part of our moral/political identity. Within the deontological proceduralism of Rawls, Scanlon, and Habermas, principles of right are defined independently of any one particular conception of the good, if this latter is taken to mean a full-blown, comprehensive view of the things that are worth pursuing, doing, loving, hating, admiring, condemning, and so on. But right is not defined independently of a conception of the good if we mean that it does not rely on contingent facts about what people in a particular society consider to be the sine qua non of the good life.

Each of the three theorists I discuss maintains that his procedural representation of right is the best way both to articulate and to protect the moral principle deeply embedded in our collective identity and way of life—namely, that we have duties toward each other which trump the particular or collective ends we might wish to pursue. This is not the only type of argument used to justify procedural justice, but it is the major one, without which these theories do not make sense.

The second sense in which these theories are a weaker form of deontology than Kant's concerns the extent to which consequences are taken into consideration. Although they are nonconsequentialists generally speaking, Rawls, Scanlon, and Habermas do in fact look at consequences. They ask themselves questions about states of affairs that

---

6. Kant's appeal to a "fact of reason" in *The Critique of Practical Reason* (p. 31), which does attempt to link ethical theory with "common knowledge," is still very different from this new interpretive model. Contemporary proceduralists appeal to meanings in our social world and not to facts buried deep within the private realm of consciousness. See Chapter 3.

could be, would be, or are brought about by adherence to a particular ethical view, and their answers are not irrelevant to their theories. Furthermore, the moral point of view to be taken up within their procedures does include "consequentialist" considerations linked to the pursuit of interests and the satisfaction of needs. Gone is the Kantian demand that the moral point of view should exclude all empirical considerations.

Thus, the distinction between deontological theories and consequentialist theories should not mean that, by definition, deontological theories disregard consequences altogether. Today, most deontological proceduralists acknowledge that in constructing a procedure to test moral principles, one cannot be blind to the concrete interests and needs of individuals or to the consequences that would follow if the principles were in fact implemented in a real social world. These considerations, however, act as side constraints, if you will, rather than the guiding concern in the construction of the theory.

Deontological proceduralism has been modified in response to two problematic aspects of Kantian theory: the unpersuasiveness of "independent" metaphysical arguments and the unacceptable consequences that arise from a principled disregard for consequences. This modification has blurred the line between the foundations of rights-based and good-based theories as well as nonconsequentialist and consequentialist theories. Nevertheless, there is still a line to be drawn. Deontological proceduralism is interested in articulating those rules that dictate right action and are binding in and of themselves.

CONTRACT

Deontological proceduralism searches for a procedure by which we can test whether or not our first-order principles conform to a standard of right. At the most general level we can describe the procedure as consisting of a set of guidelines to reach collective agreement on moral and ethical questions. At the heart of these theories is the idea that moral principles cannot be brought in from the outside. No one group, individual, or higher power, be it God or nature, can dictate right action. Instead, moral principles are the object of rational consent defined as an agreement between rational agents.

The idea of collective agreement is, of course, a very familiar argument in political theory; it is the basis for the modern contract theory of political obligation. To the extent that proceduralism is envisioned as a (binding) choice situation among equals, it has often been thought of as a type of contract theory. It is important to stress, however, that proceduralism is not synonymous with contract theory.

Both Rawls and Scanlon place themselves squarely within the tradition of contract theory beginning with Locke and running through Rousseau to Kant. Although I have no real objection to their calling themselves contract theorists, I do want to point out that this tradition uses contract in a much narrower and more specifically political sense than does either Rawls or Scanlon.

In traditional contract theory, the contract involves the establishment of a legitimate government and the promise to obey that government so long as it honors its side of the bargain. A similar type of promise plays a role in the Rawlsian model.[7] It is important that participants understand that their choices are binding. They must be fully aware that they cannot back out of the agreement if it is not to their liking at some point down the road. This is definitely a contract condition, but it is only one factor, among several, which participants should take into account. It is not the defining characteristic of the procedure. What gives the Rawlsian agreement force is not the *promise* to abide by it but the *reason* one agreed in the first place.[8] In the case of Scanlon there is no promise; indeed, there is no "contracting" between parties to speak of.

Furthermore, unlike those of traditional contract theory, the agreements proposed by Rawls and Scanlon are not directly concerned with the establishment of political authority; their concern is much broader. The question to be answered concerns moral authority.[9] Locke, when speaking about moral authority, is not a contractarian but a natural rights theorist. Locke does not use contract as a procedural test of right action, nor does he apply it to the traditional area of justice. The rules that regulate right action and just exchange already exist in the state of nature. It could be argued that if we were perfectly rational, we would choose to follow natural laws, but what makes them just is their having been sanctioned by God, not our having consented to them.

7. John Rawls, "Reply to Alexander and Musgrave," *Quarterly Journal of Economics* 88 (1974): 650–53.

8. On this issue, see Ronald Dworkin, *Taking Rights Seriously* (Cambridge: Harvard University Press, 1977), pp. 151–52.

9. Even when Rawls puts forward his theory of justice as a purely "political conception," the claim remains that it is a *moral* conception of basic political structures. John Rawls, *Political Liberalism* (New York: Columbia University Press, 1993), p. 11; and idem, "The Idea of an Overlapping Consensus," *Oxford Journal of Legal Studies* 7 (1987): 3.

It is in viewing how later contract theorists differ from Locke that we see the real legacy passed down to contemporary proceduralists. What is crucial is the shift of moral authority away from God and natural law to agreement among rational agents. In one sense, Hobbes's contract is closer to modern proceduralism than Locke's if we understand his natural laws as purely rational precepts not dependent on God. Indeed, Hobbes has inspired his own tradition of contract theory, the most recent and visible proponent being David Gauthier.[10] The similarities between the contract of Rawls and Scanlon and that of Gauthier, however, do not go beyond rejection of divine authority and appeal to human rationality instead.

The major difference lies in their respective understanding of what it means to be rational. Rawls and Scanlon are indebted to Kant and not Hobbes on this issue. Gauthier himself draws the distinction by saying that the "Kantian supposes that all men, as rational, are directly related one to another as members of a Kingdom of Ends in which each must treat his fellows not merely as means but also as ends in themselves."[11] The Hobbesian makes no such assumption. For the modern Hobbesian, rationality is associated with individual utility maximization.[12] Morality is entirely conventional and the product of an instrumental calculation.

For the Kantian, rationality is associated with reasoning in a world populated by other rational agents who are recognized as being worthy of the same consideration I am worthy of. Practical reason has an element of reciprocity built into it.[13] Although morality is based on agreement, it is not entirely conventional in the Hobbesian sense. Morality finds its underpinnings in a conception of practical reason which links the two (morality and reason) prior to the agreement. In the case of Scanlon (and Habermas), this Kantian idea is articulated in a notion of accountability or justification; the obligation to give reasons for one's actions is built into our conception of reasonableness. Being accountable to others is one way of treating them as ends and not merely as

10. David Gauthier, *Morals by Agreement* (New York: Oxford University Press, 1986).

11. David Gauthier, *Moral Dealing: Contract, Ethics, and Reason* (Ithaca: Cornell University Press, 1990), p. 343.

12. Hobbes himself had not so much a maximizing conception of rationality as a minimizing one. Human beings are motivated to minimize harm to themselves, and therefore, they pursue maximal power to guarantee that no harm comes to them.

13. The problem is not that the Hobbesian calculator has no interest in other people's ends and thus can be described as atomlike or purely asocial; the problem is that the Hobbesian calculator takes other people's ends into account only to the extent that they hinder or promote her ends, which is to say, from a strategic point of view.

means. In the case of Rawls, the situation is somewhat more complicated. The parties to his contract are conceived as being rational in the rational-choice sense of rational. Their deliberations are constrained, however, by "reasonable" limits that are intended to ensure that the outcome does not violate the Kantian injunction to treat people as ends and not merely as means.

The dispute between Hobbesians and Kantians stands and falls on the issue of which notion of rationality makes most sense. At a very general level, the Hobbesian notion makes a great deal of sense; it cannot be denied that taking efficient means to secure desired ends is a rational way of acting. There are problems, however, with applying this notion of rationality to questions of morality, for one can describe the pursuit of horrific ends as being quite rational for a utility maximizer.[14] One need only think of Hume's famous dictum, "It is not contrary to reason to prefer the destruction of the whole world to the scratching of my finger," to see the morally counterintuitive possibilities entailed in a purely instrumental preference-based conception of reason.[15] Most of us would think that there is indeed something irrational about preferring the destruction of the world to the scratching of a finger. The Kantian notion of rationality is much more difficult to defend at a general level but does offer more intuitively compelling moral outcomes. Although not without problems, the Kantian conception is defensible; indeed, this conception reflects how we ordinarily do think about rationality and morality.

For now, I will just say that the Hobbesian has more claim to the title "contract theorist" than does either Rawls or Scanlon. It is somewhat misleading to call their theories contractarian unless we want to say that all moral theories that contain the idea of agreement are contract theories. But agreement is not synonymous with contract. Contract is a certain type of agreement, which is usually entered into instrumentally and is underwritten by a promise. Perhaps we should dispense with the term *contract theory* altogether and talk about rational-choice theory (the heirs of Hobbes) and rational-agreement theory (the heirs of Kant). Choice (even if unanimous) versus agreement adequately captures the individualistic versus intersubjective starting points of these two traditions.

14. See, for example, Stephen K. White, *The Recent Work of Jürgen Habermas: Reason, Justice, and Modernity* (Cambridge: Cambridge University Press, 1988), pp. 16–17.

15. David Hume, "A Treatise of Human Nature," in *Hume's Moral and Political Philosophy*, edited by Henry D. Aiken (New York: Hafner, 1972), bk. 2, sec. 5, p. 25.

ROUSSEAU AND THE GENERAL WILL

The proceduralist tradition that interests me here finds its first expression in Rousseau's notion of the general will. Although the general will is founded on a contract, it is not itself a contract. In Rousseau's original contract there is an absolute transfer of power and right to the sovereign.[16] But this contract is not a *procedure* in the sense in which I have been using the word. It represents a promise to obey the sovereign, but it does not tell us how to discover the general will, that is, how to discover the first-order principles that will govern future interaction. In discussing the general will, Rousseau attempts to set up conditions under which agreement and consent would best reflect the interest of the community as a whole. I understand the general will to mean those principles citizens would adopt if they could factor out private and factional interests and look at issues from the perspective of the whole. What is at the center of procedural ethics is this "perspective taking."

But doesn't the moral authority of the general will reside in the original consent? That is, do we obey the general will because we consented to it or because it represents the common good? The answer lies in the distinction between politics and morality. In a political sense we obey the general will because we consented to it, but in a moral sense we obey it because it represents the common good. Simple consent cannot create the general will. For example, our individual voices converging in a "will of all" would not add up to the general will and would generate no moral obligation.[17] The original contract confers political power upon the general will; it does not create it or even justify it. Political authority is coercive and requires consent; it is created through consent. Moral authority is not coercive; it is not created through consent but is deserving of consent.

The weakness of Rousseau's procedure lies in the conditions he thought would best guarantee an impartial outcome. The exclusion of debate and exchange, combined with simple majority rule, does not do justice to the ideal of achieving a truly common perspective.[18] The dis-

16. Jean-Jacques Rousseau, *On the Social Contract*, translated by Maurice Cranston (New York: Penguin, 1968), p. 60.

17. Ibid., p. 72.

18. For a discussion of the relationship and tension between the ideal of the general will, and the procedures Rousseau appeals to in discovering the general will see Bernard Manin, "On Legitimacy and Political Deliberation," *Political Theory* 15 (August 1987): 344–47; and Seyla Benhabib, "Deliberative Rationality and Models of Democratic Legitimacy," *Constellations* 1 (April 1994): 28–30.

covery of the general will involves a "point of view" more closely associated with affective ties and commitments to the community or nation than with rationality per se. Rousseau sets up a decision procedure in which citizens are protected from factional interests, but at the expense of rational deliberation. Thus, the Rousseauean procedure, although trying to capture a general point of view, does not succeed in capturing a rational point of view; the general will is not a universal will.

KANT AND THE CATEGORICAL IMPERATIVE

Proceduralism reaches its first full expression with Kant. The categorical imperative, even in its Kingdom of Ends formulation, is not a contract.[19] Agents do not promise each other, even hypothetically, to act only on maxims that could be universal laws of nature. Furthermore, the reason why we would or should act only on these maxims has nothing to do with an instrumental calculation. If the categorical imperative is compelling at all, it is because it asks us to take up a point of view that is impartial or, to use Kant's own terminology, autonomous.

What I want to stress here is that what is central to deontological proceduralism is the idea of taking up a moral *point of view*—specifically, an impartial point of view. The idea of a contract is wholly inadequate to capture this perspective. As a justification of moral principles, a contract is designed precisely to explain why individuals who do not have a moral point of view (utility maximizers or a "race of devils") might nevertheless be bound by certain rules of justice.[20] Proceduralists, although acknowledging that we are sometimes utility maximizers (not to mention devils), maintain that morality requires rising above our self-interest and taking a different perspective on moral issues.

For Kant, the exclusion of all empirical motivation constituted such a perspective. The will must free itself from all outside influences; it must become autonomous in the radical sense of literally acting in a dimension that exists outside the causal framework of the perceived world. Only in being so radically free, could the will act in a way that

19. Kant, of course, does employ a contract in his political writings. See "On the Common Saying: 'This May Be True in Theory, but It Does Not Apply in Practice,'" in *Kant's Political Writings*, edited by Hans Reiss (Cambridge: Cambridge University Press, 1970), pp. 73–87. It is the categorical imperative, however, to which Rawls, Scanlon, and Habermas most often appeal.

20. See Gauthier, *Morals by Agreement*, pp. 306–30.

would reflect rationality per se. Autonomy, being free of all empirical influences, becomes synonymous with acting according to pure practical reason and thus acting according to a universally "fixed" and formal standard.

Impartiality, the central concept around which contemporary proceduralists build their theories, is indebted to this idea of autonomy. These contemporary theorists all assume that freeing oneself from certain empirical influences and interests moves one closer to the moral point of view. The way of doing so, however, is no longer thought to be found in subjecting one's maxims to the test of the categorical imperative: "Act only on that maxim through which you can at the same time will that it should become a universal law."[21] This imperative asks us to imagine a world where everyone did in fact (as a matter of universal law) act on the same maxim when in the same situation. But the trick for Kant is not in imagining what *kind* of a world it would be if everyone acted in a like manner; it is to ask if I could will consistently both that I act on the maxim and that everyone act on the maxim. That is, we do not ask ourselves, Do I want to live in such a world? or Would such a world be a good place to live? or Would every one be happy in such a world? Instead, we ask ourselves, Does this world make sense to me *as a rational being*? Is it even conceivable?

Kant thought that we could answer this question by appeal to the dictates of pure practical reason. A maxim failed the test if it contradicted either its own premises or an existing law of nature. Thus, a world governed by such a maxim was inconceivable in the sense that it would be a world governed by contradictory laws. This test has been subject to a great deal of debate and controversy. Contemporary proceduralists have opted for a different rationality test, albeit one that retains the idea that morally valid maxims would be chosen (willed) by agents acting rationally. Whereas Kant's procedure asks agents to check their maxims against logical rules of consistency and certain "laws of nature," modern procedures ask that maxims receive the endorsement of agents acting rationally under certain specified conditions. Agents are still asked, "Is a world regulated by your maxim conceivable?" but now the question turns on whether it is conceivable that rational agents would *agree* (or, in the case of Scanlon, have no grounds for disagreeing) to act according to this maxim.

As modern interpretations of autonomy, the rational-agreement mod-

21. Kant, *Groundwork*, p. 88.

els of moral deliberation are all less ambitious than Kant's theory. The possibility that there is a moral point of view that transcends all time and place is no longer accepted. Rawls has retreated substantially from his claim to have found an Archimedean point, which, even in its original formulation, was never as universal a claim as Kant's. In Scanlon's account, impartiality is achieved not by withdrawing from the world to a privileged vantage point but rather by entering the world and taking up many vantage points other than one's own. Habermas too rejects the Kantian view that the "good will" has no empirical interests and represents an abstractly universal perspective. Further, the attempt to give a transcendental justification for the existence and necessity of a moral point of view has been abandoned. In its place is the much less ambitious endeavor to justify this point of view by reference to existing moral values and deeply held convictions. Interpretation has replaced metaphysics as the starting point of ethics. Autonomy is no longer the characteristic of an uncaused noumenal self; rather, it is something to be *achieved* by the real or phenomenal self. Autonomy in its new guise is not something we possess which sets us apart from the contingent world; it is something that must be sought and won, sometimes through great effort, while we are part of the contingent world.

3 Proceduralism and the Recovery of Moral Intuitions

Rawls, Scanlon, and Habermas all claim that their theories articulate deeply held beliefs of moral agents in modern liberal democracies. A common theme running through all their discussions is that moral theory should reconstruct certain strong beliefs that we, as ordinary moral agents, grasp intuitively. Intuitive ideas, then, anchor these theories in our contemporary context. For example, as the starting point of his effort to develop a political conception of justice, Rawls appeals to "certain fundamental intuitive ideas viewed as latent in the public political culture of a democratic society."[1] Scanlon appeals to a commonly shared desire "to be able to justify one's actions (and institutions) on grounds one takes to be acceptable" as the intuitive starting point of his account of contractualism.[2] And Habermas claims that "the debate among cognitivist moral philosophers . . . is concerned with the questions of how and by what conceptual means the *same* intuition potential that becomes accessible to *everyone* with the transition to the postconventional level of autonomous morality can be most adequately explained."[3]

But what exactly is being appealed to when these theorists talk about "intuitive ideas," "shared desire," and "intuition potential"? For exam-

1. John Rawls, "The Idea of an Overlapping Consensus," *Oxford Journal of Legal Studies* 7 (1987): 8; idem, *Political Liberalism* (New York: Columbia University Press, 1993), p. 13.
2. Thomas Scanlon, "Contractualism and Utilitarianism," in *Utilitarianism and Beyond*, edited by Amartya Sen and Bernard Williams (Cambridge: Cambridge University Press, 1982), p. 117.
3. Jürgen Habermas, "Justice and Solidarity: On the Discussion Concerning 'Stage 6,'" *Philosophical Forum* 21 (Fall–Winter 1989–90): 34.

ple, what exactly is an intuition, and what does it mean to believe something intuitively? In what sense can we share a desire, and what does it mean for an intuition to have a potential? These questions are important because the philosophic *reconstruction* of beliefs we hold intuitively makes sense only if there is something inadequate about our intuitive grasp of them. Philosophy is shown to be useful if it can do something that intuition alone cannot do. If these theories are based on things that we already believe in some sense and if they purport to be more than simply descriptive, then we must discover what philosophy adds to intuition, and to do so, we must have a clearer grasp of what intuition is. We must have a better idea *in what sense* we already believe the fundamental premises of a particular theory.

INTUITIVE SELF-EVIDENCE

The appeal to intuitive beliefs is often an attempt to anchor an ethical theory in everyday moral experience. Intuitions are almost always understood in opposition to philosophic or theoretical understanding. In moral matters we are said to be guided by convictions or beliefs that we grasp in a spontaneous or unreflective way. Intuition somehow offers us a shortcut to knowledge: the mind immediately grasps its object without the intervening steps of reasoning or analysis, or with a minimum of reflection.

But what is the object of an intuition? We do not say, for example, that someone has an intuitive grasp of her feelings or preferences. Such a statement makes no sense because presumably we are already in direct contact with our feelings and preferences. Nor do we usually say that someone has an uncanny intuitive grasp of falsehood (except in the sense of grasping the *truth* that something *is* false). Of course, our intuitions can be mistaken, but then we feel it was not intuition at all that guided us, or perhaps not good intuition. Good intuition is insightful, something like a sixth sense. Or at least, this is one way of understanding intuition. On this model, intuition is a special faculty that when functioning properly, immediately grasps the truth.[4]

4. In ethics this view of intuition is associated with traditional intuitionism like that of G. E. Moore. Generally speaking, intuitionists of this school believe that there are universal truths, which are grasped by a special faculty of intuition as self-evident and necessary. Analogous to mathematical truths, these entities are nonnatural in that they exist independently of anything that has happened, or could happen, in the natural world. These truths are generally thought to have a peculiarly nonrational quality about them as well. It is not the

The experience of intuitive truth does seem to play a role in the way we make our moral judgments. It is not uncommon to feel absolutely certain about a moral conviction. One simply knows that something is, say, morally wrong; it appears self-evident and is in no need of rational defence. Such would be, for example, Ivan Karamazov's conviction that even the Last Judgment cannot make up for the suffering of children in this world.[5] For Ivan, the principle "children should not suffer," is truly pretheoretical, in that it is an unshakable premise *upon* which rational argument should be based. It is not a principle that needs God or reason to justify it; it appears to him to be immediately self-evident. As an unshakable first principle, it is used by Ivan as a test. Any system, whether religious, natural, or rational, which appears to violate this principle contains a fundamental ethical flaw.

Perhaps a similar moral intuition can be found behind Thomas Nagel's principle that we should not be indifferent to the suffering of others. "Justifications" for such a principle "are unnecessary. They plainly falsify the case. My reason for wanting my neighbor's pain to cease is just that it's awful, and I know it." That pain is awful is self-evident, not simply in a personal sense but in an objective or, as Nagel puts it, an "agent neutral" sense.[6] A similar argument is put forward by Judith Shklar, who claims that liberalism finds its deepest justification or raison d'être in the intuition that "cruelty and the fear it inspires" are evil. This *summum malum* needs little or no rational justification "because the fear of systematic cruelty is so universal, moral claims based on its prohibition have an immediate appeal and can gain recognition without much argument.[7]

The principle that children should not suffer or that we should not be indifferent to the pain of others does not appear to need further argument; intuition should be enough to tell us that there is something

case, for example, that this pretheoretical (i.e., intuitive) knowledge can be given a theoretical rendering by the philosopher. Morality falls outside the bounds of reason because our reasoning faculties can never "get at" these truths; they exist in some other dimension to which our moral sixth sense has the only access. The philosophical problems with traditional intuitionism are legion, and I will not rehearse them here. For a brief discussion of some of the problems with G. E. Moore's ethical philosophy and later intuitionism, see, for example, Alasdair MacIntyre, *A Short History of Ethics* (New York: Macmillan, 1966), pp. 249–55.

5. Feodor Dostoevsky, *The Brothers Karamazov* (New York: Penguin Classics, 1958), pp. 285–88.

6. Thomas Nagel, "The Limits of Objectivity," in *The Tanner Lectures on Human Values*, vol. 1 (Salt Lake City: University of Utah Press, 1978–79), p. 110.

7. Judith Shklar, "The Liberalism of Fear," in *Liberalism and the Moral Life*, edited by Nancy L. Rosenblum (Cambridge: Harvard University Press, 1989), pp. 29–30.

fundamentally right, good, or true about such principles. Or at least so we often feel. This is part of the way we experience certain strong intuitions. But what is the connection between the unshakable conviction that something is fundamentally right, good, or true and its actually being so?

Nagel says that there is something "crazy" about asking such a question. He thinks that something has gone very wrong within philosophy when we are puzzled by the foundations of strong intuitions. Their strength as unshakable convictions should be enough. Nagel is right in the sense that we do not need philosophy to convince us of the unshakableness of our unshakable intuitions. Nevertheless, we do want a philosophic account of our deepest insights. The reason for wanting to justify strong intuitions is not that we doubt that children should not suffer but that intuitions of this sort are few and far between. In looking for a philosophic account of these intuitions maybe we can come to understand their special character, and this understanding may help us in cases where our intuitions are not quite so clear.

In both Ivan Karamazov's and Nagel's examples it is not the case that there are no rational arguments to defend the moral principles; rather, rational arguments seem unnecessary. The certainty of objective principles lies in intuitive self-evidence and not rational justification, though Nagel, for example, does not deny that rational justification is possible.[8] While I am sympathetic to this view, the appeal to private experience does not get us very far. The strength of these intuitions lies not in the experience of self-evidence but in how widely the experience is shared.

There are two problems with regarding intuitions as "self-evident" moral truths that we grasp spontaneously. First, appealing to a feeling of certainty is not a convincing reason to give somebody who doubts the soundness of your conviction. We do not need reasons to support our conviction that children should not suffer only because that conviction is not seriously challenged within our cultural world. The second reason why the model of experiential self-evidence is inadequate is that it places morality in the world of private experience. What makes Ivan's and Nagel's principles compelling, however, is not how strongly Ivan or Nagel experiences them as certainties but our conviction that every-

---

8. He does not offer arguments to support the claim that pain is objectively bad because, "in arguing for this claim, I am somewhat handicapped by the fact that I find it self-evident. It is therefore difficult for me to find something still more certain with which to back it up." Nagel, "Limits of Objectivity," p. 108.

body must feel the same way about them. To express it another way, their strength lies in our conviction that every one would *agree* that children should not suffer or that we should not be indifferent to the pain of others. Strong convictions are the product of shared understandings, not the cause of them. Here is a new element in understanding moral intuitions and what makes them right, or at least appear right to us. They are moral convictions that we share with others or assume that others would agree to.

SHARED INTUITIONS

Rawls, Scanlon, and Habermas understand the object of our intuitions to be a shared value or belief. According to this view, our moral *experience* is essentially intersubjective and not private. The intuitions that form the core of this experience are moral insights we have by virtue of living in a particular world. There might be an attempt (a strong one on the part of Habermas and a weaker one on the part of Rawls) to link these intuitions to a universal standard of rationality, but the ordinary intuitions themselves are reflections of a particular way of life. Intuitions give us a pretheoretical (or unreflective) grasp of our moral world, not a pretheoretical grasp of moral truth outside our world.

The question that serves as a starting point here is what beliefs or intuitions are entailed (generally speaking) in being a member of *this* society. Rawls answers with the idea of citizenship in liberal democracies; Habermas talks about postconventional or modern society; and Scanlon simply invokes the first person plural. All three theorists are looking to find a core of shared values that constitute the heart of our modern/liberal-democratic/postconventional social order. But these values are not always easy to get at. They exist deeply embedded in a way of life made up of a complex set of practices, attitudes, beliefs, institutions, traditions, and habits, all of which are overlaid and partially hidden by a plurality of comprehensive moral views, conceptions of the good life, and competing ends. Further, these shared values are not always present to us in a fully reflective way. The objects of our intuitions are often things that we, along with a great many other people, take for granted. The problem facing the theorist who wishes to employ our deepest or constitutive values as a starting point is two-pronged: first, how to "get at" these values through the intervening density of a way of life and, second, even if we find the right method, how to determine which values are the most important. This last problem involves more than weighing the relative strength of competing convictions. As a brief look at Rawls's use of intuition will show, it also involves distinguishing between levels of intuition.

In *A Theory of Justice*, as well as his later work, Rawls brings intuitively held beliefs into play in two separate kinds of arguments. In the first, he appeals to certain moral judgments that can be used as sounding boards in the construction of a theory. In the second, he introduces intuitions that are latent in public culture as a general foundation or starting point of the enterprise of constructing a theory of justice. I would like to take up these two notions and try to draw a clearer distinction between them than Rawls does himself. The difference between these two uses of intuition is that the first appeals to first-order moral beliefs and the second refers to second-order moral principles. The second type of intuition is the more important to his theory, I bellieve, and it takes a very prominent place in his later work.[9]

In *A Theory of Justice* Rawls notes that "there are questions which we feel must be answered in a certain way." These convictions stand as "provisional fixed points" in our approach to ethics. They are beliefs we hold so strongly, are so certain about, that any theory that undermined them would automatically be suspect. As ordinary moral agents, we use these beliefs as yardsticks in judging the world around us. We employ them only "intuitively," however, according to Rawls.[10]

Intuitions, in this sense, play the role of a sounding board in theory building. We can check the outcomes of the theory against our strongly held convictions. For example, if we are certain that racial discrimination is unjust, we can test a theory to see whether its outcomes are compatible with this "fixed point." The back and forth of the testing procedure will result in a "reflective equilibrium." The result of our testing is an "equilibrium" because the intuitions and theory will eventually balance each other out. That is, our intuitions might lead us to reconstruct our theory, but the theory might also serve to correct some of our more doubtful intuitions.

9. This distinction is not unlike the distinction between narrow and wide reflective equilibrium. See Norman Daniels, "Wide Reflective Equilibrium and Theory Acceptance in Ethics," *Journal of Philosophy* 76 (1979): 256–82. I do not use the terms narrow and wide, however, because the point I want to make is that there is a qualitative and not a quantitative difference between these two types of argument. The difference is between a simple coherence argument and what I call interpretive reconstruction. See Chapter 5.

10. John Rawls, *A Theory of Justice* (Cambridge: Harvard University Press, 1971), p. 19.

Where do these intuitions come from, and how do we know which ones are the soundest? At first, Rawls simply associates them with the experience of certainty. They are convictions about which we have little or no hesitation. This association suggests the "spontaneous" model of intuitions to which Nagel and Ivan Karamazov appeal. But then Rawls changes the terms somewhat. The intuitions to serve as fixed points are not simply the ones we are most certain of but also the ones we have thought most deeply about, and thought about in a certain way. Indeed, he calls these fixed points *"considered* judgments." We are confident about our considered judgments because "we think that we have examined these things with care and have reached what we believe is an impartial judgment not likely to be distorted by an excessive attention to our own interest."[11]

But what is the source of our confidence that excluding our own interests is the best way to arrive at sound moral judgment? Is this an intuitive sort of confidence? If it is, and I think it must be, then here we have an intuition not about first-order principles such as "racism is unjust" but about a second-order procedure, about how to determine which of our first-order intuitions are solid. The intuition about impartiality is less likely to be held as an articulated belief. It exists in a way of doing something and for this reason it is often latent.

In my earlier discussion I looked at first-order moral beliefs that individuals held explicitly but for "no reason" (e.g., "children should not suffer" or "racial discrimination is unjust"). These convictions seemed to need no rational justification because they appeared to be self-evident. Now I have introduced a notion of intuition in which the unreflective nature of the intuition no longer simply means that we do not need a reason for it. These "second-order" intuitions are unreflective in a deeper sense; they involve the intuition that we should be operating according to a principle we have never fully articulated as a rule. Because it has never been fully articulated, it is not always clear to us how we go about taking up, for example, the impartial perspective. Thus Rawls is claiming, first, that we intuitively know that impartiality is the appropriate perspective to take when choosing or evaluating our first-order principles, but second, that we do not always know how to be impartial or what is entailed in impartiality. Thus philosophy comes into the picture. Philosophy sets out to reconstruct, in procedural form, what it means to be impartial.

The reconstruction of second-order moral principles is often com-

---

11. Ibid., pp. 19–20.

pared to the reconstruction used in language theory to "get at" deep grammar. In fact, Rawls himself cites Noam Chomsky in his discussion of reflective equilibrium but without making this crucial distinction between first- and second-order intuitions. Within his native language, a speaker has a spontaneous (pretheoretical) grasp of what can and cannot be said in that language. Our grasp is spontaneous in that we (intuitively) know how to construct grammatically correct sentences or immediately recognize incorrect ones without making a conscious appeal to the rules involved. Even the standard rules of grammar do not adequately explain our full range of competence. This is the job of the linguist, whose "aim is to characterize the ability to recognize well-formed sentences by formulating clearly expressed principles which make the same discriminations as the native speaker. This is a difficult undertaking which, although still unfinished, is known to require theoretical constructions that far outrun the ad hoc precepts of our explicit grammatical knowledge."[12] Analogously, the moral theoretician reconstructs the principles we use to generate our moral convictions or considered judgments. This particular language analogy has its limits, however. We do not really need Chomsky's deep grammar to help us out in speaking our native tongue, but Rawls and all the proceduralists make an implicit claim that their reconstructions can improve our moral discourse in some way, that we can learn something about ourselves from these reconstructions, perhaps something new. Nevertheless, the language analogy should not be given up just yet. It can still furnish us with some additional insights into second-order intuitions.

INTUITION AS KNOW-HOW

With the introduction of the language analogy, the type of intuitions appealed to by proceduralism can be fleshed out. Intuitions represent a "know-how" to which the philosopher furnishes the "know-that." Know-how is practical competency. An obvious, if perhaps trivial, example would be something like knowing how to ski or play tennis. We might know how to do these things even if no one has ever explained to us the principles or logic behind the activity. We might simply have pointed our skis down a hill one day and taken it from there, or grown up playing tennis. These activities can nevertheless be reconstructed in a theoretical form, perhaps in a "how-to" book to be used by those who are not "native" skiers or tennis players.

12. Ibid., p. 47.

In ethics we can also be said to grow up with a certain competency. We make moral judgments every day without consciously consulting a rule or principle. In a sense, we know how to make moral judgments even if we cannot always give a theoretical explanation of those judgments. This competency is acquired in the *practice* of making the judgments. The rules of practical competency are of a special sort. For example, if we return briefly to my sports analogy, we see that there is a difference between skiing and playing tennis. Tennis does have rules, which one must know if one is actually to play a game of tennis. Yet knowing the rules of tennis or even chess does not make one a tennis or a chess player. The kind of rules I am talking about here are not constitutive rules that determine which moves are legitimate within the instituted game, how to keep score, and so on. The rules that guide practical competencies are altogether different.[13]

The question is whether this type of rule can be reconstructed at all. For example, Bernard Williams suggests that ethics can learn a valuable lesson from Wittgenstein, who questions whether linguistic competency "can be captured in a set of statable rules." Williams says that even if our intuitive moral judgments appear to be rule governed, that does not mean that there "is some clear discursive rule" underlying our capacity to make those judgments.[14] Although I do not want to enter the unending debate about Wittgenstein's notion of a rule, I do want to take up the reasons why certain types of rules appear to be non-reconstructible, for it is just these types of rules which Habermas and, I believe, Rawls and Scanlon try to reconstruct.

The problem that Wittgenstein's later work highlights is the following: Language, being basically intersubjective and not private, must be rule governed. Not just anything can mean anything at any given time. We must be able to recognize the *misuse* of words. And for words to be misused, some kind of rule must be broken. But here is the paradox: Although language is rule governed, language can never be reduced to a set of rules, nor can the rules we apparently use every day be exhaustively stated.[15]

13. Of course, constitutive rules do play a role in moral judgments. It is the underlying competency that I am interested in here, however. Competency rules are prior to the constitutive rules that institutionally define disqualification, forfeiture, penalty, and so on, even though these can have feedback effect on competency rules.

14. Bernard Williams, *Ethics and the Limits of Philosophy* (Cambridge: Harvard University Press, 1985), p. 97.

15. Ludwig Wittgenstein, *Philosophical Investigations* (Oxford: Basil Blackwell, 1976), paras. 80–101.

One reason is that the rules of our language games change continually as meanings shift and mutate in the natural course of events. Another reason is that the rules of our language games exist in, and are fixed through, practice. A group of people using words in a certain way represents a consensus, which, in a sense, enforces the rule governing what constitutes a correct or incorrect use of words. The penalty for breaking the rule is misunderstanding. We do not, as speakers, apply the rule; rather, our successful utterances embody the rule.

It is this type of pragmatic rule to which Habermas appeals when he discusses the practical competencies people possess to make moral judgments. We do not consciously apply a rule; rather, our successful moral judgments embody a rule. Although Habermas, following Wittgenstein, takes language and consequently ethics out of private experience and consciousness and into the open spaces between subjects, from here, he departs dramatically from the Wittgensteinian paradigm. Habermas does not accept Wittgenstein's conclusion that philosophy is wasting its time trying to get behind our common practices and usages. He rejects Wittgenstein's argument that philosophy is competent to describe only the surface patterns of our talk.[16] He contends instead that although we do not consciously apply a set of rules, the philosopher can reconstruct our competencies in a rulelike form. These rules are purely hypothetical, and they do not so much govern our actions as make sense of them. That is, the meaning and significance of our actions becomes clearer when they are seen as instances of these rules.[17]

One consequence of Habermas's characterization of moral judging in terms of pragmatic rules is that he is able to distance himself from Kant's notion of a "fact of reason." Kant thought that the moral law is a component of our internal rational structure. It comes with the merchandise, so to speak, and human beings need only consult their inner selves to recognize it.[18] Habermas wants to take moral rules out of the murky and inaccessible world of private consciousness and place them in the observable world of interaction.[19] When we wish to understand

16. Ibid., para. 109.

17. I leave open for the moment the essentialist question, Do these rules actually determine the way we make judgments, or are they an interpretive framework through which we understand moral judgment? I take up this issue in Chapter 8.

18. Immanuel Kant, *Critique of Pure Reason*, translated by L. W. Beck (Indianapolis: Bobbs-Merrill, 1956), p. 31.

19. Here Habermas is much indebted to George Herbert Mead's "behaviorism," which is explicitly designed to overcome the problems of philosophy of consciousness. See Jürgen Habermas, *The Theory of Communicative Action*, translated by Thomas McCarthy, vol. 1 (Boston: Beacon Press, 1981), pp. 94–96.

normative statements, recommendations, condemnations, and so on, we ask not what is going on in our heads but what is going on between ourselves and our audience.

Habermas concludes that the practice of communicating with each other over moral issues engenders a "know-how" on which we intuitively draw in these situations. As our political and moral world has developed, become more complicated and less homogeneous, conversations about disputed norms have challenged the claims of ultimate foundations. The whole structure of moral argumentation has changed, for no longer can we resolve our disputes by appeal to the moral equivalent of "The buck stops here," which is to say, by appeal to nature, God, or a self-evident truth. But where do we turn if there is no ultimate guarantor of the soundness of our arguments? According to Habermas, the logic of speech and argumentation itself points to new ways to ground collective norms. It points toward the adoption of impartial and fair perspectives as opposed to appeal to unquestioned and shared background views of God and nature. It is not so much that we consciously apply the principle of impartiality; it is that at a certain point our conversations cannot continue if we do not adopt such a perspective. We acquire this know-how simply in doing it and, in doing it, seeing that it is successful, that is, that conversations can in fact continue only when we revise positions that others cannot share.

But if we already do this, why do we need philosophy? Or more to the point, why do we need formalized and idealized articulations of this know-how?[20] I suggest that there are five reasons why we need philosophy. For the moment, I intend simply to set them out with very little defense. As I develop a fuller picture of procedural ethics and the politics that can be derived from such an ethics, each of these five claims will be expanded and substantiated.

First, we need these articulations because the competency to make impartial judgments is often latent in our practices, and this latency can be suppressed, distorted, or derailed. An idealized articulation can

20. Sometimes Habermas implies that we do not really need philosophy except as a counterweight to skepticism and positivism, which "have misinterpreted and thus neutralized the intuitions people acquire in a quasi-natural manner through socialization." Habermas, *Moral Consciousness and Communicative Action*, p. 98. The limited role Habermas gives philosophy has more to do with a division of labor between philosophy and social theory, however, than with a purely descriptive idea of philosophy, for he adds that "in regard to providing guidance for emancipatory practice, discourse ethics can acquire a significance for orientating action. It does so, however, not as an ethics, that is, not prescriptively in the direct sense, but indirectly, by becoming part of a critical social theory that can be used to interpret situations" (p. 98 n. 81).

be used as a critical yardstick to evaluate or detect potential distortions. Second, idealized articulations are not simply redescriptions. They are potential catalysts for augmentation.[21] I mean that reflection upon the background conditions of moral judgments can sharpen and perhaps improve our competency to make moral judgments. In this sense, moral intuitions are not like deep grammar. Their articulation may give them added force or amend and modify them upon critical reflection.

Third, articulation may help us with the problem of "going on," the problem of being able to apply rules to new circumstances or to as yet unencountered moral dilemmas. Interpretations that attempt to offer a formal rendering of where we stand and what we have learned can be helpful in showing where our present moral presuppositions might lead us. Fourth, there is the problem of stability. In my view, the modern context presents some very special problems with regard to the reproduction of collective norms and principles. Without a rationalization through which latent beliefs are articulated, many of our most important collective understandings may face erosion. The need for stability may appear to run counter to the idea of critical augmentation, for augmentation implies that we add to and in some way change our collective understandings, whereas stability implies the we cement and shore them up. A properly constructed procedural theory, however, can both augment and create deeper and more lasting foundations for those insights of modern moral thinking which are undeniable.

Assuming for the moment that there is such a thing as the modern moral point of view, in what sense can insights contained within it be considered "undeniable"? This question brings up the final reason for philosophical reconstruction. Through such reconstruction we can better judge whether there is anything to these intuitions. Nagel is perhaps right to insist that philosophy has little power to shake unshakable convictions. Nothing philosophy can say, for example, will dissuade me that suffering is bad, that slavery is wrong and racial discrimination is unjust. But philosophy can investigate whether there are arguments showing that these principles are not simply modern Western prejudices but possess universal validity. If philosophy cannot establish the universal validity of such principles, that is not a reason to reject them. But if philosophy can demonstrate their validity, this gives us all the more reason to fight for and defend such principles. To put the point rather dogmatically, I believe that children should not suffer, that my

21. I thank Bonnie Honig, who introduced me to the idea of augmentation. I employ the idea of critical augmentation, however, rather than agonistic augmentation.

neighbor's pain is awful, that slavery is wrong, and that racial discrimination, intolerance, and cruelty are pernicious. If philosophy can show
that I have more than culturally specific reasons for these beliefs, so
much the better. If philosophy cannot make such a demonstration,
then the culturally specific reasons for these beliefs will have to do. To
anticipate what follows, I maintain that although the defense of universalist ethics is difficult, there are arguments that can at least give us
confidence (if perhaps not prove) that modern moral insights are not
simply one set of moral prejudices in the history of moral prejudices.

4 *Interpretive Deontology*

Rawls, Scanlon, and Habermas set out to recover our second-order moral intuitions. One way of talking about both the latency and the shared aspect of these intuitions is to say that they reflect intersubjective meanings. And because recovering meanings involves interpretation, one way to describe what these theorists are up to is to say that their reconstructions are interpretive reconstructions.

Hermeneutics is the approach most often associated with interpretation. None of the proceduralists I have mentioned so far is strictly speaking a hermeneuticist. Many readers may therefore find my introduction of interpretation odd, since Rawls, Scanlon, and Habermas are most often seen as representatives of an analytic tradition in ethics. The most obvious difference between the work of these theorists and traditional hermeneutics is that Rawls, Scanlon, and Habermas do not offer a phenomenology of moral experience. Their translation of moral experience is into a language far removed from that of hermeneutics; it is into the language of deontological proceduralism. That is, their objective is to translate intuitions into a rationalized procedure that can be employed in determining what is right or just. If I am correct about the interpretive element of these theories, then this approach can properly be called interpretive deontology.

The second difference between proceduralism and traditional hermeneutics is that proceduralism often represents a type of rationalism not normally associated with hermeneutics. Hermeneutics usually contains a form of cultural relativism. Reason can penetrate the background assumptions of a culture only so far, and at some point the authority of tradition takes over. This difference is most glaring in the case of Habermas. Indeed, Habermas distinguishes himself from people like Hans-Georg Gadamer precisely on this issue. Traditional hermeneutics denies the power of reason and reflection to disclose fully what is going on behind the scenes; discourse ethics claims not only to disclose the background of everyday life but also to reveal a universal component to that background.

The differences between what is usually thought to be involved in interpretation and what is usually thought to be involved in deontology lead to two separate types of objections to my term *interpretive deontology*. Either what these theorists are doing is not really interpretation or it is not really deontology.

Interpretive Deontology: Is It Really Interpretive?

An objection of the first sort would go something like this: What is worthwhile in interpretation, the deep and rich understanding it provides, is sacrificed when passed through the mill of reconstruction. This is how I understand Michael Walzer's criticisms of Rawls and Habermas in *Interpretation and Social Criticism*. While acknowledging that these theories are not strictly speaking "theories of invention" and that they in fact start from the very same interpretive stance as does interpretive social criticism, Walzer still thinks that there is something wrongheaded here.[1] The best way to put his misgivings is to say that he thinks these theories are unconvincing *as* interpretations. They fail because the language into which the intuitions are translated is too formal to capture the full meanings embedded in our moral experience. As Walzer puts it, these theories try to replace our comfortable homes, full of all their idiosyncratic paraphernalia, with impersonal "neutral" hotel rooms, where we see nothing familiar and certainly do not feel at home.

This criticism is wrong on two counts. As I said, Walzer thinks that proceduralism is unsuccessful as an interpretation because it translates our everyday intuitions into an unrecognizable formalism. The relatively formal language of proceduralism is not an arbitrary choice, however. Rather, there is something about the intuitions involved

1. Michael Walzer, *Interpretation and Social Criticism* (Cambridge: Harvard University Press, 1987), pp. 16–30.

which lends itself to this type of articulation. It is not as if these theorists believe that one could take *any* set of moral intuitions and translate them in this way. It is only *our* intuitions that can be translated in this way, and only *certain* of our intuitions.

For example, talk of rights and the priority of right in the moral sense is very much part of our political/moral discourses. When we ask ourselves what is being appealed to in this talk, it would be misleading to say that the appeal is to one particularly cozy feature of our shared home. When (or even if) we say it was wrong for the Chinese government to quash dissent brutally in Tiananmen Square or ethnic cleansing is an unacceptable method of dispute resolution, we usually do not think we are saying, "They would not be allowed to do that in our house!" The appeal is more often to the idea of an objective principle, indeed, a universal principle that, from an impartial point of view, should hold for everyone no matter what their "domestic" situation is.[2] This is the case even if we cannot articulate that principle or justify why it ought to be recognized as objective and universal.

Walzer, although of course in favor of human rights, has at the same time voiced a deep relativism in his work. Thus, he might answer that although human rights are good for all sorts of reasons, we are mistaken in thinking that those reasons have any kind of prior or universal claim on us. But are we mistaken? This is the question that animates interpretive deontology. We talk as if, and sometimes we act as if, there are deontological principles. Interpretive deontologists suggest that we should not dismiss this way of approaching moral issues until we have investigated how much sense we can make of it, and making sense of it involves reconstructing notions of rights, fairness, and impartiality in a principled or formal articulation.

My second objection concerns Walzer's use of the hotel room metaphor. Behind this metaphor is the idea, shared by such other critics of

2. Thomas McCarthy's response to Richard Rorty's criticism of universalism, formalism, and notions of transcendent truth makes a similar point. McCarthy says, "As a matter of fact, our ordinary, common-sense truth talk and reality talk is shot through with just the sorts of idealizations that Rorty wants to purge. In everyday talk we do not normally mean by 'true' anything like 'what our society lets us say,' but something closer to 'telling it like it is—like it *really* is.' And by 'real' we don't normally mean anything like 'referred to in conformity with the norms of our culture,' but something closer to 'there anyway, whether we think so or not.'" "Our culture," notes McCarthy, "is everywhere structured around transcultural notions of validity, and that means that Rorty's 'frank ethnocentrism' lands him in just the universalist position he is trying to escape." Thomas McCarthy, "Philosophy and Social Practice: Avoiding the Ethnocentric Predicament," in *Zwischenbetrachtungen im Prozess der Aufklärung*, edited by Axel Honneth et al. (Frankfurt: Suhrkamp, 1989), pp. 195–96.

proceduralism as Charles Taylor, Charles Larmore, and Bernard Williams, that there is something irreducible about our moral world. They say that the "density" (Walzer), "complexity" (Larmore), and "diversity" (Williams, Taylor) that characterize morality cannot be reduced to or fully captured by a procedure or any uni-theoretical packaging. "The moral world has a lived-in quality," writes Walzer, "like a home occupied by a single family over many generations, with unplanned additions here and there, and all the available space filled with memory-laden objects and artifacts. The whole thing, taken as a whole, lends itself less to abstract modeling than to thick description."[3] But in its accusation of reductionism this criticism is unfair. Proceduralist theories do not pretend to be articulating an entire way of life. A deontological procedure is not meant to be a substitute for an entire moral culture; it is an articulation of one aspect of that culture. It is not a place to live out one's whole life.

A slightly different version of the criticism I have just outlined may be more plausible. Although proceduralists do not claim that their procedures articulate all there is to say about morality, they do claim that the deontological point of view should take priority over others. Even if we acknowledge that the value of impartiality has a deeply rooted place in our social and political practices, our moral world is filled with all sorts of other intuitions and moral feelings, some of which might conflict with this one. Why, the objection goes, should this aspect of our moral world trump the others? Here we have a real dispute.

In "The Diversity of Goods," Charles Taylor describes an alternative to the deontological point of view which seems to hold at least as large a place in our moral experience. He declares that if the job of moral theory is to articulate how we see the moral world, then a better interpretation would see that much of our moral admiration and condemnation, many of our decisions and judgments, rests on a view of self which includes such elements as what we consider worthwhile goals and contemptible activities. From this point of view, morality involves taking up a perspective quite different from that called for in deontological proceduralism. Far from trying to be impartial when we look at one another's life plans and goals, we adopt a very judgmental atti-

3. Walzer, *Interpretation and Social Criticism*, p. 20. See also Bernard Williams, *Ethics and the Limits of Philosophy* (Cambridge: Harvard University Press, 1985), p. 127; Charles Larmore, *Patterns of Moral Complexity* (Cambridge: Cambridge University Press, 1987), pp. 5–21; Charles Taylor, "The Diversity of Goods," in *Utilitarianism and Beyond*, edited by Amartya Sen and Bernard Williams (Cambridge: Cambridge University Press, 1982), pp. 129–44.

tude, praising and condemning people for how they have chosen to live their lives. This way of looking at the world requires us to draw what Taylor calls "qualitative contrasts," and when employing these contrasts we think that some ways of living are clearly superior to others. The problem, according to Taylor, is that "formalisms manage to reduce these contrasts to irrelevance; ethical reasoning can finesse them through a procedure of determining what is right which takes no account of them, or allows them in merely as subjective preferences, and therefore is not called upon to judge their substantive merits."[4]

In response, I insist that a formal (or procedural) conception of fairness does not reduce qualitative contrasts to irrelevance. Say I believe strongly that the model of the independent, hardworking, and hard-hitting entrepreneur has certain morally unhealthy aspects. Perhaps I believe that our society would be impoverished if Lee Iacocca became recognized as the ideal. We argue about these sorts of things all the time, and it is important that we do argue about them and try to convince each other of the worth of certain ideals. Further, I agree with Taylor that these types of arguments do not fall outside the realm of rational discussion. There might be little chance of agreement in this sphere, but we can say more or less rational things in defense of our values and substantive ideals. These types of arguments do shape and influence the shifting qualitative contrasts that are prevalent in a given community. But there should be a few basic rules to govern these types of arguments, rules that we do agree on. We should not, for example, force our view of worthwhile ends on others. Instead, we should try rationally to persuade others of the folly or perhaps even worthlessness of their ends. The rules of justice are intended to ensure that certain very basic principles are not violated while we make our qualitative contrasts. They provide a framework (a set of background conditions) for, and not an alternative to, other moral perspectives. This is the meaning of "priority" in this context. Proceduralism, precisely because it is formal, creates the space for us to make qualitative contrasts.

And what if our qualitative contrasts conflict with the requirements of justice? This is usually thought to be the point where substantive moral theory (theories of the good) and formal moral theory (theories of the right) have their most intractable clash. I suggest, however, that substantive and formal theories converge and become complementary at precisely this point.

4. Taylor, "The Diversity of Goods," p. 139.

Although formalism is based on an idea of impartiality toward people's conceptions of the good life, it cannot achieve absolute impartiality. Deontological proceduralism is unavoidably biased against life plans that are devoid of any sense of justice or that repudiate all notions of fairness. Although we must treat these views fairly (for example, tolerate the intolerant), proceduralism cannot be said to give such life plans equal space to flourish.

Arguments for why justice should be important to us in the first place cannot be drawn from proceduralism itself. Proceduralism articulates how we go about being just once we have become interested in the question of justice. In answering the question, "Why should I/we be just?" proceduralists must borrow from good-based theories. They must declare that justice is itself a *good*; they must accept that *au fond* justice or injustice is a qualitative contrast. And what formalism can learn from good-based theories is that to defend something as a good is not to throw up one's hands and say that in the final analysis it is just a matter of preference or that the question calls for a decision that itself cannot be justified. Modern rationalism does tend toward the prejudice that goods cannot be defended on rational grounds. Nevertheless, such contemporary theorists as Alasdair MacIntyre, Taylor, Sandel, Robert Bellah, and Walzer have shown at the very least that talk about goods does not fall outside the purview of rational discourse. Which is to say that the desirability of some goods over others can be defended with reasons and is not simply a matter of preference.

Conversely, good-based theories that wish to speak to or of the contemporary context must accept that one of the goods we acknowledge in our society is that there are principles of right which trump the pursuit of other goods. The *meaning* of this good is that it constrains us in certain situations—indeed, that it has priority in the moral (as opposed to foundational) sense. It might very well be that justice is a good among other moral goods, but it is not a good like other goods, for once we have chosen justice over injustice, we have accepted that we should not violate certain basic rules about how we ought to treat each other while pursuing other goods. It is misleading to imply that because it is a good among other goods, justice will necessarily come into radical conflict with these other goods. This argument suggests that we will be faced with hard choices of the type: justice or friendship, justice or the family, justice or community solidarity, and so on. These, however, are not qualitative contrasts because the respective terms are not opposites. Justice is not like other goods, because it is a formal good; it is not a good like friendship, family, and solidarity, because it sets side constraints to these pursuits rather than offer an alternative to them. Thus, justice puts into question not *whether* one can pursue friendship, family, or communal solidarity but *how* one pursues friendship, family, and solidarity. This priority of justice does, of course, mean that certain types of friendship, family, and community are constrained, but do we want to value friendship no matter how it is understood? Do we want to exalt the family regardless of principle? Do we want to pursue community solidarity irrespective of questions of justice? I think not.

A great deal of the plausibility of my account of the relationship between the good and the right depends on how we define justice and particularly on which situations call for the adoption of an impartial moral point of view. Only after these issues are settled can we answer the question that naturally comes to mind in response to what I have just said: Do we want to be just no mater what the cost to our friends, family, and community? The details of this account are developed in the course of this book. The very general point I wish to make here is simply that good-based theories that also claim to be interpretivist must acknowledge that the priority of justice is generally part of the meaning of justice for us even if we recognize the possibility of occasional conflicts. And because of the special meaning we give to justice in the modern world, it is appropriate that the interpretation of that meaning be deontological and formal.

INTERPRETIVE DEONTOLOGY: IS IT REALLY DEONTOLOGY?

The second objection to my characterization of deontology as interpretive comes from a very different direction. It is not that deontology is too formal to be good interpretation, but that interpretation can never lead to any strong deontological claims. Interpretation radically weakens deontological theory. Caught in its own contextualist circle, interpretation is either mere description or its normative content is hopelessly relativistic.

Chandran Kukathas and Philip Pettit suggest that Rawls's later work reflects "despair as to the possibility of anything being accomplished in politics by philosophical inquiry."[5] The implication is that in focusing more on beliefs latent in our political culture and less on discovering an Archimedean point, Rawls has given up the hope that strong rational

---

5. Chandran Kukathas and Philip Pettit, *Rawls: A Theory of Justice and Its Critics* (Stanford: Stanford University Press, 1990), p. 151.

arguments can be found for a conception of justice. Instead, he is content to describe a path to political stability given our present set of beliefs. The upshot, according to Kukathas and Pettit, is that a great deal of the normative and critical force of his early theory is lost. Justice as fairness becomes a theory of accommodation and not a theory of justice at all.

In a similar vein (but from a very different theoretical vantage point), Karl-Otto Apel takes issue with Habermas's rejection of a strong transcendental foundation for ethics. He believes that Habermas's attempt to defend discourse ethics from a position within the horizons of modernity will lead him back into a relativism he claims to want to avoid. According to Apel, Habermas's denial that philosophy has a privileged access to a priori foundational truth only opens the door for the "contextualization, historicity, and contingency" of his reconstructive arguments.[6]

Both these criticisms imply that a move toward interpretation is a retreat. For Kukathas and Pettit, the retreat involves giving up normative ideals in favor of stabilizing the status quo. For Apel, the retreat involves giving up a strong universal foundation to ethics in favor of a less controversial but ultimately relative foundation. I do not think that a move toward interpretation means a retreat in either of these senses. Kukathas and Pettit are wrong to imply that an interest in consensus means that one is interested only in stability. And Apel is wrong (or perhaps unimaginative) to hold to an outdated dichotomy: either we find a way to step outside our context or we are doomed to moral relativism. Interpretation is neither a form of redescription that binds us to the status quo nor an approach incompatible with ethical universalism.

An interpretation of meaning involves getting a better or clearer understanding of what was obscure or confused in the first place. It involves "unpacking" the presuppositions or hidden premises that make sense of a common practice or shared belief. An interpreter searches out background information that might be helpful in giving us a fuller understanding of what is going on when people appeal to, say, concepts of right and wrong, fairness and unfairness, and so on.

When do we know that we have achieved a successful interpretation? The answer is maddeningly circular if we are looking for hard-and-fast

6. Karl-Otto Apel, "*Normative Begründung der kritischen Theorie: Durch Rekurs auf lebensweltliche Sittlichkeit?*" in *Zwischenbetrachtungen im Prozess der Aufklärung*, ed. Honneth et al., pp. 19–21.

methods of verification. A successful interpretation is simply a convincing interpretation. A convincing interpretation is one that really does clarify something for us. It fits with what we already understand about the case. We recognize in it an articulation and rendering of the original expression. And if we do not? Then the interpreter must bring in new arguments, expand the scope of discussion, show the coherence of the interpretation given other facts, arguments, and interpretations the objector might agree with.

When it comes to convincing an interlocutor of the coherence of one's interpretation, there is no definite end point. There is no way of breaking out of the back-and-forth of argumentation by appeal to something outside the argument itself. This is what has been called the hermeneutic circle. Hermeneutics is a closed process in that it does not rely on a higher-order criterion of verification. There are no brute facts, self-evident truths, unquestionable starting points from which we can deduce the validity of our propositions. Nature, God, and metaphysics can no longer stand outside the process of argumentation as ultimate and incontrovertible grounds. There is only the argument itself.

Interpretive deontology begins with intuitions that are latent in our cultural understanding. That Rawls, Scanlon, and Habermas do begin here is indisputable. This starting point is, of course, not peculiar to proceduralism. It characterizes much of modern ethics.[7] To start with our intuitions does not prejudice the question of universalism. We can make a distinction between the fact that they are our intuitions and the claim that they have more than relative validity.

Why start with our intuitions? Ultimately it is matter of common sense. What is the point of moral philosophy if the subject of a moral theory bears no relation to who we are or what we believe? If the point is to criticize who we are and what we believe, we do not need an external starting point to be able to do so. Interpretation is not mere description. Michael Gibbons has put this point elegantly:

> In articulating our deepest evaluations, we are attempting to clarify precisely that part of our self that is inchoate, unclear, repressed and vague. To make that which is inarticulate articulate, to clarify what is unclear, to make the repressed expressed, is to give new shape and

7. Russell Hardin notes that "much of the debate in moral theory turns on assertions of what we intuit to be true or right or good." *Morality within the Limits of Reason* (Chicago: University of Chicago Press, 1988), p. 180.

force to that which was previously undifferentiated and perhaps form-less. It is to bring the inchoate, ambivalent, and unclear into a lan-guage that embodies standards of rationality and criticism.[8]

He refers to an augmentation that interpretation can engender. Our interpretations can give a "new shape and force" to latent beliefs through rational and critical articulation. The circle metaphor, so often associated with hermeneutics, can be misleading. It suggests that the argument, being in some sense closed, goes nowhere or is stuck in the present. On the contrary, interpretation is open-ended, continually ex-panding, changing and sometimes challenging the very context in which it operates.

But even if we admit that starting with the intuitions of everyday actors makes sense and that the interpretations can critically augment these intuitions, we are still left with the problem of the status of such interpretations. Can an interpretivist model offer strong foundations for an ethical theory? Can we even characterize Rawls, Scanlon, and Habermas as employing an interpretivist type of argument?

There is no difficulty in describing Rawls's later work as interpretiv-ist. In fact, already in *A Theory of Justice* a strong interpretivist line of argument can be detected. The multiple lines of argument Rawls em-ploys there are evidence that his argument was never unidimensional, let alone deductive. He indicates that his argument is essentially con-textualist in the closing pages when he says, "It is perfectly proper, then, that the argument for principles of justice should proceed from some consensus. This is the nature of justification."[9] As I outline in more detail in Chapter 5, in *A Theory of Justice*, Rawls makes contin-uous appeals to the "fact" that justice as fairness reflects what we al-ready believe. A large part of the justification for his theory is that we recognize justice as fairness as an articulation of our deepest convic-tions concerning moral deliberation.

This justification introduces another aspect of the question, What makes a good interpretation? I said that a good interpretation is one that is convincing, but convincing to whom? Meaning is for a subject. A good interpretation is one that makes sense of X as it is understood by the subject, that is, from the participant's perspective. A convincing interpretation must in some sense be convincing to this subject. In the

8. Michael T. Gibbons, "Interpretation, Genealogy, and Human Agency," in *Idioms of Inquiry*, edited by Terence Ball (Albany: SUNY Press, 1987), p. 144.

9. John Rawls, *A Theory of Justice* (Cambridge: Harvard University Press, 1971), p. 581.

case of shared moral intuitions, the subject for whom these things are meaningful is society at large. As Michael Walzer puts it; "The interpretation of a moral culture is aimed at all the men and women who participate in that culture—the members of what we might call a community of experience. It is a necessary, though not a sufficient, sign of a successful interpretation that such people be able to recognize themselves in it."[10]

Now this is a tall order. Societies are subjects only in the loosest sense, perhaps only metaphorically. What could count as a community of experience recognizing itself in an interpretation? The need to answer this question is a constitutive element of interpretive deontology. To varying degrees, Rawls, Scanlon, and Habermas each acknowledge that if ordinary social actors do not recognize themselves in the interpretive reconstruction, then the plausibility of that reconstruction is put into question. This recognition factor involves evidence that the subjects for whom fairness and impartiality are meaningful recognize (or would recognize) the interpretations as an articulation of their intuitions.

With the idea of an overlapping consensus, this recognition factor takes on a new centrality in Rawls's later work. A complete defense of justice as fairness requires that we show that a society characterized by pluralism could nevertheless agree to (recognize themselves in) this conception of justice.[11] That citizens could or do recognize themselves in an articulation, however, is only, as Walzer notes, a necessary and not a sufficient condition of successful interpretation. There are many other aspects of a good interpretation, including, as Gibbons notes, standards of rationality and criticism. Rawls, in articulating what he sees to be our deepest values and beliefs, is not simply reporting them. One task he sees for his theory is "to originate and fashion starting points for common understanding by expressing in a new form the convictions found in the historical tradition."[12] In giving shape to our shared tradition, he gives a new shape to it. And in arguing for why this expression is one we *should* accept, he appeals to much more than peaceful coexistence. He appeals to standards of reasonableness and rationality.[13]

10. Walzer, *Interpretation and Social Criticism*, p. 30.
11. John Rawls, *Political Liberalism* (New York: Columbia University Press, 1993), p. 44.
12. John Rawls, "Kantian Constructivism in Moral Theory," *Journal of Philosophy* 77 (1980): 518.
13. Rawls, *Political Liberalism*, p. xx.

What changes in Rawls's later work is not the interpretive nature of his argument so much as the scope of the argument. In *A Theory of Justice*, Rawls tries to justify a moral point of view that is *sub specie aeternitas*. In his later work, he retreats from this claim and explains that justice as fairness represents a point of view that is situated within our cultural horizons. Rawls does not, however, retreat from the strong cognitivist argument that justice as fairness is both reasonable and rational. Now he maintains that justice as fairness is reasonable and rational for us but not necessarily reasonable and rational for everyone. This claim, if true, does not make justice as fairness any less reasonable and rational.[14] What Rawls does not undertake is a comprehensive defense of his standards of reasonable and rational. He does not try to defend the Enlightenment tradition from accusations that the standard of reason we have inherited is itself particularistic. As David Rasmussen has succinctly put it, "Rawls does not have a theory of modernity."[15] Scanlon too falls within this category. Like Rawls, although essentially interpretivist in his attempt to articulate from the inside what it means to be a moral deliberator, Scanlon retains a strong cognitivist perspective. He does not, however, enter the larger debate over why we should think that our standards of criticism and rationality are valid. Habermas does.

Habermas too begins with the ordinary moral intuitions of modern moral agents. His procedure can be understood as "a reconstruction of the everyday intuitions underlying the impartial judgment of moral conflicts of action."[16] He is also, however, concerned to show that the moral point of view to be reconstructed from our intuitions does not simply express the intuitions of a particular culture or a particular epoch but is generally valid.[17] This demonstration involves, in effect, a defense of modernity; it involves arguing that our standards of rationality and criticism can be defended as universals.

Central to this defense is the idea of a reconstructive science. Habermas often discusses reconstructive science within the context of the ongoing debate between his approach and traditional hermeneutics. It is misleading, however, to think of reconstruction as a radical departure from interpretation; it is, rather, a radicalization of interpretation. In-

14. Ibid., pp. xx, 48–54.

15. David M. Rasmussen, "Communicative Action and Philosophy: Reflections on Habermas' *Theorie des kommunikativen Handelns*," *Philosophy and Social Criticism* 9 (Spring 1982): 17.

16. Jürgen Habermas, *Moral Consciousness and Communicative Action*, translated by Christian Lenhardt and Shierry Weber Nicholsen (Cambridge: MIT Press, 1990), p. 116.

17. Ibid., p. 197.

deed, Habermas himself has called reconstructive science a type of "hermeneutical reconstruction."[18] We can get a clearer grasp of the relationship between interpretation and reconstruction if we take a brief look at the dispute between Habermas and Gadamer. The question that animates the debate is not "Critical theory or hermeneutics?" but "How critical could or should a hermeneutical social science be?"[19] The debate centers on the competing powers of tradition and reflection. Gadamer emphasizes the authority of tradition. He is skeptical of what he sees as an Enlightenment tendency in critical theory to exaggerate the power of reason and reflection to make culture and tradition transparent to the eyes of the social scientist. Habermas, for his part, emphasizes the power of human reflection to be critical, that is, to evaluate rationally the background assumptions of a culture.[20]

Where the two perspectives converge is in their united front against positivist social science. In adopting the methods of the natural sciences, positivist social science approaches its object domain from the outside. It takes up the observer's perspective and constructs theories of explanation which have little or nothing to do with how the subjects themselves, that is, social actors, understand what they are up to. Both Gadamer and Habermas insist that a truly elucidating social science must articulate the participants' perspective.[21] In this respect, reconstructive science is in the same camp as hermeneutics, for it reconstructs how social actors interpret and make sense of the world around

18. Jürgen Habermas, "Interpretive Social Sciences vs. Hermeneutics," in *Social Science as Moral Inquiry*, edited by Norma Han et al. (New York: Columbia University Press, 1983), p. 258.

19. Hans-Georg Gadamer, *Wahrheit und Method* (Tübingen: J. C. B. Mohr, 1975), pp. 261–90; and idem, "Rhetoric, Hermeneutics, and the Critique of Ideology" in *The Hermeneutical Reader*, edited by Kurt Mueller-Vollmer (New York: Continuum, 1988), pp. 274–92; Habermas, "Interpretive Social Sciences vs Hermeneutics," pp. 251–67; idem, "On Hermeneutics' Claim to Universality," in *The Hermeneutical Reader*, ed. Mueller-Vollmer, pp. 294–319. See also Jack Mendelson, "The Habermas-Gadamer Debate," *New German Critique* 6 (Fall 1979): pp. 44–73; and Dieter Misgeld, "Critical Theory and Hermeneutics: The Debate between Habermas and Gadamer," in *On Critical Theory*, edited by John O'Neill (New York: Continuum, 1976), pp. 164–84.

20. Habermas's position on this question has shifted over the years. Whereas in his earlier writings he speaks as if reason could make our cultural presuppositions fully transparent to us, in his later work he acknowledges that such a "view from nowhere" is impossible. See Chapter 9.

21. Habermas does not dismiss positivist social science in toto. He insists, instead, that it must see its limitations, particularly in regard to its claim to "objectivity." Habermas sets out to break down the artificial barrier between "scientific" investigations and normative interests. The interpenetration of these two spheres would demonstrate, on the one hand, that scientific investigation is riddled with normative assumptions and, on the other, that normative judgments are the appropriate goals of scientific research.

them. Reconstructions articulate the participants' perspective, but in doing so they go deeper into the generation of meaning than traditional hermeneutics. The reconstructive interpreter attempts "to peer through the surface, as it were, and into the symbolic formation to discover the rules according to which the latter was produced. . . . The object of understanding is no longer the content of symbolic expressions or what specific authors meant by it in specific situations but the intuitive rule consciousness that a competent speaker has of his own language."[22] Habermas calls the understanding gained by this depth interpretation "reconstructive understanding," for it attempts to reconstruct the "know-how" involved in generating meaningful utterances.

According to Habermas, social theory is unavoidably interpretive.[23] He hopes, however, that with the help of reconstructive understandings, social theory can break away from the cultural relativism that has so often characterized hermeneutics. He wants to use reconstruction to gain access to universal structures. "To the extent that rational reconstructions succeed in their search for general conditions of validity, they can claim to identify universals and thus to produce a type of *theoretical* knowledge."[24] The knowledge he seeks goes beyond the content of particular cultures and thus beyond the limits of traditional hermeneutics.

The detailed discussion of the content of Habermas's reconstructive enterprises will have to wait until Chapter 8. What is important at the moment is the intent of this approach. Habermas is involved in developing an argument able to break down a dichotomy that, as Richard Bernstein notes, has "shaped so much of modern thinking."[25] It is the dichotomy between universalism and contextualism, objectivism and relativism. Either we step outside our horizons to find an Archimedean point, an ultimate ground, an undeniable first principle, or we admit that our moral statements, recommendations, and so on simply reflect the biases of our cultural position. This dichotomy is challenged by interpretive deontology. But we must investigate the actual theories to see how successful the challenge is.

22. Jürgen Habermas, *Communication and the Evolution of Society*, translated by Thomas McCarthy (Boston: Beacon Press, 1979), p. 12.

23. Jürgen Habermas, *The Theory of Communicative Action*, translated by Thomas McCarthy, vol. 1 (Boston: Beacon Press, 1981), pp. 102–41, vol. 2 (Boston: Beacon Press, 1987), p. 153. See also idem, "Interpretive Social Sciences vs. Hermeneutics," p. 260; idem, *Communication and the Evolution of Society*, p. 13.

24. Habermas, "Interpretive Social Sciences vs. Hermeneutics," p. 260.

25. Richard Bernstein, *Beyond Objectivism and Relativism* (Philadelphia: University of Pennsylvania Press, 1983), p. 230.

II

CONTRACT OR CONVERSATION?

5 *John Rawls and the Freedom and Equality of Citizens*

Proceduralism, as I describe it in Chapter 2, involves setting out guidelines for deliberation. The central idea is to describe a point of view that deliberators should take up when considering the merits and demerits of a proposal. In his version of proceduralism, John Rawls searches for the appropriate point of view from which to assess questions of justice. What sorts of considerations and constraints are appropriate when we ask ourselves questions such as What constitutes a fair system of cooperation, or How can we achieve a just and stable system of justice given the fact of pluralism?

In *A Theory of Justice* the point of view that holds center stage is the one taken up in the original position. In *Political Liberalism* and other later work, however, Rawls wants to remind us that "it is important to distinguish three points of view: that of the parties in the original position, that of citizens in a well-ordered society, and finally, that of ourselves—of you and me who are elaborating justice as fairness and examining it as a political conception of justice."[1] Parties in the original position are called on to be impartial; citizens in a well-ordered society are called on to be reasonable; and you and I are called on to be reflective about certain "fundamental ideas seen as implicit in the public political culture of a democratic society" (pp. 13, 43).[2] Each of these three points of view serves a different function and represents different sorts of considerations and constraints. It is perhaps worthwhile to take a moment to think about these more carefully.

1. John Rawls, *Political Liberalism* (New York: Columbia University Press, 1993), p. 28.
2. See also John Rawls, "Justice as Fairness: Political not Metaphysical," *Philosophy and Public Affairs* 14 (1985): 231.

Although, as we shall see, there is some ambiguity in the relationship between the original position and citizens using public reason, some version of an initial contract is still an essential part of Rawls's view of justice. In trying to construct a theory of justice we begin with the idea of society as a fair system of social cooperation among free and equal persons. The question we ask ourselves is, How are fair terms of cooperation to be determined? Are they determined by God, by appeal to nature, by reference to an independent moral order, or are they determined by the people who do the cooperating? That is, "Are these terms established by an undertaking among those persons themselves in light of what they regard as their reciprocal advantage?" (p. 22). It is, of course, the last question that is embodied in the original position. The assumption that persons are free and equal means that principles that are to regulate their "fair system" must be agreed to by the persons themselves. As Rawls notes, however, "Their agreement, like any other valid agreement, must be entered into under appropriate conditions" (p. 23). The original position is a description of the appropriate conditions. The guiding concern is that conditions under which agreement is brought about are fair; hence, Rawls calls his conception of justice, "justice as fairness."

The constraints and conditions of the original position are the result of thinking about what sort of point of view free and equal persons would have if all they were were free and equal. As real people, we are much more. Therefore, the parties in the original position will not bear too much resemblance to us in the real world. They are supposed to represent a certain aspect of us—that is, our belief that we are free and equal—and not our whole selves. Because the original position is intended to isolate and zero in on this one feature, it is highly artificial and contrived. This is as it should be, for it is designed to untangle the freedom and equality of persons from the complexities of the real world and to model this idea into a choice situation. One of the most important ways in which this disentangling is achieved is through the "veil of ignorance." The veil ensures that existing contingencies of the social world do not influence or distort the agreement. It does so by blocking out knowledge of existing social conditions as well as knowledge about one's place within the social system and one's particular desires, goals, and interests. The veil of ignorance ensures that the point of view from which the parties evaluate principles of justice is not only free and equal but impartial.[3]

3. Rather than impartiality, Rawls now talks about rational and full autonomy. Both of these are modeled in the original position. *Political Liberalism*, pp. 72–81.

A great deal of *A Theory of Justice* is devoted to describing and justifying the fair conditions of an initial contract. Rawls has since moved on to a second problem, political rather than philosophical, which deals with the question; "How is it possible for there to exist over time a just and stable society of free and equal citizens, who remain profoundly divided by reasonable religious, philosophical, and moral doctrines?" (p. 4). This question moves Rawls from the "ideal type" contract to "real" citizens trying to achieve enough of a consensus to maintain stability. The problem is that real citizens, unlike the ideal typical parties of the original position, have deep differences of opinion on a wide variety of issues. Rawls's solution is to propose an overlapping consensus, which serves to anchor a system of rights and liberties in the political culture and thus to produce the public allegiance necessary to maintain that system over time. The consensus is overlapping because it represents not a homogeneity of moral or philosophical outlooks but rather a convergent agreement on principles of justice which is compatible with a plurality of moral and philosophical outlooks.

Stability and legitimacy require that citizens themselves are convinced that the system is just: "On matters of constitutional essentials and basic justice, the basic structure and its public policies are to be justifiable to all citizens" (p. 224). But the process of justification is complicated by the fact of pluralism. We must find guidelines that will allow these citizens to talk to one another, solve their problems, decide questions of justice, and build an overlapping consensus. Without some constraints on the public discourse, citizens risk talking past each other (or worse, fighting with each other) and thus forgoing the possibility of legitimacy. The guidelines Rawls proposes for this type of deliberation are contained in the idea of public reason. Briefly, these guidelines stipulate that when making "justifications we are to appeal only to presently accepted general beliefs and forms of reasoning found in common sense, and the methods and conclusions of science when these are not controversial" (p. 224). The point of view taken up by citizens is reasonable because, while exercising public reason, they are primarily concerned with generally acceptable reasons rather than furthering their own comprehensive moral or philosophic agendas.

What about you and me? "Here the test is that of reflective equilibrium: how well the view as a whole articulates our more firm considered convictions of political justice, at all levels of generality, after due examination, once all adjustments and revisions that seem compelling have been made" (p. 28). You and I must assess, among other things, the idea of the original position and of citizens resolving their differ-

ence through public reason from the standpoint of how well these arguments reflect things that we already hold to be convincing or true or
right. Thus, our deliberation is essentially interpretive, in the sense
that justification appeals not to a higher-order criterion of verification
but to a contextualist type of argumentation. What I propose to do is to
assess the original position and public reason from precisely this perspective. I do not challenge the appropriateness of this third point of
view. Indeed, some version of "reflective equilibrium" or "interpretive
reconstruction" is the only route to go in our postmetaphysical context.
I do say, however, that the point of view you and I must take up is
somewhat more complicated than is implied by the idea of reflective
equilibrium; that from this standpoint, the original position is not entirely adequate in articulating the freedom and equality of citizens; and
that public reason does not compensate for the inadequacies of the
original position.

From the Point of View of You and Me

Rawls puts forward justice as fairness as a theoretically sophisticated
articulation of the "basic intuitive ideas which we take to be implicit in
the public culture of democratic society."[4] In "Kantian Constructivism," Rawls explains: "What justifies a conception of justice is not its
being true to an order antecedent to and given to us, but its congru-
ence with our deeper understanding of ourselves and our aspirations,
and our realization that, given our history and the traditions embedded
in our public life, it is the most reasonable doctrine for us."[5] The object
is to construct a conception of justice that you and I—defined loosely
as citizens of liberal democratic societies—would find acceptable. Acceptable is understood in a broadly moral sense. (*Political Liberalism*, p.
147). Rawls is not looking for a modus vivendi solution to the problem
of justice. He wants to formulate a conception that is capable of strik-
ing a deeper chord; that we would accept as right and not merely as
workable. That deeper chord is found in an ideal conception of the
person which embodies, or could be recognized as embodying, our
understanding of ourselves and our aspirations.

The characteristics of the person which are of interest to Rawls are

4. John Rawls, "Justice as Fairness," 231. Rawls, *Political Liberalism*, pp. 13, 43.
5. John Rawls, "Kantian Constructivism in Moral Theory," *Journal of Philosophy* 77
(1980): 519.

those relevant to political and social relations and not necessarily to all aspects of our self-understanding. Thus, the intuitive ideas he appeals to are not tied to any one comprehensive moral or philosophical outlook. They are ideas embedded in public political culture and are compatible with a wide variety of deeper beliefs about the human condition, God, the source of moral authority, and so on. Implicit in our public culture is the idea that citizens are free and equal moral persons. Rawls believes that this idea captures how we think of ourselves, not necessarily in general but in regard to the most fundamental questions of political and social relations. This, then, is the starting premise of justice as fairness. You and I must assess how well justice as fairness articulates this widely shared belief. The next step is to flesh out what it means to be a free and equal moral person.

The moral person is characterized by two moral powers: the capacity to understand, to apply, and to act from principles of justice—what Rawls calls an effective sense of justice—and the capacity to form, to revise, and rationally to pursue a conception of the good. (*Political Liberalism*, p. 81). *Free* is understood in three senses. In the first, free citizens think of themselves as "self-authenticating sources of valid claims" (p. 72).[6] In other words, their claims are not weighted according to the social place they occupy, nor is the validity of the claims judged according to an independently stipulated set of duties or obligations. The second sense in which persons are thought to be free is that they are considered to be autonomous vis-à-vis their own conceptions of the good: "As free persons, citizens claim the right to view their persons as independent from and not identified with any particular such conception [ot the good]" (p. 30). That is, they are capable of achieving a certain distance from their own conceptions of the good in order to revise and change them. The third sense in which citizens are thought to be free is that "they are viewed as capable of taking responsibility for their ends" (p. 33). Equality is understood to mean that each person has, and conceives himself as having, an equal right to determine first principles of justice.

In defending this conception of the person, Rawls does not make direct appeal to our institutional history, public culture, or political practices. Rather, his source is Kant's view of autonomy and dignity. Kant is, of course, part of our untellectual history, but it is not clear that we, in fact, all think of ourselves in this Kantian sense. For exam-

6. Also Rawls, "Kantian Constructivism," p. 543.

ple, whereas it is undeniable that the idea of freedom has a large place in our public culture, it is not clear that a negative view of freedom might not have a stronger hold on the contemporary mind. Do we think of freedom as a right to be left alone or do we think of it as a capacity to direct our lives? Rawls does not answer this question; he poses it. More precisely, he poses the question, How do we *want* to understand ourselves?

Articulating deep self-understandings is not a simple matter of accuracy; it is not a matter of unearthing some fact about us. For this reason, the question of how we "in fact" understand ourselves is misleading. Our history and tradition, what could be called our cultural horizons, must limit the range and content of the self-understandings open to us (could we ever understand ourselves in the same way that the ancient Egyptians or African Masai understand themselves?), but within our horizons there are a number of competing, alternative, and overlapping options. For example, in defending a very different view of justice, David Gauthier also maintains that his rational-choice model of contractualism corresponds to a deep self-understanding of the modern agent. Gauthier claims that any critique of rationality as maximization would involve "transcending the conceptual horizons of our society. In questioning what not only social theory but also social practice takes to be the concept of rationality, it questions our *everyday awareness of ourselves as individuals-in-society*."[7]

In contrast, Rawls starts with an understanding of ourselves as free and equal moral persons interested in exercising our moral capacities, including the capacity to act from a sense of justice rather than a sense of benefit. Which is the more accurate articulation? Utility maximization is certainly reflected in some of our social theory, some of our social practices, and sometimes in our self-awareness. But Rawls's conception can also be found reflected in some of our social theory, some of our social practices, and sometimes in our self-awareness. Both of these conceptions are in some sense accurate. The interesting question, then, is not, Am I a utility maximizer or am I a moral person? Sometimes I think of myself as a utility maximizer and sometimes I think of myself as a moral person. The interesting question is, When ought I to think of myself as a utility maximizer and when ought I to think of myself as a moral person?

This is a question that cannot be answered by reflective equilibrium

7. David Gauthier, *Moral Dealing: Contract, Ethics, and Reason* (Ithaca: Cornell University Press, 1990), p. 169, emphasis mine.

alone. It is not possible to bring a conception of justice into reflective equilibrium with what we know to be our self-understanding, as might be done with what we know to be our considered judgments. Self-understanding, because it is multifaceted and multidimensional, is not like a considered judgment. Considered judgments, of the kind "slavery is unjust," are "fixed points." We should attempt to bring our full conception of justice into coherence with these fixed points. But self-understandings are not fixed points; they are often inchoate, unclear, and full of contradictory elements. Therefore, the theorist drawing on our self-understanding must offer an interpretation of that understanding in a way that is not required when we draw on our considered judgments.[8] Considered judgments are explicit convictions that can be appealed to as facts about us. In drawing on self-understanding or deep political culture, Rawls must reach beyond explicit convictions. Therefore, he is best understood as offering a clarification and reading of how we *might* understand ourselves given our history and tradition.[9]

The question, then, is not whether this self-understanding is accurate but rather what sort of a political and public world follows from *this* (optional) conception of ourselves and our public culture. This, in the end, is a very different type of argument from Kants. That we are free and equal moral persons was not an option but a fact for Kant. Further, it was a fact that lay at the bottom of our whole existence, not simply at the bottom of our political existence. Rawls believes that Kantian-type truth claims cannot serve as the basis of a publicly recognized conception of justice, because people could and would dispute them. Nevertheless, like Kant, Rawls believes this conception of the person must be our starting point. But why must it be our starting point if it cannot be shown to be true? The answer is that how we understand ourselves and our relation to each other has a profound

8. The appeal to considered judgments has been called narrow reflective equilibrium, and the appeal to deeper and more general intuitions, wide reflective equilibrium. See, for example, Norman Daniels, "Wide Reflective Equilibrium and Theory Acceptance in Ethics," *Journal of Philosophy* 76 (1979): 256–82. If we understand reflective equilibrium as a method or process undertaken by the theorist, then this terminology implies that we do the same thing in each of these cases, only on a narrower or wider scale. I maintain that in the case of narrow reflective equilibrium we bring considered judgments and proposed principles into coherence with each other, but in the case of wide reflective equilibrium the theorist undertakes a reconstructive interpretation of deep intuitions. This involves something more than bringing intuitions and principles into coherence with each other. Thus, I do not appeal to the term "wide reflective equilibrium."

9. Thus, a task he sets for himself is "to originate and fashion starting points for common understanding by expressing in a *new* form the convictions found in the historical tradition." Rawls, "Kantian Constructivism," p. 518, emphasis mine.

effect on how our political and social world is organized. Many types of political self-understandings are available to us. I have mentioned two, the Kantian and the Hobbesian, but there are many others.[10] Why we should see ourselves in terms of one conception rather than another is a matter not so much of truth as of consequences. Therefore, the task is not to prove that we really are free and equal moral persons, nor is it to prove that we really do think of our selves as free and equal moral persons; rather, it is to sketch a political world that follows *if* we understand ourselves as free and equal moral persons.

This way of looking at the argument is slightly different from the way Rawls sometimes characterizes his undertaking. In *A Theory of Justice*, for example, Rawls claims to be starting from uncontroversial and weak premises. The plausibility and uncontroversial character of the premises are to carry much of the weight in the justification of the theory. I see Rawls's most important contribution to political theory as working in the opposite direction. The humane, fair, and just political world he paints, justifies the starting premise that we should think of ourselves and each other as free and equal moral persons. This statement, of course, will sound horribly circular, but giving up ultimate or metaphysical foundations means giving up a deductive and linear model of justification. Thus, even talk of premises is misleading in the postmetaphysical world. We are painting pictures of ourselves and our world (or how our world could be) and these pictures must be taken as a whole. They must help us, here in the real world, *shape* our self-understanding; they cannot be deduced from that self-understanding.

I see the neo-Kantianism of Rawls, Scanlon and Habermas as offering reasons why we should think of ourselves, particularly with regard to questions of justice, as Kantian moral persons and not as attempting to prove that we are Kantian moral persons. One way to do so—indeed, what all three do—is to shape this potential self-understanding into a choice or deliberative situation. In what follows, I contend that Scanlon and Habermas have more compelling versions of this situation than Rawls. Some of the specific features of both the original position and the public use of reason are introduced not because they represent the freedom and equality of moral persons but because they constrain

10. For example, Robert Bellah et al. appeal to republican and religious self-understandings as implicit in the public life of America, in *Habits of the Heart* (Berkeley: University of California Press, 1985); and George Kateb appeals to an Emmersonian view of the self and individuality in *The Inner Ocean: Individualism and Democratic Culture* (Ithaca: Cornell University Press, 1992), to mention only two. See also Charles Taylor, *Sources of the Self: The Making of the Modern Identity* (Cambridge: Harvard University Press, 1989).

the deliberation in such a way as to produce a definite result. In the case of the original position, deliberation is too constrained to represent freedom adequately, although it does represent equality; specifically, the parties are denied the freedom to interpret their needs and interests. In the case of public reason the constraining feature that worries me is the one that limits debate to uncontroversial truths. This will effectively exclude certain citizens from debate and thus weaken the claim that the procedures of public reason embody the equality of citizenship.

THE PARTIES IN THE ORIGINAL POSITION

The guiding idea in designing the original position is that "the constraints imposed on the parties in the original position, and the manner in which the parties are described, are to represent freedom and equality of moral persons."[11] From this point of view, the representatives are to assess principles of justice and choose a scheme that will allow them to realize and exercise their moral powers.

The constraints imposed on the parties and the description of the parties themselves represent two different types of conditions. The constraints ensure that deliberation is reasonable; the parties, however, are described as rational. Participants are described as rational, that is, interested in securing the conditions for their own success, but their deliberation is "framed" by reasonable constraints, so that the outcome embodies the ideal that society is a cooperative venture among citizens who recognize each other as free and equal. The reasonable represents the intersubjective ideals of reciprocity and mutuality and includes the symmetry of everyone's position vis-à-vis one another, gained through the veil of ignorance.[12]

The veil of ignorance excludes who we are and what we want as a basis of choice. Thus, it eliminates prejudice and self-interest and guarantees impartiality and equality. The veil of ignorance causes a problem, however, if we want a definitive outcome to the procedure. Because the parties have no specific preferences, interests, agendas, or conceptions of the good, they have no grounds from which to assess their choice. The interest they have in realizing and exercising their

11. Rawls, "Kantian Constructivism," p. 520; Rawls, *Political Liberalism*, p. 72.

12. In *Political Liberalism*, Rawls introduces a slightly different terminology to characterize the deliberation of the parties versus the constraints within which these deliberations take place. Deliberation is described as embodying rational autonomy, and the constraints ensure full autonomy (pp. 72–81).

moral powers is not enough. Thus, Rawls endows them with an interest in gaining more rather than less of the primary goods society has to offer (*Political Liberalism*, p. 75). These goods include rights and liberties, opportunities and powers, income and wealth, and the social basis of self-respect. These goods are connected to the idea of the moral person in that they are put forward by Rawls as "social background conditions and general all-purpose means normally needed for developing and exercising the two moral powers and for effectively pursuing a conception of the good" (pp. 75–76).[13]

In making their choice, participants are also aware of and concerned about what happens once the veil of ignorance is lifted and real citizens must live under the principles chosen. One of the things they must take into consideration is whether the principles they choose could be the object of an overlapping consensus under conditions of pluralism. With these motivational assumptions made, the veil of ignorance in place, and the considerations that must be taken into account stipulated, the individual is presented with a problem to solve: Given that you want more rather than less of the primary goods, choose a conception of justice for the regulation of the basic structure which will best secure your interests. The particular point of view created in the original position will lead participants to choose Rawls's now-famous two principles of justice.[14] This is a highly abridged version of a very complicated and at times compelling argument, but my intention in the outline I have given is not explication. I simply want to set out, in very general terms, the main features of Rawls's procedure and assess them as interpretive reconstructions.

As Rawls acknowledges, the original position is a highly artificial choice situation. The parties do not resemble real people, and their deliberation, if you can really call it that, is far removed from how we normally go about deciding important moral questions. Rawls, however, is not trying to represent day-to-day moral/political deliberation. The original position is designed to help us articulate one very particu-

13. See also Rawls, "Kantian Constructivism," pp. 525–26. This represents a revision from *A Theory of Justice*, where Rawls implies that primary goods are things that any rational person would want whatever else she wanted (p. 92).

14. "A. Each person has an equal claim to a fully adequate scheme of equal basic rights and liberties, which scheme is compatible with the same scheme for all; and in this scheme the equal political liberties, and only those liberties, are to be guaranteed their fair value. b. Social and economic inequalities are to satisfy two conditions: first, they are to be attached to positions and offices open to all under conditions of fair equality of opportunity; and second, they are to be to the greatest benefit of the least advantaged of society." Rawls, *Political Liberalism*, p. 6.

lar, if also fundamental, moral/political dilemma: Upon what foundation can we lay the claim that the basic structure of our society is just if we no longer share an idea of ultimate foundations? That Rawls thinks about this dilemma in constructivist terms ties him to the original position, or something like it. Citizens cannot discover first principles directly; they can only construct them by means of a device that represents the free and equal agreement of ideal deliberators. Having said that, one must also add that in *Political Liberalism* Rawls appears to be more open to the idea that the device might be something like the original position rather than the original position itself (p. 226).

I want to suggest that the device of representation should indeed be something like the original position rather than the original position itself. More specifically, in the chapters that follow, I maintain that the ideal speech situation offers a more compelling representation of the freedom and equality of moral persons. I agree with Rawls that the justification of first principles is found in the agreement of free and equal moral agents under fair conditions. Furthermore, I agree with Rawls that this agreement must first be conceived as taking place under circumstances quite different from those normally found in our everyday search for agreements. To put this in a more formal way, conceptualizing what it would mean to justify first principles of justice involves a counterfactual, idealized, and hypothetical model of deliberation. Where I part company with Rawls, and where I think that Scanlon and Habermas draw better pictures of the foundational deliberation, is on the question of freedom. The original position does not adequately represent the freedom of citizens, because the parties are not free to choose in any real sense. Indeed, as some critics have suggested, there is no real choice in the original position. Bernard Manin points out that

> no real deliberation or even choice takes place in the original position. The result is already contained in the premises and is only separated from them, one might say, by the time needed for calculation. Reflection and the calculations necessary for obtaining the solution teach the individual nothing new; in particular nothing new about his own preferences. There is, therefore no *deliberation*, in the full sense of the term, to be found here. The process of forming a decision is reduced to calculation.[15]

15. Bernard Manin, "On Legitimacy and Political Deliberation," *Political Theory* 15 (August 1987): 349.

Deliberation is a process of will formation. It is a process we enter into when the answer to the question, What are fair terms of cooperation? is not self-evident. The original position is designed precisely so that the answer *is* self-evident, or at least deductively clear. Preferences, ideals, goals, and interests, the very things that moral choices are about, are not the subject of deliberation. That they are not is particularly evident in regard to primary goods. Participants are not asked to choose or evaluate the ends they are trying to secure. These ends are "given" to them. The prior stipulation of primary goods undermines Rawls's claims to have designed a choice situation in which the parties are autonomous.

One of the ways Rawls describes the freedom of the parties is through the idea of pure procedural justice, which is contrasted to perfect procedural justice. In perfect procedural justice there is "an independent and already given criterion of what is just (or fair), and the procedure can be designed to insure an outcome satisfying that criterion" (*Political Liberalism*, p. 72). A deliberative procedure modeled along these lines would not represent our freedom and autonomy, because the participants are bound by a pregiven conception of justice. Participants are not free to choose whatever principles they think are the most appropriate. Furthermore, because the criterion of justness is given in advance, parties cannot be described as truly self-governing or self-legislating. Rule utilitarianism, which designs rules so that they promote a pregiven conception of justice (say, the greatest happiness for the greatest number) is an example of perfect procedural justice.

In contrast to perfect procedural justice, Rawls defends pure procedural justice as a procedure that gives full scope to autonomy and freedom. In this case "the parties do not view themselves as required to apply, or as bound by, any antecedently given principles of justice. . . . it is up to them to specify the fair terms of social cooperation in light of what they each regard as their advantage, or good. . . . these terms are not laid down by God's law, nor are they recognized as fair by reference to a prior and independent order of values known by rational intuition" (p. 73). In pure procedural justice the parties are the final court of appeal in questions of justice: "Citizens themselves (via their representatives) are to specify the fair terms of their cooperation" (p. 72).

Rawls claims that the original position is an example of pure procedural justice. In the original position, however, parties are not given the opportunity to evaluate principles of justice in "light of what they each regard as their advantage, or good." By introducing a substantive list of goods, Rawls denies participants the freedom to interpret and understand their needs and interests in their own way. Their deliberation is bound by a prior and independent order of values. One of the things Rawls is trying to capture with the idea of pure procedural justice is a self-understanding rooted in self-direction. The original position is supposed to represent our capacity to understand, evaluate, and choose the principles we will abide by. But understanding, evaluating, and choosing are not matters of calculation, even calculation framed by reasonable constraints. The original position does represent symmetry and equality, but at the expense of freedom. An initial situation representing the freedom of pure procedural justice would have to leave the question of goods up to the deliberative process itself. The problem to be solved in the initial situation is the problem of goods. This is what it ought to be about.

In order to represent the autonomy of citizens, the procedure must be expanded to include deliberation about the premises on which choices are made. One response is to say that Rawls has in fact acknowledged as much and that the real justification of primary goods, and indeed the original position, comes when citizens using public reason evaluate the arguments and find them compelling. This idea of public reason would then make citizens the final court of appeal in questions of justice. The original position would be one possible device citizens might use in argumentation. Thus the original position would become a *reason* one could give to support an understanding of basic principles.

But the relationship between the original position and public reason is far from clear in Rawls's writings. There appear to be two versions of this relationship. The first, what I call the official version, is already contained in *A Theory of Justice*. It appeals to a "two-stage" approach to justice.[16] In the first stage one works out principles of fair cooperation through the device of the original position, and in the second stage one looks at pragmatic/political questions about how those principles could become the object of an overlapping consensus. On this view, justification is separate from and prior to issues of implementation and stability. The official version, by retaining a relatively strong role for the original position (or something like it) would avoid the accusation that justice has now become synonymous with stability.

16. Rawls still talks about two stages in *Political Liberalism*, p. 133.

The second version, what I call the political version, collapses the two stages together, with the second stage taking on a much more important role in justification. In this version public reason and not the original position takes on the burden of justifying principles of justice. An overlapping consensus brought about by an open debate limited by public reason not only stabilizes a conception of justice but also serves as the final grounds of its validity.

Both these versions can be found in *Political Liberalism*. For example, as evidence to support the official version, Rawls says that "the parties in the original position, in adopting principles of justice for the basic structure, must also adopt guidelines and criteria of public reason for applying those norms" (p. 225). The implication here is that the original position justifies public reason (and not the other way around) and that questions to be addressed by public reason are questions of application, not fundamental questions of principles. Rawls goes on to say, however, that

> accepting the idea of public reason and its principles of legitimacy emphatically does not mean, then, accepting a particular liberal conception of justice down to the last details of the principles defining its content. We may differ about these principles and still agree in accepting a conception's more general features. We agree that citizens share in political power as free and equal, and that as reasonable and rational they have a duty of civility to appeal to public reason, yet we differ as to which principles are the most reasonable basis of public justification. The view I have called "justice as fairness" is but one example of a liberal political conception; its specific content is not definitive of such a view. (p. 226)

This passage would seem to support the political version. Yet the political version is not without difficulties. Principles of justice cannot be defended solely on the grounds that they are supported by an overlapping consensus. Presumably there are conceptions of justice (based on racial hierarchies, for example) which could be made workable by an actual consensus but which we nevertheless would find unjust. So, although arguments about the empirical likelihood that a conception of justice can serve as a basis for consensus are a necessary condition for the plausibility of a theory, they are not by themselves sufficient to recommend such a theory. Consensus can ensure stability, but unless we are willing to say that stability is synonymous with justice—and I do not think we, or Rawls, are—then factual consensus by itself cannot carry normative weight.

To confer normative force on a consensus one must either stipulate the special conditions under which a morally valid consensus is formed or offer an independent argument for why the object of the consensus has some value. Habermas has pursued the first strategy, while Rawls has pursued the second. Now, however, it appears as if he is turning toward the first strategy. It is not any consensus that justifies a system of justice, but an overlapping consensus brought about through public reason. Thus, if the political version is to have any plausibility, the conditions of public reason must be evaluated from the point of view of creating a fair and equal deliberative process that can justify principles. As a procedure of justification, however, the idea of public reason contains the same problem as the original position. In both cases, Rawls is too concerned with creating conditions that will lead to a determinate outcome than with creating conditions that represent the freedom and equality of citizens.

CITIZENS USING PUBLIC REASON

Public reason sets limits on what may be appealed to in public debate in a democratic society. "We are to appeal," Rawls says, "only to presently accepted general beliefs and forms of reasoning found in common sense, and the methods and conclusions of science when these are not controversial." That is, in discussing "constitutional essentials and matters of basic justice we are not to appeal to comprehensive religious and philosophical doctrines—to what we as individuals or members of associations see as the whole truth." Instead, we must appeal to "plain truths now widely accepted, or available, to citizens generally" (*Political Liberalism*, pp. 224–25). The reason for these limits is that Rawls believes that if we are allowed to appeal to comprehensive moral views, then agreement is unlikely. Furthermore, it is important that state action be able to gain the agreement of citizens. Therefore, the reasons for state action should not appeal to ideas of moral truth which are not widely shared. These are very similar to arguments put forward by such liberal theorists as Bruce Ackerman and Charles Larmore in defense of neutral dialogue.[17] Rather than neutrality, however, Rawls appeals to the idea of the political. In public debate we should

17. Bruce Ackerman, "Why Dialogue?" *Journal of Philosophy* 86 (January 1989): 5–22; Charles Larmore, *Patterns of Moral Complexity* (Cambridge: Cambridge University Press, 1987); Rawls, *Political Liberalism*, pp. 191–95.

appeal to political conceptions that are freestanding and not dependent on comprehensive moral vision. Although these limits do appear to solve the problem of agreement under conditions of pluralism, the question I want to ask is, Are they fair? I do not think they are.

It is not always possible to retreat to accepted truths or political rather than comprehensive views in defense of one's position. I believe there are a great many more individuals than Rawls imagines who cannot substitute political grounds for morally charged ones. Samuel Scheffer, for example, notes that "the principle that ordinary citizens, when engaged in political advocacy and even when voting, must appeal only to what they regard as a political conception of justice and never to their own comprehensive moral doctrines is an extraordinarily strong one."[18] It is extraordinarily strong because it would require a great many people to exchange their controversial, morally charged reasons for noncontroversial arguments. It is not always possible to do so even when noncontroversial reasons for one's position are available. It is often the case that one cannot separate the commitment to a moral truth from the obligation to press that moral truth in the public sphere. For example, a great many people see their religious commitments as part of their public commitments; they see it as their *duty*, if not their right, to defend these positions publicly and to try to persuade others of their compelling nature. Kent Greenawalt, says that it is precisely in regard to questions that involve highly contested moral visions that religious arguments have a public role to play. He cautions liberal theorists that for many religiously minded citizens it is simply impossible to retreat to neutral ground or to employ political rather than religious arguments. Such a demand effectively excludes these individuals from participation within the public.[19] Scheffer also points out that it is not clear that these sorts of appeals are inappropriate. He cites a number of examples, including Quaker opposition to the war in Vietnam, the role of churches in the political life of the African American community,

18. Samuel Scheffer, "The Appeal of Political Liberalism," *Ethics* 105 (October 1994): 16. Thomas McCarthy, in the same issue, makes the same point, see "Kantian Constructivism and Reconstructivism: Rawls and Habermas in Dialogue," p. 51. See also Seyla Benhabib, "Deliberative Rationality and Models of Democratic Legitimacy," *Constellations* 1 (April 1994): 36.

19. Greenawalt cites several examples that illustrate the religious person's attitude toward politics: "Max Stackhouse speaks of faith and theology as inevitably 'public and political'; Jürgen Moltmann claims that a theology may be naive and politically unaware but cannot be apolitical; Lynn Buzzard urges that 'politics, art, science and philosophy are all part of the arena of activity by the believer community'; and Basil Mitchell says it is scarcely possible for anyone who takes religion seriously to acquiesce in its being treated as a private matter.'" Kent Greenawalt, *Religious Convictions and Political Choice* (Oxford: Oxford University Press, 1988), p. 35.

and religiously inspired activism against homelessness and poverty, which would appear to be precluded by the limits of public reason.[20] In addition to religiously inspired advocacy many others see their political commitments as integrally tied to highly controversial, if secular, comprehensive views. Would Aristotelians and communists have to forgo appeals to truths about human ends or the form of reasoning contained in historical materialism?

But perhaps this is the price we have to pay if we are to get along at all within a pluralistic society. If we were not willing to retreat to common ground, the argument continues, nothing would ever get decided; or worse, our disputes would escalate into open conflict. Perhaps limits of public reason are the price we pay for social peace, but if so, the cost is high. It is not simply that some, perhaps many, might be forced to exclude the things they care most about when they enter the public sphere; it is also that these preestablished limits on what may be introduced cut off many avenues of discourse and thus preempt social and political change. Defining the limits in this way ties public reason to the status quo more firmly than Rawls, I think, would want. This understanding of public reason blunts the critical potential of public discourse.

The limits of public reason are designed so that citizens may find common ground under conditions of pluralism. Pluralism is characterized by disputes and differences of opinion on a plethora of deep issues. It is important to remember, however, that the fact of pluralism is not a fact about each particular dispute or difference of opinion but a fact about our general situation. There will always be things that people disagree about; they will not always be the same things. What is disputed and contested today may not be disputed and contested tomorrow, and what is uncontroversial today may tomorrow give rise to bitter dispute. Excluding from debate what is today deeply contested assumes a fixity and permanence to the constellation of disputes and differences of opinion which just happens to prevail today. To limit the discursive agenda to "plain truths now widely accepted" is to preempt deep social and political criticism of the plain truths now widely accepted. As Seyla Benhabib reminds us, it is important to identify those power structures "which sanctify the speech of some over the speech of others as being the language of the public."[21] Public reason

20. Scheffer, "The Appeal of Political Liberalism," p. 17.
21. Seyla Benhabib, "Liberal Dialogue versus a Critical Theory of Discursive Legitimation," in *Liberalism and the Moral Life*, edited by Nancy L. Rosenblum (Cambridge: Harvard University Press, 1989), p. 156. See also E. E. Schattashneider, *The Semi-Sovereign State* (New

sanctifies the speech of political liberalism as the language of the public.

Equality and freedom of citizenship imply that the agenda, as well as what may and may not be said, cannot be set in advance. Citizens themselves must work out what is or is not a public issue. Citizens themselves must argue about which arguments are convincing and which are not. This is the model of public debate found in Scanlon's and Habermas's work. The ideal, like the ideal in public reason, is to seek common ground, but as Thomas McCarthy maintains, this common ground is not defined by an already existing consensus; rather, it is constructed in the process of public debate itself:

> *It* [the Habermasian model] *leaves the task of finding common ground to political participants themselves.* I should say, of finding, creating, expanding, contracting, shifting, challenging, and deconstructing common ground; for to suppose that the stock of shared political ideas and convictions is in some way given, there to be found and worked up, or that it somehow could be fixed by the theorist, is to hypostatize or freeze ongoing processes of public political communication whose outcomes cannot be settled in advance by political theory.[22]

It is not highly contested notions of moral truth which must be excluded from the public sphere but nondiscursive forms of persuasion such as force, threats, bribes, and deception. If there are no limits on what may be said, can we ever achieve common ground in our conversations? Does opening up public debate among citizens introduce the same problems as opening up the original position? In the previous section I said that an ideal deliberative procedure representing the freedom and equality of citizens should include the freedom to choose and agree on primary goods. Such a deliberative process would involve lifting the veil of ignorance, however. In lifting the veil of ignorance, the possibility of deducing the outcome becomes more remote. Rawls says, "The restrictions on particular information in the original position are, then, of fundamental importance. Without them we would not be able to work out any definite theory of justice at all. We would have to be content with a vague formula stating that justice is what would be agreed to without being able to say much, if anything, about the sub-

---

York, 1960), p. 71, where he talks about the "mobilization of bias" through which some issues are organized into politics and some are organized out.

22. McCarthy, "Kantian Constructivism and Reconstructivism," p. 61.

stance of the agreement itself."[23] Lifting the veil of ignorance will complicate the procedure. If moral validity hangs on agreement, how can we hope to gain agreement when we are aware of all the things that generate our disagreements in the real world? How do we retain the idea of impartiality while allowing people to know who they are and what they want? For Rawls is right to say that we want to eliminate prejudice and self-interest as the motor of moral deliberation. Something very similar can be said about public reason. If democratic legitimacy hangs on consensus about fundamental principles, how can we hope to gain consensus if we are allowed to argue from our particular conceptions of truth and good?

These are difficult problems. They are not, however, insoluble. Scanlon and Habermas describe deliberation procedures, both in the ideal and in the public sphere, in which participants must work out for themselves the appropriate premises and common ground on which to base their choices. They make a strong case to the effect that the cost of forgoing a determinate solution to the problem of justice is amply compensated by a better understanding of how we view or should be viewing questions of justice.

23. Rawls, *Theory of Justice*, p. 140.

6 *Thomas Scanlon and the Desire for Reasonable Agreement*

In the last chapter I maintained that a procedural formulation of the freedom and equality of moral agents must include deliberation about the goods they wish to see promoted within society. Participants must be free to interpret their needs and interests in their own way. Rawls excludes this aspect of moral deliberation from the original position, for two main reasons. First, including deliberation about needs and interests would involve lifting the veil of ignorance and would thus introduce bias into deliberation and threaten impartiality. Second, including a deliberation about goods would hopelessly complicate the choice situation such that no determinate solution could be achieved.

Both of these reasons are open to question. First, it is true that many of our desires, wants, and interests conflict with the requirements of morality and are anything but impartial. It is worth considering, however, whether impartiality can be achieved within a procedural model that represents a full picture of moral deliberation. If it can, then such a procedure would more accurately represent the meanings we attach to competent moral judgments.

Second, although a procedural theory that offers a definite result appears, at first sight, to be superior to one that does not, we must ask whether or not building in conditions that ensure a determinate solution does not violate the very idea of pure procedural justice. Pure procedural justice assumes that "what is just is defined by the outcome of the procedure itself. . . . [P]rinciples of justice themselves are to be constructed by a process of deliberation, a process visualized as being carried out by the parties in the original position."[1] This idea demands that we leave it up to the participants to decide for themselves what the outcome will be. Introducing conditions that in effect give them no choice in the matter undermines the ideal of pure procedural justice.

INTUITION AND THE DESIRE FOR REASONABLE AGREEMENT

Thomas Scanlon directly confronts these issues in his reformulation of the Rawlsian contract. The veil of ignorance is lifted and yet impartiality is maintained; a determinate solution is exchanged for a more compelling vision of the contract situation. Although Scanlon has yet to develop his theory fully, his contribution to the debate in ethics is important. He makes certain suggestions that can serve as correctives to the view of moral deliberation we have thus far encountered. And further, his theoretical observations can serve as a bridge between liberal theory and critical theory as it is understood by Habermas.[2]

The problem Scanlon sets out to solve in the essay "Contractualism and Utilitarianism" is one of foundations.[3] He begins by pointing out that if Kantian contractualism is to be a plausible alternative to philosophical utilitarianism, it must be able to give a deep philosophic account of itself. The intuitively compelling force of the outcomes of contract theory are not enough to sustain a strong normative claim to validity. That the outcomes seem "right" to us, given other things that we believe, is a justification that must ultimately rest on the coherence of outcomes with these other beliefs. And, as Scanlon points out, "however internally coherent our moral beliefs may be rendered, the nagging doubt may remain that there is nothing to them at all" (p. 117). The theorist must go behind the contract, so to speak, and consider its

1. John Rawls, "Kantian Constructivism in Moral Theory," *Journal of Philosophy* 77 (1980): 523.

2. Kenneth Baynes, in *The Normative Grounds of Social Criticism: Kant, Rawls, and Habermas* (Albany: SUNY Press, 1992), has also noted the similarities and connections between Habermas's work and Scanlon's contractualism (pp. 115–18). Of particular interest is his discussion of "generalizable interests" and Scanlon's theory of interpersonal comparison of individual preferences (pp. 147–48).

3. Thomas Scanlon, "Contractualism and Utilitarianism," in *Utilitarianism and Beyond*, edited by Amartya Sen and Bernard Williams (Cambridge: Cambridge University Press, 1982), pp. 103–28, hereinafter cited in the text. The position is restated with very little added in Scanlon's later essay "A Contractual Alternative," in *New Directions in Ethics*, edited by Joseph De Marco and Richard M. Fox (New York: Routledge and Kegan Paul, 1986), pp. 42–57.

presuppositions. If utilitarianism is compelling at all, it is not because the outcomes strike us as intuitively right; in fact, the opposite is quite often the case. Its strength rests instead on what appears to be a very plausible philosophical thesis, namely, that "the only fundamental moral facts are facts about individual well-being" (p. 108). According to Scanlon, utilitarianism must be challenged at this fundamental level.

Thus Scanlon begins with our intuitions about outcomes and asks, Can we make sense of them? This is, as he points out, more than a mere coherence theory. Like Rawls, Scanlon goes beyond simply bringing our first-order considered judgments into narrow reflective equilibrium with a conception of justice. He sets out to reconstruct the deeper premises of these considered judgments. Also like Rawls, he rejects a metaphysical account of the presuppositions of modern moral thinking. Instead, he finds the deep foundation of contractualism in a widely shared desire to be justified, the intuitive condition of which is reasonable agreement.

By contractualism, Scanlon does not mean that morality can be traced to some original undertaking or that it is founded on a promise between prudential actors. Morality is based on reasonable agreement, which is renewed, reformed, and reassessed every time we deliberate about moral choices. Scanlon uses the idea of a contract in opposition to philosophical utilitarianism; the general point is that "what is fundamental to morality is the desire for reasonable agreement, not the pursuit of mutual advantage" (p. 115). In addition to utilitarianism, this view also challenges Hobbesian or rational-choice contractarianism. In contrast to these two accounts of morality, Scanlon says that it is not the pursuit of collective or individual utility which motivates modern moral agents but the pursuit of intersubjective justification. The desire for reasonable agreement springs from a desire to be justified. A justified moral position is one that could not be rejected as the object of a reasonable agreement. As I see it, Scanlon's theory is not really a contract theory at all but a dialogue theory, for it places justification rather than promising at the center of morality. For the sake of clarity, however, I will use Scanlon's own terminology in discussing his theory.

THE "CONTRACT"

Scanlon begins his challenge with a contractualist account of moral wrongness: "An act is wrong if its performance under the circumstances would be disallowed by any system of rules for the general regulation of behavior which no one could reasonably reject as a basis for informed, unforced agreement" (p. 110). Although morality is rooted in agreement, the telling feature of whether something is wrong is whether no one could reasonably *reject* the agreement. This twist, however, should not obscure the fact that informed, unforced agreement, in a positive sense, is still the standard against which principles are judged. Scanlon introduces rejection not to weaken the criterion of validity but to strengthen it. There might be principles to which there are reasonable objections but which individuals nevertheless accept as the basis of agreement. For example, it is not unreasonable for particularly self-sacrificing people to agree to take on unequal burdens even when there might be an alternative set of principles under which the burdens are more equally shared. It would also not be unreasonable to object to such a set of principles, however. Thus, the criterion of rejection would disallow, in this case, a set of principles that place an uneven burden on participants. If reasonable agreement and not reasonable rejection were the standard, a set of principles that conferred an unequal burden could be excluded only if we assumed that everybody is self-interested and that no one could possibly agree to those principles. Scanlon does not want to make any such assumption about our makeup. All one must assume is that it is not unreasonable to be self-interested in this situation—not that everyone in fact is self-interested. In any event, despite the initial definition of the contract, Scanlon uses *both* measures (i.e., rejection and acceptance) throughout the article.

A valid agreement does not exist if it rests on superstition or false belief; if it was brought about by coercion or unfair bargaining tactics; or if it could be reasonably rejected by any party to the contract. This last proviso in effect confers a veto power on any and all participants in the contract. Thus, much rests on the meaning of *reasonable*. "The intended force of the qualification 'reasonable'. . . is to exclude rejections that would be *unreasonable* given the aim of finding principles which could be the basis of informed, unforced general agreement" (p. 111).

Although everyone has a veto power, this power is not arbitrary, nor can it be wielded in a clearly selfish or purely self-promoting way. It would be unreasonable, for example, *given* the end of reaching an agreement, to reject principles simply because they did not maximize one's own chances or promote one's own ends. Rejection on these grounds alone is unreasonable because the failure of principles to promote my good is not a reason that is likely to gain general acceptance.

Thus, that principles involve an unfair burden on me is a good reason for rejection, but that they do not make me better off than others is not. Reasonableness, then, involves assessing one's principles and the grounds for those principles from a particular point of view: Could they be the object of an informed, unforced agreement?

After outlining a criterion of moral wrongness, Scanlon takes up the question of motivation. Why should we be interested in finding principles that could be the basis of informed, unforced general agreement? Scanlon postulates a desire, possessed by all or most of us, to justify our actions: "The desire to be able to justify one's actions (and institutions) on grounds one takes to be acceptable is quite strong in most people. People are willing to go to great lengths, involving quite heavy sacrifices, in order to avoid admitting the unjustifiability of their actions and institutions" (p. 117). Scanlon claims that for most people the belief that something is right rests on the assumption that it is justifiable. Most people desire to be in the right; therefore they are motivated to justify their beliefs in light of possible objections. Thus, we see that justification is an essentially dialogical and intersubjective undertaking. The grounds one takes to be acceptable are grounds that no one *else* could reasonably reject. Scanlon hopes that this "fact" about us can resolve the question of motivation with which all moral theories must deal. It is one thing to give an account of moral truth; it is another to explain why we should be interested in moral truth, why we should *want* to be in the right. Philosophical utilitarianism has a strong leg to stand on in this regard because it seems absurd to wonder why I should be interested in my own well-being. Scanlon wants to say that contractualism can offer an equally strong account of its motivational premises.

On this alternative account we look at our actions from the point of view of possible agreement because we have a desire to be justified, that is, to have good reasons for our actions. And good reasons are reasons that no one could reasonably reject as the basis for agreement. It is important to note that other people's reasonable objections are not an external constraint on action. Other people's reasonable objections are an internal constraint, for in the end, to be justified in the eyes of the other is to be justified in one's own eyes.

The desire to be justified leads to the following sort of deliberation: If I believe that *x* is right, but many people disagree with me and tell me that I am mistaken, I must ask myself if their objections are reasonable. I must reflect on their grounds, evaluate their objections, try to see the situation from their point of view, and so on. But what am I doing here? I am trying to convince *myself* that the premise of my action is right because no one could reasonably reject it. If I see that some people could reasonably reject it, then the principle or premise of my action is devalued in my eyes. Moral deliberation is not a process of compromise or bargaining, where I give up a little here and modify a little there in order to reach an acceptable solution that might not be optimal for me but which I am willing to accept for the sake of mutual coexistence. It is a process whereby I come to question principles I hold but which cannot be rationally justified.

Scanlon locates the internal spring of morality in a desire to justify ourselves within the framework of general agreement. This desire leads us to view our moral convictions from different perspectives in order to assess their justifiability. We cultivate this desire "by learning what justifications others are in fact willing to accept, by finding which ones you yourself find acceptable as you confront them from a variety of perspectives, and by appraising your own and others' acceptance or rejection of these justifications in the light of greater experience" (p. 117). Rawls brackets out our moral convictions from the impartial deliberation process. Scanlon understands our moral convictions to be constituted through an impartial deliberation in which we view them in the context of what others could say about them.

When are we warranted in assuming that nobody could reject our principles as unfair? Scanlon has no hard-and-fast answer to this question. There are several different sorts of considerations we can undertake to see how acceptable, or nonrejectable, our principles are. These different sorts of considerations represent the various ways in which we try to gain an impartial perspective on the validity of moral principles. Impartiality is associated not with one particular perspective but with a range of general guidelines we employ as rough tests.

One possibility is to put oneself in the other's position and see what one's principle would look like from there. If I were in her shoes and sincerely interested in finding the basis for agreement, could I still find grounds to reject the principle? Another way might be to ask oneself, would I have reason to accept the principle no matter who I was? Or would it be reasonable to accept the principle if I were ignorant of the position I occupied in society? These types of considerations, plus the assumption that principles others could reasonably judge as unfair cannot be the basis of agreement, add up to the condition of impartiality. The end of reaching an agreement motivates us to view our principles impartially—that is, as the object of possible agreement.

I find this notion of impartiality compelling. For one thing, it allows the participant different grounds and paths to impartiality. Contemplating whether one would agree to a principle if one did not know one's place in society is simply one device among many "for considering more accurately the question of what *everyone* could reasonably agree to or what no one could reasonably reject" (p. 122). A modified version of Rawls's argument from the original position provides one ground or reason one might give oneself (or another) as a basis for a set of principles, but it is neither the only potentially good ground nor necessarily the best the ground. Argument from the original position becomes a potential subject of deliberation but does not itself define deliberation. Thus, Scanlon expands the scope of the procedure to include considerations that were, in Rawls's view, either left up to the theorist or left up to us once we emerged from the original position.

THE RATIONAL AND THE REASONABLE

What Scanlon does is to make the reasonable part of the description of the parties as opposed to part of the constraints imposed upon the parties. The reasonable incorporates mutuality and reciprocity. I understand Scanlon to be saying that our mutual life together implicates us in reciprocal accountability. The reasonable person is not simply the person who has good reasons for her actions; it is also the person who is willing to listen to objections, who is open to suggestions, who will reevaluate a position in light of new evidence, and so on. But above all, the reasonable person understands that the mutuality of common life creates an obligation to explain herself to others.

Unlike rational-choice contractarianism, in which reasoning out what one ought to do involves finding the best way to maximize one's utility, here reasoning out what one ought to do involves putting one's reasons to a publicity test. In Scanlon's model, actors find themselves situated within a collective life that creates an obligation to justify their actions in terms others could accept or not reject. Justifying our actions to others is Scanlon's interpretation of the Kantian idea that as moral deliberators we are, in a sense, legislators in a "Kingdom of Ends." Recognizing others as free and equal moral persons, or ends in themselves, leads to the conclusion that they deserve respect. Respect is conferred by taking other people's objections, positions, and interests into account when formulating one's own principles. To acknowledge this type of inherent accountability, built into the meaning of being reasonable, is to treat others not simply as means but as ends in themselves.

The desire to be justified has its source in two sorts of considerations: instrumental and moral. The instrumental consideration is that living in a world where others thought your moral positions indefensible would isolate you from the benefits of mutual coexistence. The moral consideration is that defending your moral positions in terms that others could not reject embodies the ideal that as free and equal moral persons we are all deserving of respect. As a participant in Scanlon's contract, I deliberate over principles simultaneously from the position of *my* interests and from the position of what others could say about my interests from the point of view of *their* interests. Individuals are not placed under a veil of ignorance. The contract presupposes only one very general interest, an interest in being justified, thus allowing participants the freedom to formulate their more particular interests and conceptions of the good reasonably through the process of moral deliberation itself. No doubt Scanlon would agree with Rawls that one of the meanings we attach to freedom is that we are "self-originating sources of valid claims." Where he would, and indeed does, disagree is with Rawls's contention that this idea is best represented in the initial situation "by not requiring the parties to justify the claims they wish to make."[4] In having to justify our claims to others with reasons, we come to see whether they are good claims backed by good reasons. In this way we develop our interests, self-identities, and conceptions of the good concurrently with our notions of right.

In Scanlon's understanding of the moral deliberation involved in adopting principles, successful deliberation results in a situation where we, as full persons, come to believe that a principle is right or wrong. From Rawls's perspective this is also supposed to be the outcome, but Rawls understands the path to moral conviction in a very different way. He makes a much sharper distinction between the perspective taken up in the "contract" situation and the perspective of citizens who, as full persons, must adopt principles of justice."[5] Scanlon offers a deeper understanding of moral reasoning under modern conditions by collapsing these two points of view into one conception of deliberation. In bringing these two under one conceptual roof, he has achieved

4. Rawls, "Kantian Constructivism," p. 548.
5. John Rawls, *Political Liberalism* (New York: Columbia University Press, 1993), p. 28; Rawls, "Kantian Constructivism," p. 533.

a better representation of the meanings we attach to competent moral judgments. He has articulated in a procedural and formal way what is involved in subjecting our principles to the test of reasonableness. Competent moral judgments are judgments that pass a publicity test. Unlike the publicity test of public reason, however, this test does not tie justification to preestablished limits on what can count as a good reason. Both Scanlon and Habermas leave it up to participants to construct reasonable grounds. Their arguments do not have to comply with a preexisting consensus. In this sense they are free to understand themselves and their world in new ways.

WANTING TO BE IN THE RIGHT AND BEING IN THE RIGHT

Scanlon puts forward the desire to be justified as a general fact about us. But what sort of fact is it? Considering how much hangs on this assumption, it is surprising how little time Scanlon spends explaining this built-in motivational premise. He claims that it is an "account of at least [his] moral experience" (p. 116) but does not go very far in defending it as an account of most people's moral experience. He states that it is neither a universal nor a natural fact about us but rather the product of "moral education," but the meaning of moral education is unclear. At times he implies that it is something we ought to cultivate, and at other times he implies that it is something that our culture has already (sufficiently?) cultivated. Further, he leaves unanswered the question of whether moral education refers to a long-term sociohistorical process or a shorter-term sociopsychological process.

When moral theorists introduce "facts" they make an empirical claim of some sort. Empirical claims require empirical arguments. Scanlon never undertakes such an argument, but Habermas does. Habermas's discourse ethics can be understood as an analysis of the fact about us which Scanlon has placed at the center of morality. Habermas traces out the process of moral education which has led us to the modern intuition that to be justified in our moral positions *means* that we have publicly accessible and understandable reasons for our actions. This evolution in moral thinking is linked to a progressive mastering of universal rules of communication.

It is not clear that Scanlon would accept Habermas's argument that the appropriate rules for a "contractual" publicity test can be found in the universal structure of speech. Both begin, however, by identifying the same "procedural" intuition—namely, that principles become unacceptable to *us* if we acknowledge that others could reasonably object to them. We do go to great lengths to avoid admitting that our principles are unjustifiable. To believe something is true or right is to believe that one has good reasons, and to believe one has good reasons is to believe that one's reasons can withstand scrutiny, objections, and criticisms, that is, to believe that one's principles cannot be reasonably rejected. It would be odd (perhaps psychologically impossible) to believe something was true or right and yet to acknowledge that somebody else had a well-founded objection to it.

Nevertheless, our *belief* that there are no well-founded objections to the principles we hold as right or true, does not necessarily mean that there are no such well-founded objections. How do we know, for example, that through our private deliberations we do not simply rationalize our own biases by refusing to acknowledge reasonable objections? The desire to be justified can lead, paradoxically, to a stubborn refusal to admit that we are wrong. The lengths to which we will go can and often do involve avoidance, recalcitrance, closed-mindedness, and "rationalizations." Some people do wrong knowing (and perhaps not caring) that what they do is wrong, that is, recognizing that from the standpoint of morality their action is unjustifiable. Our society could not function if everybody had such a disregard for the moral status of their actions. Other people do wrong (or do what we might consider wrong) while maintaining that what they do is right, that is, that it is justifiable from a moral point of view. They have convinced themselves that there are no telling objections to their position, although we may be equally convinced of the opposite.

One way to deal with the problem of private rationalization is to bring the process of justification itself into the public realm of real debate. Defending one's position against the actual and often unpredictable objections of real people is one safeguard against the potentially selective process of private deliberation. But the idea of having to defend one's moral positions to others is not without its problems. On the one hand, we want to say that formulating a moral position without regard to strong counterarguments or the moral convictions of those with whom we must live is unreasonable. On the other hand, we also want to say that we are entitled to formulate our own private moral convictions regardless of other people's objections to them. At some point our moral stands are nobody else's business but our own. How strong is the obligation to give others an account of our moral selves?

Bruce Ackerman, who defends a strong accountability or dialogic

theory for the public realm, believes we are under no dialogic obligation in the private realm.[6] Principles that are to govern public institutions must pass a publicity test, but private moral principles need not.
Ackerman asserts that outside of politics, moral deliberation involves
consulting "your own moral insight" and that "talking to others is no
substitute." He considers the "mature" position to be "that there is
more to moral life than mere talk."[7] Ackerman is appealing to the dictum "to thy own self be true," and there is something compelling
about this idea. Our moral principles should be nonnegotiable. We
should be guided not by others' opinions but by our own *conscience*.
That is not to say, however, that dialogue or accountability does not
have an important, indeed central, place in the process by which we
come to our own convictions. Although there undoubtedly is more to
moral life than mere talk, it is difficult to imagine how one would gain
one's moral insights in the first place independently of the "mere talk"
through which ideas, beliefs, values, and principles are transmitted,
evaluated, assessed, and so on. The structure, conditions, freedom,
openness, depth, and inclusiveness of that talk will affect the substance
of one's own moral insights. In Chapter 10, I defend the position that
the more discursive the process through which we come to our personal moral convictions, the sounder our moral deliberation. Nevertheless, the obligation to defend our stands to others is weaker in the
private realm than in the public. At some point demands for justification become intrusive and violate the immunity of private conscience.

Real dialogue is but one of the ways we test the soundness of our
private moral intuitions, but it is the only way to test the soundness of
political institutions. Scanlon makes no clear distinction between justifying actions and institutions. He is interested in asking when we are
warranted in believing something is right and not when we are warranted in institutionalizing what we believe to be right. Because principles of justice, unlike many personal moral convictions, are to be institutionalized, they require an added dimension of justification.
Believing that no one could reasonably object to one's principle is not
enough in this case. Political institutions are basically coercive and so
require that objections be voiced and listened to. This is the democratic core of liberal democracy. Scanlon's contract must be actualized

6. Rawls also takes this position. Public reason, and the model of accountability that
goes along with it, is understood to apply only to a narrowly defined political sphere. See
Chapter 12.

7. Bruce Ackerman, "Why Dialogue?" *Journal of Philosophy* 86 (January 1989): 6.

in some way if it is to serve as a procedure appropriate for the public realm.[8] Habermas's discourse theory of legitimation is an example of how one might translate Scanlon's contractual accountability into political terms. Like Scanlon, Habermas makes accountability to others the centerpiece of his theory. Like Scanlon, Habermas collapses the impartial point of view of the original position into the reasonable point of view of citizens to come up with one overarching procedure.

8. Scanlon's quantitatively small contribution to the philosophical debate about justice and morality has spawned a great deal of interest within political theory, and although he does not elaborate the politics of "reasonable agreement," many others have done so. See especially Charles Beitz, *Political Equality* (Princeton: Princeton University Press, 1989), pp. 99–107; Thomas Nagel, *Equality and Partiality* (Oxford: Oxford University Press, 1991), pp. 36–40; Brian Barry, *Justice and Impartiality* (Oxford: Oxford University Press, 1995).

7 Jürgen Habermas and Practical Discourse

At the center of Habermas's moral theory is a strong cognitivist claim. Moral statements are open to rational evaluation and are not mere statements of preference or "decisions" for which there are no further grounds. In *The Theory of Communicative Action*, Habermas begins his defense of cognitivism with an analysis of everyday speech and the meanings we attach to such utterances as "X is rational" or "So and so is acting rationally." Habermas maintains that what we mean when we say something is rational is that it could be defended with reasons.[1] When there appears to be no good reason for an action or no good reason to believe a proposition we say that the person is not acting rationally or that the proposition is not rational. Further, people whose actions, beliefs, and statements appear to be backed by good reasons are the people whom we usually describe as being rational.

On this view, rationality is embedded in essentially public practices of communication. A statement or an action is rational to the extent that it could be *explained to others*, that is, to the extent that its grounds could be intersubjectively recognized. What Scanlon referred to as reasonable, Habermas brings under one overarching conception of rationality. In this way, instrumental rationality is seen not so much as an alternative to communicative rationality as contained within it. Instrumental considerations of efficiency and utility are one sort of reason a person could give to someone to explain an action. Habermas never denies that there are many situations where instrumental reasons are

1. Jürgen Habermas, *The Theory of Communicative Action*, translated by Thomas McCarthy, vol. 1 (Boston: Beacon Press, 1981), pp. 9–10.

good reasons. His point is that instrumental reasons are not the only sort of reasons that can make an action "rational."

Habermas tells a similar story with regard to the meaning of our normative utterances. When we say, "You should do x," or, "It is right to do x," what we mean is, "There are good reasons to do x." Moral utterances are inextricably linked to the rational process of proffering reasons for our actions, recommendations, or commands. Every time we make a statement with normative content we are implying that we have good reasons to hold the moral position that would support it.

One conclusion to be drawn from the appearance of everyday speech is that in this domain the skeptic is on weak ground. The skeptical position, summed up by the sentiment that "moral controversies cannot, in the final analysis, be decided with reason because the value premises from which we infer moral sentences are irrational," is one to which it is difficult if not impossible to adhere in practice.[2] If one took this position seriously then one would have no reason to enter into arguments about norms, and the fact of the matter is, we all enter into these kinds of arguments every day. It makes no sense to denounce apartheid, defend the equal rights amendment, advocate prayer in school, or even justify a private action to a friend, if I assume that the reasons behind such a position are irrational or at best arbitrary. In arguing over moral matters, I act as if good reasons supported my moral sentences. Not only do I act as if I had good grounds, in entering into arguments *with others*, I act as if these grounds could be generally recognized. If I thought that convincing the other person of the soundness of my moral position was impossible, I would have no motive or need to enter into argument.

Thus the skeptic is challenged on three fronts: as an observer of moral phenomena, as a participant in moral discourse, and as a proponent of skepticism at a metaethical level. As observers, even skeptics cannot deny, as Habermas remarks, "that people quarrel over moral issues all the time in everyday life as if such quarrels could be decided on the basis of good reasons."[3] Skeptics must answer the question, If we are not really trying to convince each other of the rational validity of our moral stands, then what are we trying to do? What function does moral argumentation play if the only premise that would give it

2. Jürgen Habermas, *Legitimation Crisis*, translated by Thomas McCarthy (Boston: Beacon Press, 1975), p. 102.

3. Jürgen Habermas, *Moral Consciousness and Communicative Action*, translated by Christian Lenhardt and Shierry Weber Nicholsen (Cambridge: MIT Press, 1990), p. 54.

meaning, that is, that we *can* convince each other with our reasons, is an illusion? From Habermas's point of view, the onus is on the skeptic to explain why it is that we all seem to act like cognitivists.[4]

The problem for the skeptic as participant is that in order to maintain a consistent position she would have to abstain from arguments about norms. If questions of right and wrong cannot be answered rationally, then there is no real point in sitting down and arguing about these things. Why should one give reasons for one's actions if one reason is as good as another? Skepticism takes the point out of argumentation. But, says Habermas, arguments about norms are a constitutive part of our social world.[5] In the long run, avoiding such argumentation would erode any common foundation to ethical intuitions.

Consistent skepticism would involve a withdrawal of radical proportions. It is not impossible to imagine an individual who refused to defend her actions or beliefs or who defended her moral positions by claiming that it was simply her "preference" in the matter, but it is impossible to imagine a whole society of such individuals. Giving reasons for our ethical stands, arguing about our moral convictions, justifying our actions or condemning others' actions are all core communicative activities. They are constitutive of social interaction. A thoroughgoing skeptic would have to isolate herself from such activity, or in refusing to justify her actions, she would be isolated by the community at large. Refusing to offer an explanation or give a reason for a questionable action is at odds with our general expectation regarding normative interaction. Thus, to Scanlon's idea that most people desire to be justified, Habermas adds the correlative proposition that most people expect to be given a justification at least for controversial actions or principles.

The skeptic is challenged on a third front as well—as a defender of skepticism at the metaethical level. Here Habermas, following Karl-Otto Apel, introduces the idea of performative contradiction, which is generated when the content of an utterance contradicts the pragmatic presupposition that makes it possible actually to utter the statement in the first place. Thus, for example, to say "I doubt that I exist" is possible only if there really is someone existing to say this. The skeptic's attempt to persuade someone with reasons that moral assertions (or

---

4. Jürgen Habermas, *Justification and Application: Remarks on Discourse Ethics*, translated by Ciaran P. Cronin (Cambridge: MIT Press, 1993), p. 20.

5. Jürgen Habermas, "A Reply to My Critics," in *Habermas: Critical Debates*, edited by John B. Thompson and David Held (Cambridge: MIT Press, 1982), p. 227.

factual utterances) cannot be grounded rationally presupposes the very thing that is being denied in the utterance, that is, that reasons can be brought to bear to support or criticize moral assertions (and factual statements).

By themselves these three arguments make something less than an airtight case against the skeptic, although they do make an important point: The search for a cognitivist account of ethics does not begin from an arbitrary starting point. Rather, it has its basis in ordinary practical reasoning because, as one moral theorist has put it, "the ordinary process of deliberation, aimed at finding out what I have reason to do, assumes that the question has an answer."[6] We operate under the assumption that there are right answers to moral questions, which is to say, that there are answers that are right independent of our personal preferences and even of our actually finding them. The important point is that cognitivism sets out to *account* for these ordinary moral intuitions; it begins from the presumption that there is something to our intuition that there are right answers to moral questions.

The weakness of the first two arguments against the skeptic (as observer and participant) is that acting as if we had good grounds does not necessarily mean that we have good grounds for moral positions. The skeptic might respond that the assumption that there are right answers to moral questions is simply a subjective illusion. Or perhaps, like Hume, she might say that being skeptical about our ability to find rational foundations does not require skepticism in our practical day-to-day activities. Or again she might reply cynically that we enter moral argument for instrumental and self-interested reasons, not because we believe that our positions are morally right and can be demonstrated to be right. In order to counter the skeptic's objections, Habermas must go farther than the observation that we act *as if* we had good grounds; he must offer an account of what a good reason might be.

The performative-contradiction argument is somewhat stronger in that it points to an inherent problem facing any skeptic who sets out to criticize using argumentation. Skeptical premises must undermine the skeptic's arguments just as much as anybody else's arguments. This is one of the major themes in Habermas's criticism of postmodernism.[7] If we are to accept some of the specific criticisms leveled at modern ratio-

<hr>

6. Thomas Nagel, "The Limits of Objectivity," in *The Tanner Lectures on Human Values*, vol. 1 (Salt Lake City: University of Utah Press, 1978–79), p. 100.

7. Jürgen Habermas, *The Philosophical Discourse of Modernity*, translated by Frederick Lawrence (Cambridge: MIT Press, 1987), pp. 238–65.

nalism as compelling, we must reject the larger skeptical claims or else we have no grounds for finding one set of criticisms more compelling than another. Benjamin Barber describes the self-referential problem of postmodern skepticism well when he says: "Reason can be a smoke screen for interests, but the argument that it is a smoke screen itself *depends on reason*—or we are caught up in an endless regression in which each argument exposing the dependency of someone else's argument on arbitrariness and self-interest is in turn shown to be self-interested and arbitrary."[8]

As Habermas himself has pointed out, however, the performative-contradiction argument is useful only to the extent that it highlights problems internal to skepticism. What is involved in ethical cognitivism itself "can certainly not be decided by a direct recourse to performative self-contradiction."[9] Instead, the theorist who wishes to defend cognitivism must give an account of how we decide moral questions in a rational manner. Habermas does so by reconstructing the presuppositions of communication, which then furnish the formal conditions under which a moral statement can be said to be rationally justified.

THE PRESUPPOSITIONS OF COMMUNICATION

"When we discuss moral-practical questions of the form 'what ought I to do?'" writes Habermas, "we presuppose that the answers need not be arbitrary; we trust our ability to distinguish in principle between right norms and commands and wrong ones.[10] Through an investigation of what lies behind this trust, Habermas traces our everyday intuitions back to the structure of speech itself. In this way, he tries to convince the skeptic that our (and her) intuitions are not subjective illusions but rather pretheoretical knowledge of the rules of communication and, further, that by reconstructing this pretheoretical knowledge we can find a procedure through which the norms that stand behind moral utterances can be rationally evaluated. This procedure is the argumentative redemption of normative validity claims under conditions of undominated discourse.

The reconstruction of everyday intuitions leads Habermas to a now-

8. Benjamin Barber, *An Aristocracy of Everyone: The Politics of Education and the Future of America* (New York: Ballantine, 1992), p. 109 (my emphasis).

9. Jürgen Habermas, *Autonomy and Solidarity: Interviews with Jürgen Habermas*, edited by Peter Dews (New York: Verso, 1992), p. 259.

10. Habermas, *Moral Consciousness and Communicative Action*, p. 56.

familiar set of presuppositions which actors "naively" assume every time they enter into communication, that is, every time they enter into symbolic interaction oriented to reaching an understanding. In order for normal communication to continue uninterrupted, we must presuppose a background consensus whereby we take for granted that utterances fulfill certain conditions. Not only must we share the same natural language in order to understand each other; we must share or assume we share the same objective world, the same normative world, and commensurable subjective worlds. It is precisely under conditions where these assumptions are impossible to make that communication becomes muddled and understanding difficult. I begin to lose the sense of what is meant when my dialogue partner refers to an objective world I have no knowledge of, appeals to norms I have never recognized, or represents himself in blatantly inconsistent or insincere ways. Our utterances appeal to these shared contexts by way of implied validity claims raised by any speech act. A communicative utterance contains the claims that it is true, that is, corresponds to a state of affairs in the objective world; that it is right, that is, appeals to legitimate norms in the social world; that it is sincere, that is, accurately represents the inner state of the speaker's subjective world.[11] The three validity claims reflect a differentiation we make between the objective/external world of facts, the intersubjective/social world of norms, and the subjective/inner world of feelings and dispositions.

My interest here is the intersubjective/social world of norms. How does Habermas link up the universal presuppositions of communication with the idea of good grounds for holding a moral belief? At this point a simple example might be useful. The communicative routine of giving and taking commands can proceed smoothly only so long as there is a general consensus as to who is to issue commands and who is to follow them. Our understanding of who may direct (traffic, a classroom, the nation, attention, the battlefield, and so on) and who may not, represents a complicated web of reciprocal expectations which is reinforced every time the illocutionary act of commanding is successfully followed through. In issuing an order with the expectation that it will be understood and carried out, the commander raises the claim that the norm to which the speech act appeals is valid. In voluntarily obeying this order, hearers act as if the commander could make this claim good.

11. Ibid., p. 58; see also Habermas, *Theory of Communicative Action* 1:149.

This presupposed consensus breaks down when the assumed ability to justify one's actions is brought to an explicit level and one or more participants challenges the commander's right to command. If the commander cannot immediately dispel doubt by appealing to a recognized norm, such as "I am a policeman" or "you chose me as your leader," and instead appeals to a questionable or obsolete norm, as in "I am taller than you" or "I have Divine Right," then the normal activity of giving and taking commands breaks down.[12]

At this impasse interlocutors are faced with several options. They may simply part company and refuse to be involved with one another; one party may use coercive force to impose her idea of the appropriate norm on others; they may attempt to influence each other strategically to "go along with" the proposed norm through the threat of sanctions or the prospect of rewards; or they may attempt to convince each other that there are (or are not) good reasons to recognize the proposed norm as right.

In the real world of social interaction, talk of options is slightly misleading, however, for in the long run, if disassociation is not possible (and it rarely is), then some form of persuasion must be undertaken.[13] Following Emile Durkheim and Max Weber, Habermas contends that social and political institutions cannot be maintained solely through force or strategic manipulation.[14] Although the threat of sanctions or the prospect of rewards is often part of what motivates citizens to play by the rules, by themselves such inducements cannot guarantee mass loyalty and thus stability. Stability requires that "reasons for obedience can be mobilized" which "at least appear to be justified in the eyes of those concerned."[15]

When the fragile maintenance system of a norm falls apart, then this mobilization must be either regenerated or shifted to an alternative norm. And mobilizing reasons for obedience is achieved through the communicative practice of convincing each other that there really are (or are not) good grounds to recognize a norm. Without such a regenerating process not simply at our disposal but constantly in use, the

12. Jürgen Habermas, *Communication and the Evolution of Society*, translated by Thomas McCarthy (Boston: Beacon Press, 1979), p. 99.

13. As Hume noted, the idea of being free to withdraw from one's social and political context is often like being free to jump overboard "into the ocean and perish." David Hume, "Of the Original Contract," in *Hume's Moral and Political Philosophy*, edited by Henry D. Aiken (New York: Hafner, 1972), p. 363.

14. Habermas, *Communication and the Evolution of Society*, pp. 178–205.

15. Habermas, *Moral Consciousness and Communicative Action*, p. 62.

shared background to our social world which makes communication possible would fall apart.

According to Habermas this process often takes place unreflectively, in what he calls the "negotiation of a new situation definition." The negotiation is informal and partial, and is characterized by a "diffuse, fragile, continuously revised and only momentarily successful communication in which participants rely on problematic and unclarified presuppositions and feel their way from one occasional commonality to the next."[16] Thus the image is of a world where we continually renegotiate, in small and sometimes big ways, the normative backdrop to our actions. The decisive force in these renegotiations is communication. We reach partial understandings through dialogues in which we justify, convince, defend, criticize, explain, argue, express our inner feelings and desires while interpreting those of others. Without partial understandings between members of a community, normative regulation cannot be said to take place. But partial understandings are, after all, only partial. These understandings are neither fully reflective nor fully rational. What I mean is that they often do not go very deep into the background presuppositions that maintain a way of life, what Habermas calls the lifeworld context. Further, they are not fully rational in the sense that within everyday communication other influences filter into the process such that the outcomes are not exclusively the result of reasoned dialogue. We also cajole, threaten, subtly persuade, bribe, exploit, manipulate, and lie our way into new situation definitions. Our conversations are rarely exhaustive. We recognize norms that perhaps we would not under other circumstances.

The "negotiation of new situation definitions" is the process through which the social validity of a norm is reproduced. But a socially valid norm, that is, a norm that is recognized by a certain group of people, cannot claim to be right simply on the grounds that it is in fact recognized. The task of a discursive moral theory is to formalize, clarify, and universalize the unavoidable presupposition that behind every valid norm stands a good reason and, in doing so, to proceduralize the "diffuse, fragile, continually revised, and only momentarily successful communication" by which we unreflectively renew social norms. In this way we arrive at a constant, rational, and dependable method to validate moral norms reflectively. Practical discourse is this formal, universal, and ideal form of communication.

16. Habermas, *Theory of Communicative Action*, 1:100–101.

Practical Discourse

Practical discourse is focused in a way that day-to-day communication is not. If the norm to which a commander appeals in defense of her right to command is not recognized by those who are expected to obey, then normal communicative action comes to an impasse. To resolve this impasse discursively, the participants suspend the norm by giving it a hypothetical status until its validity has been redeemed. The norm is no longer taken for granted as the background to action but is brought to an explicit level and made the object of discourse. One might say that discourse cuts into communicative action vertically in order to reestablish a background consensus so that normal communication can resume.[17]

Practical discourses are highly specialized discussions. Once engaged in discourse, participants have one thing on their minds: resolving the normative dispute to the satisfaction of all. Thus, as in Scanlon's work, the motivational premise is a desire to reach agreement. Participants undertake a cooperative search for a common understanding of the principles that are to regulate their interaction. Given that common understanding is the end of discourse, certain conditions of discourse suggest themselves. These conditions are intended to ensure that the resulting understanding is indeed genuinely common and that the agreed-upon norms are considered valid by all.

In his most formal account of these conditions, found in the essay "Discourse Ethics: Notes on a Program of Philosophical Justification," Habermas proposes three sets of rules applying respectively to three levels of argumentation. In each case, the claim is that the rules represent "a reflective form of communicative action," or an explicit rendering of the assumptions that stand behind our everyday attempts to reach situation definitions.[18]

The first set of rules requires that we speak the same natural language according to the same general conventions. Habermas has in mind here logical and semantic rules that state, for example, that a speaker may not contradict herself, that predicates must be used consistently, that various meanings should not be attributed to the same expression, and so on.

---

17. Habermas has sometimes used a different metaphor to describe the relationship between discourse and communication: "Discourses are islands in a sea of practice." See "Reply," p. 235.

18. Habermas, *Moral Consciousness and Communicative Action*, pp. 87–89.

The second set of rules is drawn from the premise that participants desire to reach agreement. These rules stipulate that participants state and defend only what they believe to be the case—what they believe to be factually true; what they believe to be right norms; what they know to be their inner dispositions. On their side, hearers must respect the intent behind the claims even if they cannot accept the claims themselves. In discourse a participant must recognize his dialogue partner as responsible and sincere in her desire to reach agreement, even if he disputes the validity of her claim, for if mutual understanding is the goal, then what would it mean to defend a proposition one knew to be false, to champion a moral principle one believed to be wrong, or to express feelings and desires one did not feel or desire? A sincere interest in reaching authentic agreement presupposes that participants are not interested in deception, manipulation, misdirection, or obfuscation.

These rules are derived from the goal of communication, but the final set of rules formalizes the process of communication itself. In communicative action participants search for agreement by offering arguments that could command assent. As opposed to strategic action, where participants are primarily interested in bringing about a desired behavioral response, in communicative action, participants are interested in bringing about a "change of heart." For example, in strategic action participants often attempt to sway each other by introducing influences unrelated to the merits of an argument, for example, threats, bribes, or coercion. Such inducements can bring about the desired behavior even in situations where the other player is not convinced that there are any inherently good reasons to act that way. Communicative actors are primarily interested in mutual understanding as opposed to external behavior. Therefore, they attempt to convince each other that there are inherently good reasons to pursue one course of action over another. Only the "force of the better argument" should have the power to sway participants. Practical discourse, as an idealization of this kind of activity, must set conditions such that only rational, that is, argumentative, convincing is allowed to take place. It must be "immunized" in a special way against repression and inequality."[19]

The immunization is gained through a set of rules designed to guarantee discursive equality, freedom, and fair play. No one with the competency to speak and act may be excluded from discourse. Everyone is

19. Ibid., p. 88.

allowed to question or introduce any assertion whatever as well as to express her attitudes, desires, and needs. No one may be prevented, by internal or external coercion, from exercising these rights.[20]

Discourse under these conditions will be successful only if participants adopt equally respectful and impartial attidues. The rules of discourse stipulate that we must treat each other as equal partners in the process of deliberating about and choosing principles that will govern our collective interaction. Thus, each individual must be given the opportunity to speak her piece and stand up and say yes or no to a proposal. In addition to the negative requirement that individuals be given the space and opportunity to speak, moreover, productive discourses contain the positive requirement that individuals listen to each other, respond to each other, and justify their positions to each other. To treat each other as equal dialogue partners means that we must start from the assumption that each participant has something worthwhile to contribute to the discourse. This assumption embodies the Kantian idea that respect involves treating people as ends in themselves and not merely as means. Strategic actors view their dialogue partners as means—as either limiting or facilitating the pursuit of their ends. Communicative actors view their dialogue partners as ends in themselves—as autonomous agents whose capacity for rational judgment must be respected. Most day-to-day interaction is a combination of these two orientations. Practical discourse, as an idealization of communicative action, asks participants to exclude from the conversation all strategic and instrumental attitudes toward interlocutors.[21]

Impartiality is achieved by putting oneself in the position of the other and trying to see the situation from her perspective. Only in trying to understand how the world looks to other people will participants be flexible and open enough to undertake a genuine evaluation of their opinions. Discourse is directed at mutual understanding, which, at a minimum, means understanding the real issues that divide you from your interlocutor and at a maximum, means coming to a shared understanding. Even the minimum case calls for impartiality. Deep disagreement is not always or even primarily a case of misunderstanding. Deep disagreement is often a case of understanding too well the

20. Ibid., p. 89.
21. It is not entirely correct to say that discourse does not contain any instrumental calculation. Discourse is goal oriented in the sense that participants are looking for the best means of attaining the goal of mutual understanding. Thus, it is not means/ends rationality that is excluded from discourse but only viewing one's dialogue partner as the means to attaining one's own ends.

gulf that separates you from others. But disagreement, like agreement, can be more or less rational depending on the reasons one has. Rational disagreement requires that you understand the claim you are rejecting, and it calls for putting yourself in the other's place. If participants are unwilling to make a sincere effort to assess their motives, ends, and needs in light of the motives ends and needs of their interlocutors, the discursive process, no matter how structurally equal, will go nowhere. Thus, impartiality is achieved not by a withdrawal from the concrete interests of particular people but rather by becoming more attached to the concrete interests of particular people. That is, it is not a view from nowhere but rather a view from the perspective of each other person.

Although the requirements of equal respect and impartiality contain substantive moral assumptions about how we should be talking to each other, they are still formal in that they do not determine how the conversation will turn out or even what we should be talking about. Instead, they set up a framework within which we can search for common ground. That common ground may very well be an agreement to disagree, but it also might represent substantive interests we share with our interlocutor/s.

Generalizable Interests and Moral Deliberation

The final question to ask in this preliminary sketch of practical discourse is, What would participants agree to (if anything) and why? The desire for agreement itself is not enough to generate agreement. Just as Rawls needs to assume an interest in primary goods to get any outcome at all, because people who have no interests (needs, desires, goals, and so on) have no basis for preferring one option over another, so too must Habermas assume that people enter into discourse with interests and needs they wish to see satisfied by the agreed-upon norm. The desire for agreement cannot itself be the basis of preferring one option over another if everyone has this same desire.

If people deliberate from the point of view of furthering their own interests, then the possibility of agreement rests on their sharing an interest or on the convergence of their diverse interests to support one alternative. Rawls dealt with this issue by postulating a set of goods necessary to exercise our moral powers and then attributing to each participant an identical interest in pursuing these goods. Habermas, however, is unwilling to stipulate in advance which interests are to motivate the participants, for as he says, "the individual is the last court of appeal for judging what is in his best interest."[22] Interests are not fixed in advance by the theorist, nor are they understood to be fixed in the sense of being "brute facts," which need only be consulted but not justified. Interests and needs are not "givens" within the procedure but are open to criticism, interpretation, and revision.[23] Part of what discourse is about is judging what is in my/our best interest.

It is here that many commentators, as well as Habermas himself, note the most significant difference between the original position and practical discourse.[24] By introducing a substantive list of goods, Rawls denies participants the freedom to interpret and understand their needs and interests in their own way. Like Scanlon's "contract," practical discourse asks participants to deliberate about needs and interests and thus focuses the procedure on questions that were excluded from the original position.

The idea here is that we cannot ignore the sorts of people we are when we evaluate normative questions. The sorts of people we are provide the very subject matter of discussion: "If actors did not bring with them, and into discourse, *their* individual life-histories, *their* needs and wants, *their* traditions, memberships, and so forth, practical discourse would at once be robbed of all its content."[25] If each of us deliberates from the point of view of what we need and want, then the possibility of agreement rests on our discovering things that we need and want in common. Thus, deliberation is really about working out interests we share with each other which can furnish a reason for collectively recognizing a norm. According to Habermas, what we search for in practical discourse are generalizable interests. There are a few things to keep in mind about generalizable interests in order to avoid misunderstanding.

First, a generalizable interest need not rest on identical particular

---

22. Habermas, *Moral Consciousness and Communicative Action*, p. 67.

23. Habermas, *Communication and the Evolution of Society*, pp. 63–64, 198; idem, *Theory of Communicative Action*, translated by Thomas McCarthy, vol. 2 (Boston: Beacon Press: 1987), pp. 95–96. Needs and interests are interchangeable; see Stephen K. White, *The Recent Work of Jürgen Habermas: Reason, Justice, and Modernity* (Cambridge: Cambridge University Press, 1988), p. 69.

24. Kenneth Baynes, *The Normative Grounds of Social Criticism: Kant, Rawls, and Habermas* (Albany: SUNY Press, 1992), p. 151; White, *Recent Work of Habermas*, p. 72; Habermas, *Communication and the Evolution of Society*, pp. 198–99; Habermas, *Moral Consciousness and Communicative Action*, pp. 66–67.

25. Habermas, "Reply," p. 255.

interests. I could have an interest in peace and security and you could have an interest in a Christian concept of *agape* and these two separate interests could lead us to agree on a norm of religious toleration. We could say that it was in both our interests to see the state guarantee religious freedom—me, because religious intolerance leads to social disorder and I do not want to live under conditions of social disorder, and you, because religious intolerance violates the principle of universal love and you do not want to live in a society that violates this principle. Thus, a generalizable interest can be understood as representing overlapping particular interests.

But one might want to ask what kind of an interest is an interest in *agape*. This question leads to a second aspect of generalizable interests. They are not understood in exclusively materialist terms, nor are they tied to a narrow concept of individual benefit. We may be said to have interests that involve attaining ideals rather than securing our own benefit. There are good reasons for expanding our idea of interest and need to include the pursuit of moral ideals. As Stephen White has pointed out, splitting up the interest to pursue some goal from the belief that that goal is worthwhile, creates the difficulty of explaining why anyone would be motivated to pursue the goal: "If this difficulty is to be overcome, it means that ideals . . . must gain their capacity to move people by virtue of their place within a conception of what is important for the flourishing of human life; in saying this one is saying that they must be tied to some sort of need interpretation."[26]

Finally, the appeal to generalizable interests does not presuppose a set of universally true human needs which we attempt to discover in discourse. Except for the most basic physical needs such as food and shelter, interests and needs are understood to be socially and culturally constituted. We do not acquire our needs and interests in isolation, nor do they stay static over a lifetime. Our inner selves (who we are and what we want) are shaped through the communicative relationships we enter into. Practical discourse rationalizes this process by asking participants to reflect upon and evaluate their needs and interests rationally from the point of view of their generalizability. Most of our needs and interests are not generalizable, but some of them are, and practical discourse asks participants to search for such points of commonality to serve as foundations for legitimate norms. This search may lead to the revision and reinterpretation of needs and interests in light of criticism

26. White, *Recent Work of Habermas*, pp. 70–71.

and argument. Through criticism and argument, revision and rein-terpretation, we deliberately arrive at generalizable interest. Thus, it is not a discovery of our "true" interests which is made in discourse but a collective interpretation of how we will *understand* our most important interests. As the product of collective need *interpretation*, a generaliz-able interest is open to revision. Our choices are not set in stone for all time.

Habermas does not fall into the problematic position of denying that people's interests are what they say are, although this view has been attributed to him.[27] The individual is the last court of appeal for judg-ing what is in his best interest. The process of "judging," however, is not understood as a simple internal consultation. Judging what is in our best interest is a critical deliberative process in which we proffer reasons for why something really is in our interest, or why one interest is more generalizable than another, or why our particular interest de-serves special protection, or why someone else's need interpretation is unsound, and so on. And some reasons will be better than others. Does this mean that people can be mistaken about what they think they need or what they believe to be in their interest? The answer is, yes. They can be mistaken, but such mistakes cannot be identified independently of the procedure itself. Discourse ethics does not offer an external vantage point from which an observer can conclude that actors are suffering from false consciousness in their need interpreta-tion.[28] Here I take Habermas at his word when he says that the individ-ual is the last court of appeal for judging what is in his best interest. Discourse ethics does, however, offer an internal critical vantage point from which participants can come to believe with good reason that an earlier need interpretation was mistaken, ill conceived, shortsighted, inconsistent, or generally indefensible.

The discursive model of moral deliberation precludes the possibility of hypothetically working out, let alone deducing, what participants would agree to. Individuals in discourse have too much information and there is too much room for learning for us to "predict" how they would interpret their needs and what agreements they would come to. Thus, discourse ethics is open to the charge that it is an empty theory of justice. Are we left, to use Rawls's words, "with a vague formula stating that justice is what would be agreed to without being able to say much, if anything, about the substance of the agreement itself"?[29] The countercharge is that introducing procedural constraints that would allow us to say something about the substance of the agreement distorts the idea that parties to a rational agreement are free and equal moral persons. What flows from the procedural component of modern ethics ought to forbid us from trying to anticipate how people will understand themselves and the needs and interests that must be answered by a system of justice. In a discursive model of procedural ethics we are free to interpret our interests in new ways; we are equal partners in the process of will formation; and we are full moral persons because the process by which we come to have and understand a conception of justice as well as a conception of the good is part of the procedure itself.

Finally, the procedure is not empty because the process itself is designed to engender a point of view that has normative content. The pursuit of uncoerced agreement within the rules of discourse initiates a learning process through which participants come to see that certain discursive attitudes are essential to the success of the process itself. In Chapter 12 I discuss this learning process in more detail. For now, what is important to stress is that the rules of discourse describe a moral point of view to be taken up within deliberation; they do not determine the outcome in advance. Participants are free to work out for themselves what is in their general interest.

29. John Rawls, *A Theory of Justice* (Cambridge: Harvard University Press, 1971), p. 140.

III

DISCOURSE AND MODERNITY

8 *Universalism in*
   Reconstructive Science

"Should one party make use of privileged access to weapons, wealth or standing, in order to wring agreement from another party through the prospects of sanctions and rewards," Habermas says, "no one involved will be in doubt that the presuppositions of argumentation are no longer satisfied."[1] At a general level this statement makes a great deal of sense. We assume that consent under duress does not count as real consent and that the use of deception and fraud to gain agreement is illegitimate. We recognize that with the introduction of threats, bribes, blackmail, pressure tactics, and so on, something has gone wrong with a process whose end is supposed to be agreement. Put this way, the rules of discourse are intuitively compelling; they do seem to articulate rules that we presuppose when we enter argumentation. It is the strong claim that Habermas makes on behalf of these rules that many people find hard to swallow. The consciousness of these rules might be tied up with *our* historically specific intuitions, but the rules themselves transcend context; they are universals.[2]

Habermas believes that if his theory of communicative rationality is to be objectively valid, then the presuppositions of communication "would have to be shown as *universally* valid, in a specific sense." And although he never actually admits that such a requirement is impossible to fulfill, he does concede that it would be very difficult to fulfill "for

---

1. Jürgen Habermas, "A Reply to My Critics," in *Habermas: Critical Debates*, edited by John B. Thompson and David Held (Cambridge: MIT Press, 1982), pp. 272–73.
2. Jürgen Habermas, *Moral Consciousness and Communicative Action*, translated by Christian Lenhardt and Shierry Weber Nicholsen (Cambridge: MIT Press, 1990), p. 89.

someone [like himself] who is operating without metaphysical support and is also no longer confident that a rigorous transcendental-pragmatic program, claiming to provide ultimate grounds, can be carried out."[3] Does he mean that he cannot prove the universal validity of the presuppositions in a specific sense? Are they then universally valid in an unspecific sense? Despite how odd this phrase sounds, it is, I think, exactly what he means.

On the one hand, metaphysical arguments seeking ultimate grounds are no longer convincing. On the other hand, we do not have, nor will we ever have, direct empirical access to the underlying rules of communication. Thus, the rules can never be shown to be universally valid in a specific sense. That they cannot, however, is not a reason to dismiss the possibility that they are universally valid. Such a dismissal would involve succumbing to a common temptation of modern positivist social science; allowing established standards of verification to drive the sorts of questions social scientists ask. Our questions should not be driven by our methods; our methods should be driven by our questions. Thus, Habermas, in asking a question that cannot be answered directly by standard methods in the social sciences, has attempted to develop an alternative method of investigation. He calls this method reconstruction. And as with any attempt to carve out a new research domain, there are still many ambiguities and difficulties to be worked out.

Hypothetical and Fallible Universalism

Habermas describes his method sometimes as quasi-transcendental reconstruction, sometimes as reconstructive science, sometimes as hermeneutical reconstruction, and sometimes as rational reconstruction. It is not always clear what he means by all these terms. What is clear is that he wishes to steer a new and middle course among three types of argument: a transcendental deduction, a nomological-deductive model found within positivist social science, and a hermeneutical interpretation.[4] A reconstructive approach resembles a transcendental deduction

3. Jürgen Habermas, *The Theory of Communicative Action*, translated by Thomas McCarthy, vol. 1 (Boston: Beacon Press, 1981), p. 137.

4. Often overlooked in the literature is this *three*-way methodological distinction. For example, David Rasmussen characterizes reconstructive science as steering a middle course between transcendentalism and contextualism, and Fred Alford sees it as a middle course between explanation and description. David M. Rasmussen, "Communicative Action and

but is not a transcendental deduction; it uses knowledge gained by positive social science but differs from positive social science; it borrows from hermeneutical method but is not identical with hermeneutical method. In what follows I try to sort out some of these claims.

I start with the claim that reconstruction uncovers "quasi-transcendental" presuppositions. Transcendental arguments are those that seek the conditions of possibility for some given phenomenon. At the most rudimentary level they are transcendental in the obvious sense that they "transcend," or go beyond, the phenomenon to uncover what must be presupposed if we are to make any sense of the phenomenon whatsoever. So, for example, Kant, in his most famous transcendental argument asks the question; How is experience possible? Kant sets out to discover what must be presupposed if we are even to conceive of human knowledge and science as possible. In contrast to Hume, who sets out to deconstruct our claims to knowledge, Kant can be described as taking a reconstructive approach. He says, in effect, let us assume that human knowledge is possible. Can we reconstruct what would have to be the case for this assumption to be true? His answer is that we must presuppose certain mental structures, the categories of the understanding, to make sense of human experience.

Habermas asks a question similar in form to Kant's; How is communication possible? What must be presupposed in order for two human beings to understand each other? Again, like Kant and in opposition to skeptics, Habermas begins with a presumptive claim. Let us assume that human beings really do understand one another and that they can come to a full understanding with one another. What would have to be the case for this assumption to be true? As we saw in Chapter 7, Habermas's answer is that everyday communication presupposes an ideal form of communication which can be articulated in a set of rules governing the production of a rational consensus or a full mutual understanding.

Despite initial similarities between the Kantian and Habermasian enterprises, there are also important differences, which lead Habermas to use the term "*quasi*-transcendental." The first major difference is that Kant's question is much bigger and more fundamental than Habermas's. Indeed, Kant's question is unavoidably metaphysical in that it seeks the first principles of our knowledge of the world—*all* our knowledge of the world. Thus, Kant's investigation is fully transcen-

Philosophy: Reflections on Habermas' *Theorie des kommunikativen Handelns*," *Philosophy and Social Criticism* 9 (Spring 1982): 3–28; Fred Alford, "Is Jürgen Habermas's Reconstructive Science Really a Science?" *Theory and Society* 14 (May 1985): 321–40.

dental, for it goes not just beyond a particular phenomenon but beyond the phenomenal world as such to uncover what makes our experience of phenomena possible. In searching for what makes experience of the world possible, Kant must abstract from all experience. Habermas's question encompasses only a certain type of experience.[5] Therefore, his answer need not be found in a priori principles as Kant's must. Habermas can draw on our knowledge of the world, including scientific knowledge, in answering his question.

The second major difference between Kant's transcendental argument and Habermas's quasi-transcendental reconstruction is that Kant claims his argument is a deduction. The connection between the categories of the understanding and the possibility of human experience is a logical one: the categories of the understanding are an absolute necessity for the possibility of knowledge.[6] In contrast, the rules of argumentation are not defended as logical necessities. Indeed, Habermas says that they are fallible and hypothetical.

By fallible, he means that the strength of his claim rests not on logical necessity but on the absence of any equally plausible account of the phenomenon to date. This understanding does not preclude the possibility that there might be a better account or a corrected account at some future date. Kant must preclude this possibility because the scope of his claim implies that any future account—indeed, any account of anything in the world—must presuppose his categories. By hypothetical, Habermas means that one first hypothesizes that these rules underlie all communication and then one goes in search of evidence to support this hypothesis. They are not self-evident a priori truths like Kant's categories of the understanding. These differences represent a substantial gap between Kant and Habermas. Transcendental and reconstructive arguments might possess a family resemblance in form, but the claims are qualitatively different. Reconstructed rules of argumentation do not represent logical conditions of possibility. Instead, I believe, they represent a plausible description of what is going on when two or more people communicate with one another.

What Habermas tries to do is to shift the status of the deep structure of communication from a transcendental ultimate ground (a position that Karl-Otto Apel holds, for example) to a fallible and hypothetical

5. For a good discussion of this issue, see Stephen K. White, *The Recent Work of Jürgen Habermas: Reason, Justice, and Modernity* (Cambridge: Cambridge University Press, 1988), pp. 128–32.

6. Immanuel Kant, *Critique of Pure Reason*, translated by L. W. Beck (Indianapolis: Bobbs-Merrill, 1956).

ultimate ground. In this way he hopes to avoid the dangers of foundationalism while maintaining a foundation for his theory. Habermas is adamant that his theory should not be taken as foundationalist. He thinks he can avoid the accusation of foundationalism by stating that the universal structure he is appealing to as a "first principle" is neither undeniable nor immune to revision. At times he is quite generous in entertaining the possibility that the reconstruction of the presuppositions of speech might require revision. He admits that the "transcendental flavour" of his type of approach has "often seduced philosophers into mistaking some sort of reconstructions for ultimate foundations, or *Letzbegrunden*. It is important to see that rational reconstructions, like all other types of knowledge, have only hypothetical status. They may very well start from a false sample of intuitions; they may obscure and distort the right intuitions; and they may, even more often, overgeneralize particular cases. They are in need of corroboration."⁷ Transcendental arguments do not need corroboration; they are self-contained arguments. In contrast, Habermas's reconstructed "first principle" is not defended as being in any way self-evident or undeniable. Rather, it is defended by appeal to a vast array of interdisciplinary "corroboratory" research which converges in support of the reconstruction. No single strand is enough to sustain the claim that the reconstruction is "true," but the whole taken together contributes to the plausibility of the reconstruction. This is the strategy he adopts in *The Theory of Communicative Action*. What he does in this book is to offer a theory premised on a universal concept of communicative rationality. One then judges the plausibility of the premised concept on the coherence and explanatory value of the theory. Habermas suggests some research paths, which include studying universal pragmatics and checking this reconstruction against speakers' intuitions; assessing the "empirical usefulness of formal pragmatic insights" in the areas of psychology, social evolution, and the identification of social pathologies; and looking at the history of social theory "with the systematic aim of laying out the problems that can be solved by means of a theory of rationalization developed in terms of the basic concept of communicative action."⁸ Most of the two-volume work is devoted to this last research path, although throughout the work he makes suggestions as to how the others might be pursued and prove fruitful.

7. Jürgen Habermas, "Interpretive Social Sciences vs. Hermeneutics," in *Social Science as Moral Inquiry*, edited by Norma Han et al. (New York: Columbia University Press, 1983), p. 261.

8. Habermas, *Theory of Communicative Action* 1:139–40.

Habermas's *Begründung* (grounding) strategy is, in the end, the mirror image of the one adopted in *A Theory of Justice*. Rawls proposes to start from uncontroversial and weak premises and build from there. The plausibility and uncontroversial character of the premises are to carry much of the weight in the justification of the theory. Habermas starts with rather controversial and strong premises but gives them a weak or hypothetical status within the theory. The plausibility of the various theoretical and empirical insights these premises make possible is to carry much of the weight.

This *Begründung* strategy implies that Habermas's foundational premise regarding communicative rationality can never be directly verified. Is this a serious flaw? Some philosophy of science suggests not only that this is not a flaw at all but that any progress in the sciences will inevitable involve unverifiable "theories" of this type. For example, Larry Laudan offers a useful distinction that can help us make sense of the relationship between the foundational component of Habermas's theory and the theoretical and empirical insights offered, not only by Habermas, but by a growing army of researchers and theorists using his model. Laudan says that the term *theory* is often used to denote two quite different enterprises, the first of which he calls theory proper and the second, a research tradition.

A theory refers to a specific set of doctrines and hypotheses which can be used to make relatively precise predictions, generate detailed explanations of phenomena, and offer exact pictures of events. Examples of theories in this sense are Maxwell's theory of electromagnetism and Marx's theory of value.[9] In contrast, a research tradition refers to a much less easily testable set of doctrines or assumptions—"assumptions about the basic kinds of entities in the world, assumptions about how these entities interact, assumptions about the proper methods to use for constructing and testing theories about these entities."[10] Examples of research traditions include such things as the atomic theory and the theory of evolution, and I would include the theory of communicative rationality.

The individual theories constituting the tradition will generally be empirically testable for they will entail . . . some precise predictions about how objects in the domain will behave. By contrast, *research*

9. Larry Laudan, *Progress and Its Problems: Toward a Theory of Scientific Growth* (Berkeley: University of California Press, 1977), p. 71.
10. Ibid., p. 97.

traditions are neither explanatory, nor predictive, nor directly testable. Their very generality, as well as their normative elements, precludes them from leading to detailed accounts of specific natural processes. . . . *A successful research tradition is one which leads, via its component theories, to the adequate solution of an increasing range of empirical and conceptual problems.* Determining whether a tradition is successful in this sense does not mean, of course, that the tradition has been "confirmed" or "refuted." Nor can such an appraisal tell us anything about the *truth* or *falsity* of the tradition.[11]

No one can deny that the theory of communicative rationality has opened up and created many interesting and innovative avenues of research, interpretation, normative criticism and theory building.[12] It is through the success or failure of these enterprises that a reconstructed understanding of communication must be evaluated. The standard for evaluating a research tradition is not truth or falsity but rather adequacy or inadequacy of the problem-solving capacity of the various theories and research programs that are spawned by it. Thus, a comprehensive evaluation of Habermas's hypothesis would entail an extensive review of the conclusions and methods of these studies in comparison with alternative approaches to the respective object domain. I cannot furnish such an evaluation here. Instead, I take up a single line of inquiry: the question of democratic legitimacy. Communicative rationality is particularly useful in understanding the relationship between democracy and justice. Thus, part of what I do in the remainder of this book is offer a defense of communicative rationality by way of a theory of democratic legitimacy premised on this concept.

Although thinking of Habermas's theory of communication as a research tradition is the most fruitful way of making sense of his *Begründung* strategy, Habermas is also interested in a more direct approach, which can be seen as motivated by the question, But is it *really* true? Here Habermas wants to put forward the reconstructed understanding of communication as a "theory" in the narrow sense I have described, as opposed to a research tradition. He often appears drawn to the idea that a

11. Ibid., pp. 81–82.

12. It would be impossible to cite all the work that Habermas has inspired. Instead, I will just mention some of the fields in which his theoretical approach has been thought useful: social action theory, aesthetics, jurisprudence, ethics, applied ethics, developmental psychology, feminist theory, pedagogy, linguistics, and of course, democratic theory. Although many of the theorists who appeal to communicative rationality or discourse ethics also criticize Habermas in many of the details of his argument, they all accept that a reconstructive understanding of communicative rationality is a powerful theoretical tool.

reconstructive science can replace the mumbo jumbo of Kantian meta-physics with straightforward "scientific" arguments. He wants recon-structive science to have the respectability of a "science" but at the same time avoid the pitfalls of positive social science. This desire leads him to make some strong and, I think, implausible claims about reconstructive science.

RECONSTRUCTION AS DESCRIPTION

Habermas claims that reconstructive science sets itself apart from normal or positivist social sciences in being descriptive.[13] Normal sci-ence explains more than it describes. Normal science begins with a hypothesis or law derived from general principles and then goes out into the world to test that law. So, for example, from general principles about rationally self-interested behavior we might derive a hypothesis that economic development leads to democratization.[14] Armed with this hypothesis, the social scientist then goes in search of empirical evi-dence to confirm or disconfirm it.

There are two potential problems with this model of social science. The first is that it could be argued that it is just not good social sci-ence. It is not good because, in the name of parsimony, it misses a large part of what is really going on out there in the world. As Clifford Geertz says, "Things get lost."[15] The social scientist peers at reality through the lens of her hypothesis and is interested only in those facts that support or contest the hypothesis. This model of social science can indeed explain things and often predict things, but the question is whether or not these explanations and predictions really give us insight into social reality. The world is a messy place that perhaps cannot be adequately captured in elegant and parsimonious explanations. This is, of course, a common criticism of social science understood narrowly on a nomological-deductive model. Evidence that this criticism is correct is that few really good positivist social scientists can be described as narrow hypothesis testers, despite claims to the contrary.[16]

13. For a good discussion of this issue, see Alford, "Is Habermas's Reconstructive Science Really a Science?" pp. 321–40. My interpretation differs from Alford's in making a stronger distinction between falsifiable and fallible.

14. This is the argument that Seymour Martin Lipset makes in *Political Man: The Social Bases of Politics* (Baltimore: Johns Hopkins University Press, 1981).

15. Clifford Geertz, *Local Knowledge* (New York: Basic Books, 1983), p. 10.

16. The work of such people as Karl Deutsch, Barrington Moore, and Seymour Martin

The second criticism is normative. It is not just that this type of social science is not good or interesting social science; it is that this type of social science dehumanizes its subject. In studying, for example, the nomadic patterns of the Masai in the very same way one studies the migration patterns of the caribou—that is, by correlating behavior to natural variables—we do some sort of injustice to the Masai; or if we reduce democracy to the variable of economic development we do an injustice to those people who fight for and even die for democracy. This is not to deny that economic development can be correlated to democracy; that is, this very well may be a good explanation. It is to say that a social science that believes this type of explanation to be the pinnacle of its achievement is a social science that objectifies human relations. And what is wrong with objectifying human relations if by doing so we actually come up with good explanations? This question brings us back to the first criticism, for the two criticisms are not unrelated. Human beings are, in some fundamental sense, not like caribou or the movement of particles. To study them as if they were like caribou is to miss something important about human life. It is to miss the role that human agency, self-understanding, and meanings play in events. And a social science that misses something important is not a good social science. What is and is not important about human life, however, is itself a normative question that informs social science. It is not discovered by social science.

There is another and potentially darker side to this kind of social science. To study human beings as one would study external nature is to develop a whole body of scientific knowledge that, in addition to offering explanations, also offers ways and means to control and manipulate human behavior. Think, for example, of Jeremy Bentham's efforts to design a humane rehabilitation system for criminals, which resulted in his panoptikon—a form of control that can be seen as more invidious and dehumanizing than brute force. This is an extreme example. Less extreme, but no less troubling, is the way in which voting behavior studies can be used by politicians to manipulate elections. A social science that focuses on the external causes of human behavior teaches us how to manipulate those causal factors to bring about the desired behavior.

Habermas, along with a great many other people, has made a career

---

Lipset shows that these social scientists are more interested in research into what is really going on than in simply testing their models.

of criticizing positivist social science for its objectifying stance and the inherent dangers of control and manipulation in a nomological-deductive model. Thus, a clear distinction between reconstructive "science" and positivist social "science" is very important to him.

Habermas claims to be describing a certain type of human experience from the point of view of the participant. In this way, he thinks he frees reconstructive science from the two problems I have mentioned. First, reconstructive science does not view its object domain through a model. The hypothesis (communication presupposes a universal structure) is not a theoretically derived causal hypothesis but rather a hypothetical description of the presuppositions that must be appealed to when two or more people attempt to communicate with each other. As a description, it is supposed to reflect reality rather than to organize reality along pregiven theoretical lines. Second, as a description of the participant's point of view, it does not objectify human experience. It tries to give a rendering of communication that corresponds to how actors actually experience communication. But what exactly is reconstructive science describing?

Description can be used in either an essentialist or an interpretivist sense. Description in an essentialist sense is what one might find in zoology: the two-toed sloth is an arboreal mammal with two toes on its forefeet, found in Central and South America, and so on. The description claims to correspond to a set of brute facts about the world. Obviously, we do not need a reconstructive approach to describe the two-toed sloth. An example of an essentialist description that would require reconstruction can be found in Noam Chomsky's linguistic theory. Chomsky asserts that ordinary learning processes cannot account for the speed with which children master complex grammatical structures. If children were born with a kind of grammatical tabula rasa, they would never be able to acquire such grammatical competency. Chomsky says that the only thing that can account for this competency is the existence of an innate deep grammar. This is an essentialist description in the sense that Chomsky claims to be describing a brute fact about how the human brain works, independent of context and culture.

The second sense of description is interpretivist. Here, one sets out to give a fully articulated understanding of the participant's point of view. This type of description will also require a form of reconstruction. The interpreter must reconstruct background knowledge that is not always explicit for the subject but is nevertheless essential if we want to have a full understanding of what is going on. Although the interpretivist is not making things up, there is no essentialist claim in the sense I have described. The reason is that the interpretivist does not accept the idea that there are any brute facts that can serve as a source of independent verification. Although good interpretations should correspond to a "reality," a good interpretation is checked not against that reality but against other interpretations of that reality.

If Habermas is using description in the second sense, then he is offering a deep semantic analysis of terms such as communication, rationality, and agreement. To communicate means that we seek to understand and convince; to be rational means that we offer reasons that can be understood and can convince; to be in agreement means that we understand each other fully and have been freely convinced. The rules of discourse would then be a way of articulating these meanings: we have a better understanding of communication, rationality, and agreement when we understand them as being structured by these rules. If this is what Habermas is doing, then we would see a strong family resemblance between reconstruction and hermeneutics. The difference would be that Habermas is interested not in the content of particular meanings but in the communication of meaning as such. When Habermas uses such terms as reconstructive understanding or even hermeneutical reconstruction he is appealing to this interpretivist sense of description. If this were all he were saying, his theory of communicative action would be much less controversial than it is. But in addition to the semantic argument, he wants to make an essentialist one as well. He says, for example, that if reconstructions "are true, they have to correspond precisely to the rules that are operatively effective in the object domain—that is, to the rules that actually determine the production of surface structures."[17]

The problem with this claim is that the rules of argumentation cannot be shown to be true or false in this correspondence or essentialist sense. The reconstruction of the rules of discourse represents a fallible hypothesis, but it is not a falsifiable hypothesis in the same way that interpretations are not falsifiable. A description in the essentialist sense can be true or false in that (in principle anyway) it can be checked against the brute or independent facts being described. Furthermore, these descriptions are independent of the brute facts in the sense that the description of the two-toed sloth or of innate deep grammar does

17. Jürgen Habermas, *Communication and the Evolution of Society*, translated by Thomas McCarthy (Boston: Beacon Press, 1979), p. 16.

not feed back on or affect the objective attributes of the two-toed sloth or a child's competency to acquire a language.

Interpretivist description cannot be true or false in this sense because what is a fact is part of the description. The description, for example, of an intersubjective meaning that helps us make sense of a certain practice cannot be checked against the brute fact of that meaning because there is no meaning independent of our or our subject's understanding, of it. We can check our understanding as social scientists against our subject's understanding but this is not the same thing as checking it against an independent brute fact. Furthermore, interpretations are internally related to their object domain in such a way that they can feed back on and affect the very thing they are describing.

The analogy between innate grammar and the presuppositions of communication breaks down here. While it is true that we need neither Chomsky nor Habermas in order to make well-formed sentences or to communicate with one another, it is also true to say that Chomsky's analysis of language is not related to our self-understanding in the same way that Habermas's analysis of communication is potentially related to our self-understanding. There is an undeniable normative and feedback component to a theory of communicative rationality which is not part of a theory of innate grammar.[18] What we understand by terms such as rationality, communication, and argument, affects how we reason, communicate, and argue. This is one of the reasons why Habermas has now rejected maieutic testing (eliciting recognition of the rules through question-and-answer sessions) as a direct method of verification. There is no way to separate the self-understanding of the subject, which can be affected by the very questions the researcher asks, from the rules themselves.[19]

The conclusion to be drawn is that reconstruction is best characterized as reconstructive *understanding*. Thus, we act *as if* the rules of discourse stand behind our communicative interaction. This is less than Habermas wants, but I think it is strong enough to do the work

18. Mary Hesse, "Science and Objectivity," in *Habermas*, ed. Thompson and Held, p. 112.

19. Fred Alford argues that with the essentialist claim, Habermas cannot maintain the distinction between normal science and reconstructive sciences he wishes to. An essentialist description is a description from the observer's point of view. It must take the brute fact as an independent object that can in principle falsify the original hypothesis. But if Habermas's hypothesis is falsifiable in this sense, then he too must be approaching reality with a model and selecting the information that will fit into the model. See "Is Habermas's Reconstructive Science Really a Science?" p. 336. This problem does not arise if we understand the hypothesis as fallible rather than falsifiable.

he intends for his "first principle." Thinking about communication as if it were structured according to these rules makes sense of our world and gives us a meaningful point of comparison to view development. That the rules of discourse cannot be shown to be a "fact" of reason in the Kantian transcendental sense or a brute fact of cognition in the Chomskian essentialist sense should not lead us to conclude they are not real. We do not carry these rules around in our heads. These rules describe something that goes on between communicators, not within a solitary thinker; or rather, they describe how we experience what goes on between ourselves and our interlocutors. The plausibility of the rules rests ultimately not on proof but rather on how much sense this description makes to us as communicators, given other things that we believe, know, and understand.

Does this reading of Habermas make the argument relativist? I believe the answer must be no. A reconstructive understanding of communicative rationality is universal in the sense that it is a conception of rationality which can account for changes through history and be applied without damage to other cultures—indeed, can be applied universally. Instrumental conceptions of reason also claim to be universal in this sense. Which is the more adequate conception of reason is not a matter of proof, transcendental or otherwise. It is a matter of adequacy. Which conception gives a more coherent account of our intuitions and interaction, of the relationship among speech, language, and culture, of developments in science and politics, of our understanding of truth and justification, of the rise of modernity and the decline of tradition, and so on? This type of question will not yield a neat, parsimonious answer. Indeed, it really represents a set of interlocking questions that span a great many divergent fields of study.

Habermas's work can be understood as a set of interlocking answers that add up to a somewhat messy and expansive theory of rationality, but one that has many plausible elements. Adequacy and plausibility may appear to be a weaker sort of defense than verification. That a theory is plausible means that it makes a certain amount of sense, that it is not blatantly false, contradictory, or counterintuitive, and that we give it the benefit of the doubt until such time as it is shown to be mistaken. That a theory is adequate means that in comparison with other theories it is more effective in solving problems and answering questions. If we add up the various specific arguments that Habermas makes, none of which by itself can fully justify the universality of communicative rationality, we find that the theory rests on this idea plausibility and adequacy. That it does, does not weaken Habermas's claims, however. In the final analysis, any and every theory of rationality must ultimately rest on plausibility and adequacy, not proof. For some, this is perhaps a reason not to bother making universal statements about rationality which cannot be proven. But if we, as social scientists, talk only about things that we can prove or disprove, then we are being led by our methods.

Communicative rationality is a plausible reconstruction of the presuppositions that speakers must make when they communicate with each other. To think that something has or could go wrong with communication is to assume that there is a form of communication in which nothing goes wrong; it is to presuppose an ideal form of communication that stands as a counterfactual background to our conversations. In the following chapters, I hope to show that the theory of communicative rationality is not only plausible but also adequate in solving some long-standing problems of political theory.

9 Defending Modernity

The most ambitious claim put forward on behalf of discourse ethics is that it contains a moral principle that is universally valid. With this claim and its defense, Habermas moves beyond Scanlon and Rawls. Like Habermas, Scanlon is interested in furnishing his moral theory with strong philosophical foundations, but unlike Habermas, Scanlon has not undertaken a comprehensive account of these foundations. In the end, the status of Scanlon's "foundation"—the desire to be justified—is left vague. It is neither a universal fact nor a natural fact but rather the product of moral education. The meaning of moral education, however, is never made clear.

With regard to universalist claims, Rawls's position is somewhat puzzling. In "The Domain of the Political and Overlapping Consensus," he contends that although his conception of justice "may not apply to all societies at all times and places, this does not make it historicist, or relativist."[1] This is a defensible position and, as we will see, one that Habermas takes up. What is puzzling in Rawls's case is that although it is defensible, he never defends it. While it is true that a theory need not apply to all societies at all times and places to avoid relativism, it is also true that a theory that claims to be articulating "basic intuitive ideas which we take to be implicit in the public culture of a democratic society"[2] must substantiate its claim not to be relativist. On the face of

1. John Rawls, "The Domain of the Political and Overlapping Consensus," *New York University Law Review* 64 (May 1989): 251.
2. John Rawls, "Justice as Fairness: Political not Metaphysical," *Philosophy and Public Affairs* 14 (1985), 231; and see Rawls, *Political Liberalism* (New York: Columbia University Press, 1993), pp. 13, 43.

it, articulating intuitions embedded in democratic society looks historicist and relativist, and most commentators have read Rawls as such. Rawls has made very little effort to dispel this reading, apparently for the reason that he simply does not want to get mired in a "metadebate"; he is more interested in theories of justice than in theories about theories of justice. Furthermore, he believes that the persuasiveness of his argument does not depend on vindicating a universal claim about reason. It is enough that justice as fairness be reasonable and rational *for us*. The plausibility of the argument does not depend on showing that our standards of reasonable and rational are themselves universal. He remains agnostic about these metaquestions and does not see his role as manning the barricades against skepticism and relativism.

This strategy, however, smacks somewhat of preaching to the converted. Given the rise of both postmodern and antimodern attacks on modern conceptions of reason, not to mention doubts about the public culture of democratic society, expanding the scope of the argument into "meta" questions would seem in order. Habermas undertakes such an expansion. He attempts to defend modern moral intuitions from the accusation that they are simply one set of historically specific preferences in a long history of such preferences. The first step in this defense is the introduction of a theory of moral development.

LEARNING TO BE MODERN

Habermas's theory of discourse ethics begins with general presuppositions underlying all communication and ends with a procedure for the resolution of normative disputes. This procedure can be understood as a "reconstruction of the everyday intuitions underlying the impartial judgment of moral conflicts of action."[3] Habermas draws a connection between speaking a language and adopting a particular moral point of view, namely, a deontological point of view, which sees justice as primary and impartiality as central to justice. But does speaking a language, any language, necessarily lead to deontological ethics? At some level this clearly cannot be the case. The moral intuitions to which Habermas refers are *our* intuitions. Impartiality is a modern (perhaps only Western) point of view. The connection between universal pragmatics and deontological ethics must be supplemented

---

3. Jürgen Habermas, *Moral Consciousness and Communicative Action*, translated by Christian Lenhardt and Shierry Weber Nicholsen (Cambridge: MIT Press, 1990), p. 116.

with an argument that can account for the historical specificity of deontological intuitions.

Habermas supplies this argument in the form of a theory of moral development which is interwoven with nothing less than a full-blown theory of social evolution. The introduction of social evolution as a complement to the reconstruction of the presuppositions of moral discourse adds a dimension to Habermas's ethical theory which is lacking in the two liberal accounts I have reviewed thus far. Habermas, Rawls, and Scanlon are all interested in articulating intuitions embedded in our political and moral culture. Habermas, however, introduces a detailed account of how these understandings come to be part of our shared background.[4] In this way he expands the purview of interpretive reconstruction to include an analysis of modernity itself. This expansion lends a richness to his description of modern morality which is missing in the purely synchronic accounts of moral judgment offered by Rawls and Scanlon.

Investigating the evolution of moral understandings lends more than richness and detail to a theory, however. It can counter the objection that, without ultimate grounds, metaphysics, or self-evident first principles—that is, without the ability to step outside our horizons—we must accept some version of moral relativism. Moral relativism assumes that cultural value systems are incommensurable. They have their beliefs; we have our beliefs; who's to say which is better? One way to counter this argument, while still accepting that we cannot step outside of our context, is to maintain that the horizons that limit our view are not arbitrary. Our horizons are the product of learning about and becoming aware of the problems and limitations of earlier horizons. Here we have the idea that accumulated knowledge is the stuff of which horizons and contexts are built. Tracing learning processes over time can shed light on the question, What leads us to believe that our moral intuitions are sound? The answer to this question is found in a progressive development of moral consciousness over time through which intuitions become ever more rationally defensible.

Although the plausibility of this type of argument is a necessary (but

4. Rawls, of course, is not blind to the history of our intuitions. For example, he suggests that modern notions of fairness and impartiality can be seen as developing out of sixteenth- and seventeenth-century ideas of toleration. What was once a modus vivendi to escape devastating religious wars, he says, turned into a commitment to public impartiality. "Justice as Fairness," pp. 225–26; *Political Liberalism*, p. xxiv. This is a plausible reading of our past, but Rawls tells us very little about the process of moral education that led from a modus vivendi on toleration to a principled commitment to fairness and impartiality.

not sufficient) condition if we are to avoid relativism, there are many dangers and problems associated with developmental theory. The most obvious objection is that it is inherently ethnocentric and devalues past and contemporaneous cultures that appear to be less developed than our own. A second common objection is that developmental theory rests on a naive (utopian) notion of progress passed on to us by an Enlightenment tradition that has been largely discredited. Finally, even if the argument can be sustained, it adds up to less than a full defense of modernity. At best, developmental theory can show that we have learned something over the course of time. Unless we want to talk about the end of history, we cannot conclude that we have learned all there is to know. In this and the next chapter, I show that the first and second objections are unwarranted and that the third is no objection at all.

RATIONALIZATION OF THE LIFEWORLD

Habermas develops his theory of communicative action and social evolution as, among other things, a corrective to the Marxist tradition that saw labor as the driving force in social evolution. In the Marxist view, social reproduction is defined and given content through our interaction with nature; inquiry focuses on how we remake our external world generation after generation. Habermas says that the overarching place of labor within this theoretical approach has produced a one-sided view of social dynamics which leaves out what he calls the lifeworld.[5] Not only do we remake the external/natural world through labor, but we also remake, generation after generation, our inner/sociocultural world through symbolic interaction or communication.

The lifeworld is the background against which all social interaction takes place. It is a repository and contains the accumulated interpretations of past generations, how the people who went before us understood their world, themselves, and each other; their duties, commitments, and allegiances; their art and literature; the place of science, religion, and law; and so on. As social actors, we draw upon these understandings when trying to make sense of the things that go on around us (or even inside of us). This is what Habermas means when

5. Habermas borrows the concept of the lifeworld from phenomenology and most particularly Husserl. See Jürgen Habermas, *The Theory of Communicative Action*, translated by Thomas McCarthy, vol. 2 (Boston: Beacon Press, 1987), p. 119.

he says that the "lifeworld background serves as a source of situation definitions."[6] Sometimes individuals simply reproduce background assumptions unreflectively. For example, one understands a situation in exactly the same way as did one's parents, and their parents before them, and so on. At other times individuals or groups revise these assumptions to fit new circumstances. For instance, a group reinterprets its religious understanding in light of historical circumstances (religious wars, say). At other times again, an individual or group may consciously reject background assumptions embedded in the lifeworld. For example, one puts a urinal on the wall and calls it art, or one refuses to fight for one's country when it is expected, and so on. Even these rejections, however, must draw on some other part of the lifeworld in defining a situation in a new way. We can never fully transcend our own horizons.

All symbolic or meaningful action draws upon the lifeworld. Every time we engage in such action we are taking up an attitude toward part of the given lifeworld. The range of ways in which we bring the background assumptions into play in our interactions can be understood to lie on a continuum between the attitudes expressed in the terms *yes* and *no*. We say yes to aspects of our lifeworld every time we consciously or unconsciously reproduce them. We say no to other aspects every time we reject them. Most of our interaction, however, falls somewhere in the middle. We gradually and slowly reinterpret our lifeworld and pass it on to the next generation in a slightly altered form.

Rather than interpret the substantive content of particular lifeworlds, Habermas wishes to begin by uncovering "structures that, in contrast to the historical shapes of particular lifeworlds and lifeforms, are put forward as invariant."[7] What he is really interested in is seeing if we can identify a logic at work in the way we alter and revise our lifeworld over time. The first "invariant" element is communicative action and the raising of validity claims presupposed by that action. Wherever there is social interaction there is communication, and wherever there is communication there are people who do (or could) ask, Is that true? Ought I to do this? Do you really mean that? Although there are all sorts of others we can ask, these are core questions when it comes to the constitution of the lifeworld. It is through meaningful answers to these questions that we gain access to a shared objective

6. Jürgen Habermas, *The Theory of Communicative Action*, translated by Thomas McCarthy, vol. 1 (Boston: Beacon Press, 1981), p. 70.

7. Habermas, *Theory of Communicative Action* 2: 119.

world, a shared normative world, and commensurable subjective worlds.

In understanding how lifeworlds change, the focus is not on the substantive answers to these questions. That we answer the question, "Is it true that the world is flat?" with a no, whereas earlier cultures answered it with a yes, does not represent an interesting difference. The interesting difference arises when we go one step further and ask, "*Why* is/is not the world flat?" This is a question that asks for reasons. Habermas says that the fund of background knowledge and information we draw on in answering the "why" question has undergone a process of rationalization such that reason giving is a very different thing for moderns than for premoderns. Thus, it is not so much that we have different answers to the questions, as that we have a different way of answering the questions.

The rationalization of background information involves progressive differentiation (*Ausdifferenzierung*). Actors begin to differentiate between different types of information which are drawn upon in different types of situations.[8] For example, in primitive societies it is often the case that people appeal to a core set of understandings in almost all situation definitions. There is little differentiation between information appropriate to understanding a social situation and information appropriate to understanding natural phenomena. In both cases an individual may appeal to, say, magical beliefs. At this stage, her world view is "centered," in that making sense of the world is tied to one central set of meanings.

Habermas suggests that as societies develop we can see a "decentering" taking place.[9] A central core of meanings can no longer serve as the organizing principle for all the situations individuals find themselves in. Social actors begin to differentiate between different types of

8. Habermas is more interested in describing this process than in explaining why it happens. Thus, he rejects "the idea of evolution as a causally unfolding law-like process." See Jürgen Habermas, "History and Evolution," *Telos* 39 (Spring 1979): 25; also Habermas, *Theory of Communicative Action* 1: 67.

9. Habermas's understanding of social evolution is indebted in many ways to Jean Piaget's theory of cognitive development. While admitting that the analogy between individual cognitive development and sociocultural development is *only* an analogy and cannot be taken too literally, Habermas borrows heavily from Piaget's terminology, in particular the concept of "decentering." In Piaget's theory this concept refers to a child's progressive movement away from an egocentric understanding of the world. As the infant confronts the external world it must learn to differentiate between the internal universe of subjectivity and the external world of objects. Later, this external world is differentiated "into the world of perceptible and manipulatable objects on the one hand and the world of normatively regulated interpersonal relations on the other." Habermas, *Theory of Communicative Action* 1: 68.

situations which call for different types of explanations and meanings. For example, people begin to recognize that the question of how one goes to heaven is distinct from the question of how heaven goes and that the latter can be answered independently of the former.[10] This recognition serves to exclude religion as an appropriate reference in explaining the movement of planets. Thus, actors begin to grasp the world in a differentiated way; different things need different sorts of explanations. The process of differentiation places a more complex lifeworld before our eyes. We see the growing autonomy of the spheres of science, morality, religion, law, and aesthetics. Each of these spheres comes uncoupled from traditional interpretations and thus requires new interpretations to underpin it. It is important to remember that although a differentiated lifeworld can be described as more complex than an undifferentiated lifeworld, this does not mean that centered world views are not multifarious and intricate in the sense of accounting for innumerable interconnected factors of life in a coherent way. Primitive world views can indeed be very complex; but the complexity is of a different type.

As cultural understandings become decentered, the power of culture over social actors is weakened. As parts of our daily life break away from the central world view—that is, can no longer be explained or understood in the terms that world view offers—social actors must seek out their own explanations and understandings: "The more the worldview that furnishes the cultural stock of knowledge is decentered, the less the need for understanding is covered *in advance* by an interpreted lifeworld immune from critique, and the more this need has to be met by the interpretative accomplishments of participants themselves.[11] Decentering is a destabilizing force, which calls into question "givens"; less and less of the lifeworld is simply taken as given. With the rise of modernity, then, we see the attempt to penetrate more deeply than ever before into the lifeworld and bring to light the background information contained within it. Thus, although the lifeworld can never become fully transparent to us, it has become progressively less opaque.[12] For example, we as moderns have become aware, in a

10. In "Letter to the Grand Duchess Christina," Galileo, appealing to Cardinal Baronius in his defense of science, quotes the cardinal as saying "that the intention of the Holy Ghost is to teach us how one goes to heaven, not how heaven goes." *Discoveries and Opinions of Galileo*, translated by Stillman Drake (Doubleday Anchor, 1957), p. 186.

11. Habermas, *Theory of Communicative Action* 1: 70.

12. In an earlier essay Habermas implies that discourse could potentially make our lifeworld fully transparent to us. Through discourse, we could "rise above" our contingent situa-

way that premoderns were not aware, that there is something like the lifeworld, or that our arguments draw upon background and hidden assumptions within our culture. The reasons we offer for our beliefs and principles must penetrate more deeply into the lifeworld precisely because we are conscious of all the things (interests, ethnocentricity, cultural bias, unexamined assumptions, socialization, domination, and so on) that can lie hidden behind arguments. Decentering and differentiation create a different and, I believe, a more demanding context in which to answer such questions as, Why is this true? or Why ought I to do that?

RATIONALIZATION AND MORAL DEVELOPMENT

One question that immediately comes to mind with Habermas's claims about decentering and differentiation is the one David Rasmussen asks: "Does modernity represent a *higher* level of rationality and rationalization, or does modernity represent a *different* modality of rationalization?"[13] According to Rasmussen, not only is it unnecessary to claim that modernity represents a higher level of rationality, but such a claim is tied to an outmoded and discredited view of progress. For example, he claims that Habermas displays a "tendency to assume that myth is either a form of limited rationality or that it is pre-rational altogether. At any rate, it is assumed that, in juxtaposition to modernity, myth is a confused form of linguistic expression." Appealing to Claude Lévi-Strauss's analysis of the Oedipus myth, Rasmussen maintains that "rather than being a form of confused thinking, myth can be said to represent a quite legitimate and valid form of thinking with its own rubrics and properties." For example, the Oedipus myth, "when considered as an anthropological document, explains social integration

<hr/>

tion and achieve the view from nowhere. Jürgen Habermas, "*Wahrheitstheorien*," in *Wirklichkeit und Reflexion: Walter Schulz zum 60 Geburtstag*, edited by H. Fahrenbach (Pfüllingen: Neske, 1973), pp. 211–263. In the twenty years since this essay was published, Habermas has significantly retreated from this position but without altering the fundamental core of his theoretical position. Now he maintains that we can never fully step outside our own horizons, but we can come to have a deep knowledge of our horizons. "*Wahrheitstheorien*" contains many strong claims about discourse ethics which Habermas has softened over time. Many critics nevertheless still return to this piece to criticize Habermas.

13. David M. Rasmussen, "Communicative Action and Philosophy: Reflections on Habermas' *Theorie des kommunikativen Handelns*," *Philosophy and Social Criticism* 9 (Spring 1982): 21. See also, Michael Schmid, "Habermas's Theory of Social Evolution," in *Habermas: Critical Debates*, edited by John B. Thompson and David Held (Cambridge: MIT Press, 1982), pp. 162–80.

and the phenomenon of taboo."[14] Habermas would not disagree. Myths help people make sense of the world, often good sense. The problem with myth is not that it is a confused form of thinking but that it is often embedded in a world view that is undifferentiated in the sense that participants do not clearly differentiate among the objective world, the social world, and the subjective world. The real question is, Why is a differentiated world view higher or more rational than an undifferentiated world view?

It would be a mistake to understand Habermas's answer to this question as an essentialist answer. He is not saying that we have come to grasp the world as it really is and therefore we are more rational than myth believers. Habermas is not making a substantive claim about the content of our knowledge and understanding; he is making a procedural claim about how open or closed is the process through which we acquire our knowledge and understanding. Thus, he is not saying that reasons given to justify an action or statement which appeal to myth are nonrational because myths are fictions (are not real). He is saying that world views that *limit* acceptable reasons to myth are less rational because they preempt a more extensive search for reasons. Decentering or differentiation frees norms (or propositional statements) from preestablished limits on what counts as an acceptable justification. Myth itself is not devalued; rather, it is the exclusivity of myth that is devalued.

At its most basic, the claim to a higher level of rationality simply means that accepting claims (to truth or whatever) reflectively can be described as a more rational *process* than accepting claims unreflectively. This claim does not necessarily affect the substance of beliefs. For example, that people might accept the taboo against incest unreflectively—that is, without really thinking about and evaluating the reasons—does not necessarily undermine the sensibleness of the taboo, for which many reasons could be offered. The deeper and more extensive the opportunity and possibility of reflection, however, the more rationality plays a part in the process. The more a culture allows for an open environment of questioning and criticism, the more we can describe the process of inquiry involved in answering such questions as Why is this true? or Why ought I to do that? as rational. And conversely, belief systems that work against the possibility of rational reflection—that is, cultural traditions that "predecide which validity

14. Rasmussen, "Communicative Action and Philosophy," pp. 19, 20.

claims, when, where, for what, from whom, and to whom must be accepted"[15]—are less rational. Again, this does not mean that the substance of beliefs is necessarily irrational, false, or indefensible. It means that the substance of beliefs has not been rationally tested in a rigorous way. For example, Habermas does not object to Zande belief in witchcraft because it is incompatible with scientific rationality. "Rather, the belief in witches exhibits a structure that binds the Zande consciousness more or less blindly to inherited interpretations and does not permit consciousness of the possibility of alternative interpretations to arise." Following Ernest Gellner and Robin Horton, Habermas characterizes the difference between mythical and modern world views as being a difference between closed and open belief systems and maintains that comparison on these grounds "seems to provide a *context-independent standard for the rationality of worldviews.*"[16]

The intuitive idea behind communicative rationality is that an action or statement is rational to the extent that the actor or speaker can give good reasons for the action or statement. Applying this standard of rationality across cultures means that the extent to which a cultural belief system opens up the possibility of searching for the best possible reason—which means allows for revision, corrigibility, criticism, and so on—the more rationalized is that culture.

What then is the connection between rationalization and claims that modernity has reached a higher level of moral development? The theory of the progressive rationalization of the lifeworld avoids the most obvious danger involved in defending modern moral understandings: a blanket cross-cultural standard of moral behavior. It answers, for example, the objection of Raymond Geuss, who contends that the "quasi-transcendental deduction" of Habermas's theory burdens "the pre-dynastic Egyptians, ninth-century French serfs, and early-twentieth-century Yamano tribesmen with the view that they are acting correctly if their action is based on a norm on which there would be a universal consensus in an ideal speech situation."[17] This is clearly not the case. In all the cultures Geuss mentions norms have yet to detach themselves from totalizing world views and so have yet to *require* the legitimating force of an "achieved" consensus.

Ninth-century French serfs, for example, would view themselves as

15. Habermas, *Theory of Communicative Action*, 1: 70.

16. Ibid., 61, 62.

17. Raymond Geuss, *The Idea of a Critical Theory* (Cambridge: Cambridge University Press, 1981), p. 66.

acting correctly when their actions conformed to internal standards of conduct. Appropriate behavior would depend on whether the reasons they could offer for their conduct would be the sort of reasons that would be acceptable given the makeup of their lifeworld. The difference between our culture and the ones Geuss mentions is that our idea of what constitutes a good reason has shifted with the shifting structure of our lifeworld.[18]

What kind of reasons are acceptable to us given the make up of our lifeworld? Because there are no agreed-upon first principles, unquestioned moral truths, or unimpeachable moral authorities, a good reason cannot be substantively stipulated in advance; it can only be procedurally stipulated. That is not to say that as moderns we have no substantive reasons for our moral stands. Many of us appeal to religion, natural rights, or conceptions of the good in defending our actions. Any of these might be a good reason. But none of them represents unquestioned shared assumptions in our lifeworld; therefore, none of them can be taken for granted as a good reason.

The devaluation of traditional justifications and interpretations opens the door to discursive justifications and interpretations. When the traditional foundation of social norms erodes, we are, so to speak, thrown back on our own resources. When shared religious beliefs no longer form the unquestioned foundation of certain social arrangements, we are forced, if social cooperation is to continue, to construct new foundations. The rationalization of the lifeworld leads us to search deeper and deeper for good reasons. What happens in this search for reasons is that the structure of moral argumentation changes. We begin to see that we can no longer resolve our disputes by appeal to the moral equivalent of "the buck stops here," which is to say, by appeal to God, or nature, or self-evident truth. In premodern society, moral argumentation proceeds against the background assumption that the buck does stop somewhere. Even if there is disagreement about where it stops, it is assumed that discovering some final point is the *way* of resolving the dispute. We no longer share that assumption. The changing background assumption, then, is not about the truth of God or the existence of self-evident truth (many of us still believe these things). The changing assumption is about whether these sorts of appeals can resolve our moral disputes; it is a changing assumption about the *way* the argument ends.

18. Habermas, *Theory of Communicative Action*, 1: 55.

One way to express this difference is to say that premodern moral conversation sets out to discover truths; modern moral conversation sets out to test claims. Modern conversations that try to answer the question, Why ought I to do that? seek a type of warranted assertability rather than a "buck-stopping" device. This warranted assertability is achieved in conversations that criticize, challenge, analyze, and question proposed norms. The demise of ultimate foundations has made life more complicated and messy, with many more arguments and disputes about morality, but at the same time, it has produced a more demanding context of justification for moral claims. To use a scientific analogy, rigorous attempts to "falsify" norms strengthens their claim to rightness, just as rigorous attempts to falsify scientific hypotheses strengthen their claim to truth. The more the context we live in opens up the potential for criticism, the more confident we can be that the norms that survive this criticism are well founded. Argumentative criticism must proceed along certain lines and under certain conditions, however, for this confidence to have any foundation. Thus, we fall back on the rules of speech and argumentation, rather than ultimate truth as the background assumption of moral discourse.

This argument is expanded in the next chapter. For the moment it is important to remember that the claim being made here is about structural components and potentialities of the lifeworld and not about the substance of all our beliefs. The rationalization of the lifeworld opens up the structural possibility of testing norms rationally through critical argumentation; it does not guarantee it. There are also crosscutting influences in society that work against the possibility of exploiting that potential. Further, as we will see in the next chapter, the claim that modernity has opened up the opportunity to rationalize the foundations to norms is not synonymous with the claim to have found moral truth.

Defending Modernity

With his idea of communicative rationality Habermas believes he can avoid the commonest criticisms of Enlightenment notions of progress. Skepticism about modernity's claim to represent a higher stage of development finds expression in several theoretical approaches. One of the most popular is the incommensurability or hermeneutical thesis, which postulates a multiplicity of "rationalities" or languages through history and across cultures. On this view, for example, the Azande belief in witchcraft appears irrational only from our vantage point.[19] From within the Azande lifeworld, witchcraft makes perfect sense, and making sense of the world is what rationality is all about. Therefore, we must understand the Azande culture and language as expressing their own form of rationality. Another popular objection finds expression in the "wrong turn" or anti-Enlightenment thesis. Those who hold this view, most notably Alasdair MacIntyre, maintain that far from representing a higher level of rationality, a modern conception of rationality is the result of a wrong turn taken somewhere in the seventeenth century.[20] Modernity, denuded of substantive content by such people as Descartes and Hobbes, has been left a confused, impoverished, and morally dubious conception of rationality. Finally, the critique of reason or post-Enlightenment thesis, is also popular. Those who support it contend that modernity does indeed represent a higher level of rationalization, but far from freeing us from the irrational yoke of unquestioned myth, such a rationalization places a much more insidious and invidious yoke on our shoulders.[21] Rationality becomes the unquestioned myth dominating our lives and understandings.

Habermas's defense of a universal standard of rationality accepts a certain plausibility in all three of these arguments, but Habermas maintains that these criticisms are more properly applied not to modernity as such but to a particular development of modern thought, an uncritical understanding of rationality which is fixated on instrumentality and on knowing and mastering external nature. Thus, in answer to the incommensurability thesis, Habermas acknowledges that judging the Azande world view to be irrational because the belief in witchcraft is unscientific is a form of cultural imperialism. Following hermeneutical anthropology, Habermas agrees that from an internal perspective, world views are totalities because "for members of the same culture the limits of their language are the limits of their world." As totalities, languages and the world views they express are not better or worse, true or false, confused or clear. Propositional statements

19. See, for example, Peter Winch, "Understanding a Primitive Society," in *Rationality*, edited by Bryan Wilson (Oxford: Oxford University Press, 1970), pp. 78– 111.

20. Alasdair MacIntyre, *After Virtue* (Notre Dame: University of Notre Dame Press, 1981).

21. See, for example, Michel Foucault, *Power/Knowledge: Selected Interviews and Other Writings* (New York: Pantheon, 1980), pp. 83– 85.

made within a language might be false, but languages themselves are not propositional statements. World views are, says Habermas, like portraits, which claim to "represent the person as a whole."[22]

The project of tracing learning over time does not devalue world views as totalities, nor does it impose an external and alien standard of rationality on other cultures. The idea that one is acting rationally or reasonably when one has a good reason for an action is a standard that all "communicators" share. The implication of this argument is that although the Azande appeal to different sorts of reasons than we do, they would nevertheless recognize this idea of communicative rationality as an acceptable standard from within their lifeworld. Although there is a certain plausibility to the idea that the Azande believe themselves to be acting reasonably if they have good reason for their action, it is unlikely that they would accept the next step in the argument, that is, that the more one's context opens up the process of reason giving to alternatives, the more rational is the process. Presumably, the Azande believe that they have hit upon the best possible reasons for their actions. Thus, from inside their lifeworld, the Azande can be described as acting rationally, that is, with good reasons. But from outside their lifeworld, we can question whether or not they have the best possible reasons for their actions. In this way the Azande belief system, to the extent that it does not allow for criticism, can be described as less rational than our own. This is not to devalue the Azande world view as a totality; rather, it is to judge that along one dimension, a dimension of rationality, it is less developed than our own.

In answer to the anti-Enlightenment thesis, Habermas would say, among other things, that MacIntyre's criticism of modernity is one-sided. MacIntyre contends that a modern instrumental conception of rationality offers the modern moral agent no way of rationally determining right from wrong, good from bad. We are left with emotivism, "the doctrine that all evaluative judgments and more specifically all moral judgments are *nothing but* expressions of preference, expressions of attitude or feeling." He goes on to say that "emotivism has become embodied in our culture."[23] MacIntyre acknowledges that we often talk as if we could defend our moral statements with reasons but says that modern culture offers no resources from which to draw such a defense. Like MacIntyre, Habermas is interested in refuting emotivism, but unlike him, Habermas believes that emotivism can be refuted from within

22. Habermas, *Theory of Communicative Action*, 1: 58.
23. MacIntyre, *After Virtue*, pp. 11, 21.

the Enlightenment tradition, which is to say that he denies that "emotivism has become embodied in our culture." Our culture offers many more resources than MacIntyre is willing to acknowledge. Instrumental rationality is only one strand of modernity. The development of a theory of communicative reason is designed precisely to overcome the weakness and narrowness of instrumental reason. Therefore, MacIntyre's criticisms apply to a caricature of the Enlightenment only and not to all that the Enlightenment contains.

Habermas uses a similar argument against post-Enlightenment or postmodern criticism. The postmodern critique of reason hits its mark when applied to the instrumentalization of human interaction, an undeniable product of modernity. Modernity has brought with it new forms of domination in the guise of technological liberation and "rationalization."[24] Rationalization is a two-edged sword. For example, on the one hand, modernity has brought a rationalized rule of law which frees individuals from arbitrary and unpredictable incursions. On the other hand, the development of the modern legal system has also brought an instrumentalization of human interaction in which we talk to each other as if through our lawyers. This way of interacting represents an internalization of discipline, which shapes the way we present ourselves in the public and private sphere and reproduces hierarchical relations of domination. Thus, the modern legal system is both a form of emancipation and a form of domination. Postmodernism, in its blanket attack on rationalization, fails to recognize this Janus-like quality of modernity. In denying that modernity contains any emancipatory potential, Habermas claims, postmodernism undermines its own critical perspective.

Rationalization is more than instrumentalization. Rationalization involves the intensification of publicity requirements, the increased visibility of underlying and hidden arguments, the proliferation of challenges to the status quo, and the growing power of argumentation itself. Postmodernism is part of this process of rationalization. Postmodernism engages in argumentation, challenges validity claims, publicizes hidden disciplines. All these activities presuppose communicative rationality; that is, all these activities presuppose that argumentative criticism has an emancipatory force. If we deny that it has, if we say that rational argumentation is just another form of discipline and domination, then postmodernism can offer no reasons why its criticisms, arguments, and

24. Jürgen Habermas, *The Philosophical Discourse of Modernity*, translated by Frederick Lawrence (Cambridge: MIT Press, 1987), pp. 238–65.

contributions to discourse are not one more form of domination. We take postmodern criticism seriously because we believe that we can *really* find out something about our selves and our society through such criticism. But the deep skepticism that can be found in some postmodern authors puts into question this very belief.

Habermas is concerned with the deep skepticism underlying much of postmodern thought and not with the particular critical studies that emerge within that tradition. This skepticism, along with the hermeneutical and anti-Enlightenment critique, are one-sided and fail to recognize the contradictory forces at work within modernity. The Enlightenment legacy is far from monolithic; it contains more than the rise of science and instrumental reason. Modernity is not tied to one strain of thought or tradition; it is better characterized as the rise of criticism of any one defining strain of thought or tradition. Criticism is here understood as argumentative criticism, a questioning of received wisdom in order to uncover deeper insights, a demand for justification in order to find the best possible reason, an inclusion of new voices and perspectives in the debate, and so on. This is not a naive faith in progress. This is a recognition of the potentials offered within the modern world.

10 *Universalism in Morality*

"An ethics is termed *universalist* when it alleges that this (or a similar) moral principle, far from reflecting the intuitions of a particular culture or epoch, is valid universally," Habermas writes, and he adds, "I must prove that my moral principle is not just a reflection of the prejudices of adult, white, well-educated, Western males of today."[1] Habermas believes that discourse ethics is a universal ethics in this strong sense. Applied to a moral theory, the adjective *universal* can refer either to an idea of "universalizability" or to an idea of objective validity. One of the characteristics of "modern" moral theory is that it is universal in the first sense.[2] Moral agency is universalized in that it is no longer tied to specific group membership or natural attributes. If it is wrong for me to do x in a certain situation, then it is wrong for anyone to do x in this situation.

One can hold that moral principles must be universalizable in this first sense (that is, that they must apply irrespective of natural, ethnic, or class differences) but at the same time doubt their universal validity (that is, doubt that they are universal in the second sense). For example, "Every human being is deserving of respect" universalizes the moral idea of respect. Whereas "Greeks (or the very brave, or the morally righteous, or the true followers of God) are deserving of respect" attaches respect to a particular group and in this sense is not universal. The very strange thing about modernity is that as the content of our

1. Jürgen Habermas, *Moral Consciousness and Communicative Action*, translated by Christian Lenhardt and Shierry Weber Nicholsen (Cambridge: MIT Press, 1990), p. 197.
2. Of course, not all contemporary moral theory is "modern."

moral intuitions has been universalized to include everyone, the foundations appear to have been relativized to include only us. For example, many people (indeed most of the undergraduates I teach) feel that there is no contradiction in stating that they believe in a principle of universal respect but that this principle is merely a modern Western value (opinion, preference) and cannot be defended as a universal truth. For premoderns the relationship was often reversed. Particularist content was defended as universal truth discovered in nature or sanctioned by God.

Habermas sets out to reunite universalist content with universal validity while avoiding the dogmatism of ultimate foundations found in premodern appeals to nature or God. He wants to attach our universal intuitions (of the type, all human beings are deserving of respect) to claims of general validity. They are attached at the point of convergence between the reconstruction of the presuppositions of communication and the evolutionary theory of moral development. Practical discourse is an articulation of *our* intuitions concerning the reciprocal conditions of moral deliberation and agreement; however, these intuitions can be understood as the product of a learning process whereby the *universal* structure of communicative reason comes to fruition.

The U-Principle

Habermas says that viewing moral deliberation as being governed by the pretheoretical rules of argumentation leads to a moral principle that is universal in both of the senses I have described. The principle, which Habermas calls the *Universalierungsgrundsatz* (U-principle), declares that a norm can be said to be valid when "*all* affected can accept the consequences and the side effects its *general* observance can be anticipated to have for the satisfaction of *everyone's* interests (and these consequences are preferred to those known alternative possibilities for regulation)."[3] Practical discourse, or what Habermas calls the *Diskursgrundsatz* (D-principle), requires that all participants treat each other as free and equal partners in the process of rational argumentation. The U-principle stipulates the criterion of success for moral argumentation: a valid outcome is achieved when we have full and autonomous agreement from all those affected by a proposed norm that it is in their interest.

There are two separate moral claims here. The first has to do with

3. Habermas, *Moral Consciousness and Communicative Action*, p. 65.

how we treat people or ought to treat people within moral discourse. The second is a strong claim about the moral validity or moral truth of the outcome. It is the second claim that has come under a great deal of criticism. For example, Albrecht Welmer argues, among other things, that the U-principle relies on an incoherent consensus theory of truth.[4] Truth, according to a consensus view, is what people in an ideal communication community, that is, people with full information, unlimited time, no other concerns but arriving at the truth, and in a situation of equality with one another, would agree was the truth. In our everyday search for truth, we try to arrive at true propositions that would be agreed to by this ideal communication community. The consensus theory of truth appeals to the intuition that for something to be true then there must be good reasons for it. The idea of having good reasons entails the idea that given enough time and information, given interlocutors of goodwill, and a constraint-free environment, everyone would agree with these reasons.

The problem with the consensus theory of truth is that it confuses having reasonable grounds for believing something to be true with what the truth is. When we say something is true, the idea that everyone would agree that it is true (given enough time, etc.) might very well be entailed, but their agreement does not make it true. They agree presumably because it *is* true. Truth should be able to gain the agreement of reasonable people, but truth cannot be defined as the agreement of reasonable people. As Welmer points out, rational consensus can tell us if we have good reasons for our judgments, but the rationality of a consensus has no necessary bearing on the truth: "Why should the consensus among physicists of the nineteenth century about the truth of Newton's theories not have been *rational* (in the sense of the conditions of the ideal speech situation)? . . . The truth of consensus cannot follow from their rationality any more than their *untruth* can automatically follow from their lack of rationality.[5]

In response to this and other criticism of the consensus theory of truth, Habermas has since modified his position. He now makes the distinction between the meaning of truth and the criterion of truth. When we say that p is true, what we mean is that we have good reason to support the proposition p, and good reasons are reasons that can withstand the critical force of undominated debate. This view would

4. Albrecht Welmer, *The Persistence of Modernity* (Cambridge: MIT Press, 1991), pp. 113–231. For a very clear and more accessible discussion of Habermas and theories of truth, see Jane Braaten, *Habermas's Critical Theory of Society* (Albany: SUNY Press, 1991), pp. 19–29.

5. Welmer, *Persistence of Modernity*, p. 161.

make discourse theory compatible with various theories of truth. For example, we might hold a correspondence theory of truth which says that p is true when it corresponds to a state of affairs in the real world. In many cases the truth of p can be established simply by pointing. The truth of "It is raining" can usually be established by pointing to the state of affairs to which it is supposed to correspond and saying something like, "Look for yourself; it really is raining." In more complicated and perhaps more interesting cases, however—for example, the truth of a theory—there is often no equivalent to simple pointing. Here we might say we have good reason to assert that p is true (i.e., that it corresponds to a state of affairs in the real world) when no one within an open and undominated discourse has been able to show convincingly that p is not true (i.e., does not correspond to state of affairs in the real world). We could make the same sort of argument for a coherence theory of truth. The point here is that we make a distinction between what the truth is and our reasonable grounds for holding something to be true.

If we try to make the same distinction with regard to moral validity we have the problem of how to fill in what appears in the parenthesis. For example, we might want to say that we have good reason for asserting that q is morally valid (i.e., . . .) when q commands the consent of all those affected that it is morally valid (i.e., . . .). But it is not clear what could possibly be a candidate to put within the brackets. Without something within the brackets, it is also not clear what people are consenting to. Are they consenting to the idea that everyone would consent to it? But this is an empty sort of reason for holding something to be morally true. It would come up against the same problem I outlined in questions of propositional truth. Moral truth, if there is such a thing, is not created through agreement; it is deserving of agreement. We would then have to say something like, people are consenting to the idea that everyone would consent to it because it really *is*, on some other grounds, morally true. But what are those other grounds?

With the plurality of moral conceptions that coexist in our world it would appear that we would have to leave it up to each individual to fill in the blank. The U-principle cannot be understood as restricting the moral principles that may be brought forward within discourse. The rules of discourse themselves stipulate that "everyone is allowed to introduce any assertion whatever into the discourse,"[6] necessarily including moral principles the content of which runs counter to the U-princi-

---

6. Habermas, *Moral Consciousness and Communicative Action*, p. 89.

ple. For example, participants must be able to appeal to natural rights theory, utilitarian principles, even religious experience as a basis of moral validity if they wish. Not only do the rules themselves guarantee that anything may be appealed to, but as a procedural ethics, discourse does not generate maxims or principles; it tests them. The actual generation of our principles must rely on more substantive grounds than proceduralism offers.

Thus, the U-principle as criterion of moral truth runs into two problems: that it must rely on a consensus theory of truth which is unpersuasive and that it runs up against the plurality of conceptions of moral truth. Although within the philosophy of science there is also a plurality of conceptions of propositional truth, the question of what is truth (as opposed to what is the truth of this or that matter) is relatively unproblematic for scientists themselves and, I would say, the general public. As Thomas McCarthy has pointed out, for most people the truth simply means "telling it like it is—like it *really* is."[7] Despite its philosophical problems, most scientists and people in general operate with something like a correspondence theory of truth. The idea that there is a "reality" out there to which our propositional statements should conform creates a commonality from which people can discuss anything from the weather to DNA structure without having to problematize what they mean by "It really is raining outside" or "DNA really is a double helix." But the statement "It really is right that you should do *x*" cannot rely on the same commonality.

People fundamentally disagree not simply on what is the right thing to do but on what makes it right in the first place. In fact, on many issues there is more agreement on what is the right thing to do (one should keep one's promises) than on what makes it right (because it is in your self-interest, because it promotes the good life, because everyone would agree to it, because the Bible tells you, and so on). The U-principle, as a definition of moral truth, must inevitably run up against these competing visions. And for this reason, many theorists sympathetic to the idea of discourse ethics have tried to distance themselves from any claims about moral truth.[8]

7. Thomas McCarthy, "Philosophy and Social Practice: Avoiding the Ethnocentric Predicament," in *Zwischenbetrachtungen im Prozess der Aufklärung*, edited by Axel Honneth et al. (Frankfurt: Suhrkamp, 1989), pp. 195.

8. Seyla Benhabib, *Situating the Self: Gender, Community, and Postmodernism in Contemporary Ethics* (New York: Routledge, 1992), pp. 23–67; Welmer, *Persistence of Modernity*, pp. 113–231; Jean L. Cohen and Andrew Arato, *Civil Society and Political Theory* (Cambridge: MIT Press, 1992), pp. 351–60; Alessandro Ferrara, "A Critique of Habermas' Diskursethik," *Telos* 64 (Summer 1985): 45–74.

These theorists say that discourse and the U-principle offer a theory of political justice and democratic legitimacy rather than a theory of general moral validity. The argument here is that what we mean by moral truth is highly contested but what we mean, generally speaking, by political justice and democratic legitimacy is not. A just system is one that regulates society fairly and in the general interest. The democratic legitimacy of a just system means that citizens freely consent that their institutions indeed do regulate society fairly and in the general interest.[9] Discourse can then serve as a test for such free consent. Moral validity by definition should transcend concrete communities, but democratic legitimacy is situated within concrete communities. Thus, consent need not encompass an ideal communication community but only those people who will have to live under the laws. Public institutions are the proper subject matter of discourse. Private morality, it is argued, is a matter of conscience, not debate and discourse. Alessandro Ferrara adopts this position when he maintains that discourse ethics "should not be seen—as Habermas sometimes presents it—as an exhaustive reconstruction of our ability to correctly evaluate norms and conduct in all spheres of life, but as a specification of the standards of legitimate decision-making in the public sphere of a participatory democracy."[10] Jean Cohen and Andrew Arato agree with this view and suggest that discourse ethics is "overburdened" if applied outside the realm of politics. They set aside the question of which general moral theory is appropriate to the realm of private moral judgments and insist that it is possible, "to defend the discourse ethic as a political ethic without committing oneself to a specific moral philosophy." Because of questions of privacy and conscience, discourse ethics must grant autonomy to other modes of moral reasoning.[11]

MORAL TRUTH AND MORAL DELIBERATION

Although I agree that discourse ethics makes its strongest showing as a theory of political justice and democratic legitimacy, I also think that

9. See, for example, Seyla Benhabib, "Deliberative Rationality and Models of Democratic Legitimacy," *Constellations* 1 (April 1994): 27.

10. Ferrara, "Critique of Habermas' Diskursethik," p. 74.

11. Cohen and Arato, *Civil Society and Political Theory*, pp. 351–60. See also Jean Cohen, "Morality or *Sittlichkeit*: Towards a Post-Hegelian Solution," *Cardozo Law Review* 10 (March–April 1989): 1398. Although Seyla Benhabib distances herself from Habermas's strong universalist claims, she does not exclude morality from the scope of discourse ethics.

it offers insight in to the world of morality. To say that discourse theory does not offer a coherent view of moral truth is not to say that it does not offer a coherent view of moral deliberation. The U-principle does not make sense as criterion of moral truth, but it does make sense as a criterion of democratic legitimacy. That a norm is in everyone's interest and can be shown to be in everyone's interest is a plausible and defensible definition of legitimacy. In politics both the D-principle and the U-principle have a place. In questions of morality, however, only the D-principle applies. For this reason discourse ethics has more to say about politics than about private morality, but it nevertheless has something to say about both.

Welmer's argument points to a gap between rationality and truth. It does not undermine the claims of rationality. The reason why there is no necessary connection between rational consensus and truth is that what counts as a good reason is ultimately bound up with a particular context. Although the idea of being persuaded by reason can be given a procedural and universal form, the actual arguments we undertake within this framework are contextualist arguments. But this does not mean they are bad arguments. Indeed, Welmer himself maintains that which principles we take to be morally binding will depend on "interpretations, convictions, and our understanding of ourselves, and *these* things can be more or less 'rational,' i.e, appropriate, justified, correct or even truthful."[12] Thus, rational discourse might not guarantee moral truth, but it can guarantee that our principles and maxims are at least reasonable given what is accepted as true, correct, and justified within our context.

This discussion sounds contextualist, and contextualism is often considered synonymous with relativism. I do not think it is. Borrowing from Charles Larmore, I take contextualism to be "the view that a disputed belief is sufficiently justified if justified by appeal to other beliefs not challenged by the particular dispute."[13] On a contextualist view of justification, we can never completely transcend our context; in one conversation we can never make explicit all the presuppositions and assumptions that make communication possible. There will always be "givens" and unquestioned shared assumptions standing behind our conversations. Thus, in all cultures and societies what counts as a good reason will always be tied to one's context. But having said so, we do

12. Welmer, *Persistence of Modernity*, p. 159.
13. Charles Larmore, *Patterns of Moral Complexity* (Cambridge: Cambridge University Press, 1987), p. 29.

not have to say that every context is the same as every other context. Because our arguments proceed contextually, just as the ancient Egyptians' arguments proceeded contextually, does not mean that our arguments are no better or worse than those of the ancient Egyptians.

The argument that I want to make here is that our context possesses two features that allow us to distinguish between our form of contextualist argumentation and other forms of contextualist argumentation. The first is the ubiquity of criticism, and the second is the universalization of criticism. Within the modern context, fewer and fewer things are immune from criticism, doubt, dispute, and challenge. One of the defining features of modernity, I would say, is that nothing is in principle "beyond question." Indeed, the very idea that there are things beyond question invites the modern mind to question it. This assertion will perhaps be disputed by postmodern thinkers, who often imply that modernity is characterized by blindness to hidden forms of domination. But the very fact that people such as Michel Foucault and Jacques Derrida *criticize* the assumptions of modern thinkers is evidence that very few assumptions can lie hidden for long. As William Connolly has put it, "The aspiration to become postmodern is one of the paradigmatic ways to be modern. . . . the aspiration to delineate the frame of modernity is a paradigmatic idea of the modern age."[14] There will, of course, always be unproblematized assumptions at work behind our conversations, but our very concern for the role of hidden assumptions leads us to expose as many as possible.

Thus, one of the ways our context differs from other contexts is that we are more aware, indeed painfully aware, that we are caught in a context. The reasons we offer for our beliefs and principles must meet a higher standard of justification precisely because we are conscious of all the things (interest, ethnocentricity, cultural bias, unexamined assumptions, socialization, domination—the list is very long) that can lie hidden behind arguments.

But it is not only that criticism is deeper within the modern context, it also that criticism is wider. Our contextualist arguments must respond to a wider array of objections from a plethora of viewpoints. This is particularly true in moral discourse because modernity has brought with it the idea that moral claims cannot be evaluated on the grounds of who makes them. The universalization of the content of morality to which I referred at the beginning of this chapter leads to a

14. William Connolly, *Political Theory and Modernity* (Oxford: Basil Blackwell, 1988), p. 3.

universalization of criticism. Thus, if we are interested in justification and responding to criticism, then the social position, race, religion, and so on of the objector are irrelevant. That they are signals that our context requires that we respond to a more exacting type of criticism. The universalization of criticism, although driven by contextually specific reasons, attempts to transcend context. Take, for example, the inclusion of future generations in the debate about the environment. Here, the reasons we find convincing must also meet objections that could possibly be made by those who must live with our decisions down the road. At a more general level, we can say that the universalization of the content of moral intuitions leads to a form of deliberation in which we make universalist-type criticisms. We ask ourselves such questions as, Could anybody agree with this principle regardless of his context? or Would I agree if I had no knowledge of my position in society? or Could I imagine everyone agreeing? The answers might never be definitive, because such questions must always be asked counterfactually, but they attempt to gain a maximum distance from and self-consciousness about the distorting factors of context.

The ubiquity and universalization of criticism must be understood as potentialities that have been opened up within modernity and not necessarily as fully realized actualities. We often do not exercise the opportunities to criticize which have been extended to us, or we take things for granted, or we are silenced, or we dismiss criticism without fully considering its merit, and so on. Nevertheless, the age of reason really has turned out to be the age of criticism. Criticism does not lead, as Nietzsche thought it would, to nihilism. It leads instead to a search for reasons that have the widest and deepest support, given our horizons.

The point here is that although we cannot avoid contextualism, we can avoid relativism. We have good grounds for claiming that beliefs and principles that survive the exacting type of criticism characteristic of modernity are indeed rational in a nonrelativist sense. They are rational given our context, but our context itself leads to a radicalization and universalization of the reasons that are acceptable. This facet of modernity does not allow us to say that we have arrived at the moral truth, but it does allow us to say that principles that are widely accepted at the same time as being widely debated (for example, human rights) have a more rational foundation than principles that have not been able to survive critical examination (for example, racial hierarchies).

Discourse theory does have something to say about the rationality of our beliefs, including our private moral beliefs. As Donald Moon puts it,

> When we agree, when we are able to respond to criticism and win over doubters, we have good (indeed the best possible) reason to act on our judgments. But agreement obviously does not mean that we have the truth, let alone the Truth, for we might discover later that we were wrong. . . . if we can never get the Truth, if we only have our judgments, the failure to reach agreement should at least give us pause: If we have such good grounds for our beliefs, why have we been unable to convince others.[15]

Subjecting our principles to a discursive test might not be definitive of their truth, but it does give us grounds for their reasonableness. Even if I believe that moral truth is revealed through religion, what particular principles of action follow from that belief is a matter of judgment. And this judgment can be more or less reasonable. How else can we distinguish between a "Son of Sam" who claimed that his crimes were ordered by God and more "reasonable" understandings of what follows from religious belief? Without some way to test our moral beliefs, to bounce them off something other than our belief in their validity, we always risk falling into what Hegel called the problem of "pure conviction." Here our only standard is what "each individual allows to rise out of his heart, emotion and inspiration."[16] The strength of our feeling becomes the justification of our positions. But strong feeling, as Hegel points out, equally justifies the morally motivated criminal and the morally motivated humanitarian.

If we believe that moral principles are the sorts of things that people should deliberate about, then I think we are committed to something like Habermas's and Scanlon's understanding of reasonableness. That is to say, deliberation is essentially intersubjective, not in the sense that all our moral principles must acquire the consent of every other person but in the sense that our honest deliberations must include what others could, would, or do say against our positions. At the very least, deliberation is internal argumentation, and sincere argumentation, as we have seen, has certain structurally invariant components.

In *Interpretation and Social Criticism*, Michael Walzer tells an interesting Talmudic story about moral argumentation which illustrates this

15. Donald Moon, "Constrained Discourse and Public Life," *Political Theory* 19 (May 1991): 202.

16. G. W. F. Hegel, *Philosophy of Right*, translated by T. M. Knox (Oxford: Oxford University Press, 1967), p. 5.

point, although he would no doubt disagree with my universalist reading. Two rabbis are arguing a point of law. Rabbi Eliezer, in order to convince his colleagues of the soundness of his position, appeals to heaven to vindicate his interpretation. Sign after sign is sent in answer to Rabbi Eliezer's appeal, but Rabbi Joshua does not think these signs constitute proof. Or rather, he does not think that backward-running streams and tumbling walls have any business interfering in the dispute. Finally, God himself steps in and cries, "Why do you dispute with Rabbi Eliezer? In all matters the law is as he says." But Rabbi Joshua is still not moved and exclaims, "It is not in heaven!" From this story Walzer concludes that "morality, in other words, is something we argue about. . . . No discovery or invention can end the argument; no 'proof' takes precedence over the (temporary) majority of sages. That is the meaning of, 'It is not in heaven.' We have to continue the argument: perhaps for that reason, the story does not tell us whether on the substantive issue, Rabbi Eliezer or Rabbi Joshua was right. On the procedural issue, however, Rabbi Joshua was right.[17] The conclusion that a procedural rule could have been broken presupposes the notion of an argument in which no procedural rules are broken. Despite Walzer's criticisms of procedural ethics, he seems to be appealing to the very same intuitions to which Scanlon and Habermas also appeal. Not only that, but the procedural rules appear to be universal in that they apply equally to ancient rabbinical conversations and to our own conversations.

And what is the procedural issue? What is the procedural rule that Rabbi Eliezer was trying to circumvent? It is the rule that stipulates that attempts to bypass the argumentative process (in this case, by appeal to external authority) distort the processes that underlie the acceptance of moral principles. Morality is something we argue about, says Walzer. Robbing us of the opportunity to engage in this argumentation robs us of the means to establish (perhaps temporarily) reasonable grounds for our beliefs. What can be said of the argument between two rabbis can also be said of internal argumentation. The internal suppression of argument can also rob us of the opportunity to establish reasonable grounds for our beliefs.

If Rabbi Eliezer had won the day instead of Rabbi Joshua a procedural premise of moral argumentation would have been broken. Would the outcome carry the same weight? No. Why not? Presumably because bringing in God as a trump card to force the issue is not itself

17. Michael Walzer, *Interpretation and Social Criticism* (Cambridge: Harvard University Press, 1987), p. 32.

an argument; rather, it is an external authority to *backup* an argument. As Rabbi Joshua points out, making the river run backward is not a relevant reason; it does not represent an appropriate argument. But why do we need arguments as opposed to signs? Because when we say that morality is something we argue about, we mean that each one of us must be convinced that there are good grounds for a moral principle we ultimately accept. That acceptance should not be forced or pressured out of us; it should spring from our finding the relevant arguments compelling.

The preceeding discussion points to the relevance of discourse theory in the area of private morality if we are interested in having reasonable grounds for our moral beliefs. Moral deliberation is sounder and more reasonable when we assess our positions in light of the objections others, with whom we must live, might have. Conversely, formulating a moral position without regard to strong counterarguments or the moral convictions of those with whom we must live is unreasonable. But why should we be interested in being reasonable? One answer to this question is to say that although people do ultimately have a right to be unreasonable in their private opinions, this strategy lacks common sense and can be self-defeating. When asked to justify our private moral stands, we are often well within our rights to say "none of your business." But why should we? Perhaps it is because these questions can be intrusive, but if we believe they are intrusive shouldn't we try to explain to our questioner that they are intrusive? That is, shouldn't we try to give reasons for why we do not want to talk about our private conceptions? This response seems more likely to result in our being left alone than stony silence.

Silence itself can be more or less reasonable. Silence motivated by the fear that your beliefs will not stand up to criticism is unreasonable. It is unreasonable because the fear presupposes that you already believe that there might be good reasons, reasons that you yourself will find convincing, against holding the belief that you do. We often have cherished beliefs the undermining of which can put our whole world and identity into turmoil. Thus, we often go to great lengths, as Scanlon says, "to avoid admitting the unjustifiability" of our principles and beliefs.[18] But immunizing our beliefs from criticism involves immunizing ourselves from the possibility of moral development, of learning from

---

18. Thomas Scanlon, "Contractualism and Utilitarianism," in *Utilitarianism and Beyond*, edited by Amartya Sen and Bernard Williams (Cambridge: Cambridge University Press, 1982), p. 117.

others, of gaining deeper insight into ourselves, of benefiting from communication, and of having a richer moral life. We may choose to forgo all these possibilities and hold tightly to our unexamined beliefs, but we lose a great deal in this trade.

There is another reason why being reasonable makes good sense. The more plural and various are moral conceptions within a society, the more we need to talk about them. So many of the things we say and do are informed by our private conceptions that if we want our statements and actions to be understood we must make some attempt to explain and justify the moral positions from which they spring. The desire for recognition or respect or understanding leads to communication about who we are, what we stand for, and where we are coming from. Again, we may choose to forgo this type of communication, but doing so cuts us off from the benefits of recognition, respect, and understanding.

Once we have decided to be reasonable, we are bound by certain procedural rules. Moral justification entails a sincere effort to justify one's position in terms that one's interlocutor can understand and relate to. Moral persuasion entails the prohibition on coercion, manipulation, and deception. At the beginning of Chapter 8 I quoted what I thought to be a compelling illustration of our intuitions concerning argumentation. This intuition, if correct, must hold no matter what the substance of the argument: "Should one party make use of privileged access to weapons, wealth or standing, in order to wring agreement [that slavery is wrong, that children should not suffer, that pain is bad] from another party through the prospects of sanctions and rewards, no one involved will be in doubt that the presuppositions of argumentation are no longer satisfied."[19] Why is it that when we hear of religious cults using brainwashing techniques on new members we are uneasy, even morally incensed? It is not always or even primarily because the substance of what is being taught is false or immoral. It is because the procedure through which members are acquiring their beliefs and convictions violates our idea of freedom of conscience. Freedom of conscience implies not only that people be allowed to believe whatever they want but also, to paraphrase Locke, that faith cannot be commanded by force.[20] Faith and conscience heed persuasion not force. Force does not always come in the form of a state with a big stick. It can also come in the form of

19. Jürgen Habermas, "A Reply to My Critics," in *Habermas: Critical Debates*, edited by John B. Thompson and David Held (Cambridge: MIT Press, 1982), pp. 272– 73.

20. John Locke, *A Letter concerning Toleration* (Indianapolis: Hackett, 1983), p. 27.

deception, psychological pressure, subtle forms of domination, and emotional manipulation. Freedom of conscience is appealed to when rejecting discourse ethics as criterion of moral truth. I maintain that freedom of conscience implies the relevance of discourse ethics as a model of moral deliberation. Discourse ethics gives us a picture of non-coercive persuasion. It can arm us against the manipulation and domination of others.

We enter into moral disputes all the time. They are one of the defining features of pluralism. It is because we disagree so much that we should have rules to guide our disagreements, rules that safeguard freedom of conscience and respect our dignity as moral agents. If we maintain our stony silence and withdraw from moral conversation, we are not bound by its rules, but if we participate in the moral life of our community, then these rules make a great deal of sense.

IV

DISCOURSE AND
POLITICS

11   *From the Ideal to the Real*

The reconstruction of the presuppositions of speech produces a speech situation in which all elements extraneous to the end of reaching a reasoned agreement are excluded. In effect, what we have so far is an "ideal speech situation." And of course, Habermas himself has used this term to refer to the formal conditions under which validity claims are redeemed. In his most recent work, however, Habermas very rarely uses the term and appears to be distancing himself from his earlier uncompromising formalism. The reason is that the idea of an *ideal* speech situation is too rigid, narrow, and indeed ideal to capture all that is entailed in a collective evaluation of the appropriateness of a norm.[1] In particular, it does not capture the idea that practical discourse is primarily intended to be an undertaking in the real (less than ideal) world by real (less than ideal) social actors. This idea is often overlooked and has led to considerable misunderstanding about the role an ideal speech situation plays in a discursive theory of political justice. It is to some of these misunderstandings that I now wish to turn.

DISCURSIVE UTOPIA

One of the ways discourse ethics can be and has been misinterpreted is that the conditions of discourse are thought to apply generally to all meaningful interaction. In this view, the ideal society would look some-

1. Jürgen Habermas, *Autonomy and Solidarity: Interviews with Jürgen Habermas*, edited by Peter Dews (New York: Verso, 1992), p. 163.

thing like the ideal communication community. We would strive in all spheres of life to achieve consensus, to resolve disagreement, to find a rationally grounded way of life. The good life would be realized through convergence; that is, as far as is humanly possible we should try to bring our interests, needs, tastes, preferences, values, ideals, plans of life, and so on into consensual harmony with those of others.[2]

One source of this misunderstanding can perhaps be found in Habermas's 1971 reference to the ideal speech situation as prefiguring a form of life (*Vorschein eines Lebensforms*).[3] He has since retracted this formulation in several places.[4] Even before the retractions, however, there was no evidence that the ideal speech situation was intended as something to be realized in an ideal communication community.

The ideal speech situation is a presupposition of argumentation, never fully realized in the real world but approximated in a sincere search for consensus within a practical discourse. The rules of practical discourse are not guidelines for all social interaction; they are guidelines for collective deliberation regarding disputed norms—not rules of action but rules of argumentation. Practically speaking, nothing would ever get done in a purely discursive world. We suspend normal interaction when we enter discourse. That is, we suspend the activities, concerns, interests that guide us in our day-to-day life and concentrate on one concern and interest—resolution of a disputed claim to right. Our daily concerns and interests may inform our arguments, but we do not actually pursue them in discourse. One cannot make a living, write a book, teach a class, or run a business discursively, although each of these situations might require, at one point or another, that we enter into discourse to resolve normative impasses. Discourse ethics might contain the ideal of a consensually *steered* society but not the ideal of a fully rational and entirely consensual society.[5]

There is, however, a slightly different version of this criticism which is perhaps more plausible. Even if we admit that practical discourse is a model of argumentation only and not a model way of life, there still appears to be a questionable and perhaps utopian privileging of agree-

2. For an interpretation of Habermas along these lines, see, for example, Steven Lukes, "Of Gods and Demons: Habermas and Practical Reason," in *Habermas: Critical Debates*, edited by John B. Thompson and David Held (Cambridge: MIT Press, 1982), p. 144. Also see Wolfgand Schluchter, *Religion und Lebensführung* (Frankfurt: Suhrkamp, 1988), 1:322–33.

3. See Jürgen Habermas and Niklas Luhman, *Theorie der Gesellschaft oder Sozialtechnologie: Was leistet die Systemforschung?* (Frankfurt: Suhrkamp, 1971), pp. 140–41.

4. See Jürgen Habermas, "A Reply to My Critics," in *Habermas*, ed. Thompson and Held, p. 262; and Habermas, *Autonomy and Solidarity*, p. 260.

5. Habermas, "Reply," p. 262.

ment over disagreement. Habermas himself has said that he takes "the type of action aimed at reaching understanding to be fundamental" and starts from the assumption that "other forms of social action—for example, conflict, competition, strategic action in general—are derivatives of action oriented to reaching an understanding."[6] This privileging of consensus (the reaching of full understanding between actors) puts into question the place of pluralism, diversity, and difference within discourse ethics. Are these pathologies to be overcome? Some critics have thought this to be the implication of Habermas's position.

The most extreme versions of this criticism equate consensus formation with an updated but still dangerous form of collectivism. The worry of some liberal pluralists, for example, is that talk of consensus and generalizable interests has authoritarian or at least elitist implications. It implies that a great many people in our competitive market-oriented societies, who continue to disagree with one another on deep issues, are laboring under a form of false consciousness.[7] Given the lack of consensus in modern society, the critical theorist must be wedded to the idea of "liberating" people from a false understanding of their interests. For many liberal pluralists, this idea of liberation is inherently authoritarian, inasmuch as an individual's true interests are simply what that individual believes her true interests to be. From the postmodern perspective the criticism is sometimes no less extreme, as, for example, when consensus is equated with a collective subjectivity that is inherently totalitarian or when consensus through discourse is thought to be a type of disciplinary action ("consensual disciplines") aimed at taming and bringing order to a world of unruly differences.[8] Here, consensus formation is understood not as constraint-free but as imposing constraint on those who do not wish to be "reasonable." And

6. Jürgen Habermas, *Communication and the Evolution of Society*, translated by Thomas McCarthy (Boston: Beacon Press, 1979), p. 1.

7. Quentin Skinner, "Habermas's Reformation," *New York Review of Books*, October 7, 1982, pp. 35–38. Even some sympathetic readers have implied that there are potential authoritarian dangers to Habermas's theory of generalizable interests. See, for example, Jean L. Cohen and Andrew Arato, *Civil Society and Political Theory* (Cambridge: MIT Press, 1992), pp. 360–74.

8. Jean-François Lyotard, *The Postmodern Condition: A Report on Knowledge*, translated by Geoff Bennington and Brian Massumi (Minneapolis: University of Minnesota Press, 1985), p. 66. Michel Foucault, "Politics and Ethics: An Interview," *The Foucault Reader*, edited by Paul Rabinow (New York: Pantheon, 1984), p. 380; idem, "The Order of Discourse," in *Untying the Text: A Post-Structuralist Reader*, edited by Robert Young (Boston: Routledge and Kegan Paul, 1981), p. 66. Michael Walzer makes a similar criticism when he says that discourse is designed "to press the speakers towards a preordained harmony." "A Critique of Philosophical Conversation," *Philosophical Forum* 21 (Fall–Winter 1989–90): 186. For a defense of Habermas against these criticisms, see Stephen K. White, *Political Theory and Postmodernism* (Cambridge: Cambridge University Press, 1991), pp. 132–42.

even sympathetic readers of Habermas worry that discourse, in its quest for consensus, community, and commonality cannot deal adequately with the problem of "otherness" or the inherent paradoxes of the human condition.[9] The suspicious harbor a fear that rational consensus represents a dangerous homogenization of differences. The sympathetic critic has the opposite fear: in the face of the inherently messy, discordant, contingent, and tragic nature of our collective life together discourse has less power and relevance than Habermas's optimistic rationalism assumes.

Consensual will formation represents neither an overly optimistic rationalism nor a totalizing suppression of difference. A discursive approach to the dilemmas, conflicts, and tensions of modern society stands somewhere between the view that all problems are amenable to rational solutions (it is only a matter of time) and an approach that accentuates the intractability of the dilemmas, conflicts, and tensions of collective life. Discourse ethics offers no theoretical guarantee that discourse will be successful or somehow always *could be* successful if only we were all of goodwill. Even men and women of goodwill, especially men and women of goodwill, are caught in tragic dilemmas, are faced with questions for which there is no right answer, find no common ground with the "other."[10] Tragedy, no right answer, the problem of otherness, and disagreement are permanent features of our collective life. Nevertheless, we cannot draw the conclusion that all the problems we face are tragic, insoluble, unbridgeable, or irreconcilable. Admitting that reason has limits calls for an investigation of where those limits lie. We are left with a question: Which dilemmas can we solve through rational discourse and which are impenetrable?

But does the very attempt contain hidden dangers? Does the cooperative search for agreement devalue heterogeneity, difference, and nonconformity? Does the requirement that participants be reasonable place an unacceptable constraint on the exercise of free subjectivity? This way of construing the search for agreement ignores that disagreement, conflict, dispute, argumentation, opposition, in short, naysaying, are essential aspects of the discourse process. Pluralism, diversity,

9. White, *Political Theory and Postmodernism*, p. 22; William E. Connolly, *Identity/Difference: Democratic Negotiations of Political Paradox* (Ithaca: Cornell University Press, 1991), pp. 162–63.

10. Seyla Benhabib makes a similar argument in *Situating the Self: Gender, Community, and Postmodernism in Contemporary Ethics* (New York: Routledge, 1992), pp. 76–82. Benhabib, however, is interested in distinguishing between the integrationist approach to conflict adopted by communitarians and the participationist approach of discourse ethics.

and difference, far from being antithetical to discourse ethics, furnish the very conditions that make universalized norms possible. Habermas, for example, notes that "as interests and value orientations become more differentiated in modern societies, the morally justified norms that control the individual's scope of action in the interest of the whole become ever more general and abstract."[11] Norms become more general and abstract because their justification must satisfy a wider and more profound set of criticisms and objections in a pluralistic, democratic society. Points of agreement within a highly homogeneous or conventional society will not be subjected to the same range and depth of scrutiny. And as society moves from a conventional to a postconventional stage, those norms that cannot withstand the critical force of pluralism, diversity, and difference will pass away. Only those that represent principles that are generalizable within pluralism and despite difference, that is, which can generate the support of all, will survive.

But even if there is no conflict in principle between consensual will formation and pluralism, is there perhaps a practical conflict? We may agree in theory that the more varied our private interests and identities, the more general and impartial will be those points upon which we do agree. But it might also be that, as a practical matter, the more pluralistic our society becomes, the fewer points there are upon which we *can* agree. Is the very idea of convergence of opinion through discourse utopian and unrealistic?[12] One can assume that the expanding diversity of particular lifestyles and conceptions of the good decreases the chances of finding anything to agree on only if one believes that there is a zero-sum relationship between these two aspects of our moral life. "But," Habermas says, "there are enough counter-examples—from traffic rules to basic institutional norms—to make it intuitively clear that increasing scope for individual options does not decrease the chances for agreement concerning presumptively common interests. The discourse ethical way of reading the universalization principle does not rest—even implicitly—on assumptions about the quantitative relation between general and particular interests."[13] The fact of pluralism by itself does not stand as a reason why people might not find things to agree about in addition to the things that they disagree about. As

11. Jürgen Habermas, *Moral Consciousness and Communicative Action*, translated by Christian Lenhardt and Shierry Weber Nicholsen (Cambridge: MIT Press, 1990), p. 205.

12. This is the argument put forward, for example, by Adam Przeworski in *Democracy and the Market: Political and Economic Reforms in Eastern Europe and Latin America* (Cambridge: Cambridge University Press, 1991), pp. 15–18.

13. Habermas, "Reply," p. 257.

Rawls has pointed out, pluralism is simply a fact about us, and pluralism is characterized by disputes and differences of opinion on a plethora of deep issues.[14] We must resist the temptation to take all our disputes and disagreements as given, however. Taking them as given implies that the interests and beliefs that inform these disputes are fixed and, in turn, that individuals are unable or unwilling to reevaluate, modify, or alter their interests and beliefs self-consciously. Not only does this assumption deny an essential aspect of human autonomy, but it is also clearly false. People alter and modify their interests and beliefs all the time. Life would be much simpler and more predictable if they did not; economic models of political choice would be much more successful if they did not; but they do. Furthermore, as Adam Przeworski notes, using the established social science lingo, preference alterations are not exogenous to the deliberative process; rather, "deliberation is the endogenous change of preferences resulting from communication."[15] But the real question, according to Przeworski, is whether deliberation leads to convergence. Echoing many critics of discourse ethics, he thinks that Habermas's assumption that it does is unrealistic, because it assumes that there is a unique or "true" solution to political disputes, that people will accept the truth when confronted with it, and that people will present their arguments in a disinterested way.

Przeworski believes that there is no evidence to indicate that there are unique solutions to political conflicts, no reason to assume that people would, anyway, accept the truth if there was one, and finally, that people are much more likely to present their arguments strategically. He concludes that "the coup de grace against theory of democracy as rational deliberation was administered in 1923 by [Carl] Schmitt, who argued that not all political conflicts can be reconciled by discussion."[16]

There are several responses to this criticism. The first is to say that discourse ethics does not assume that *all* political conflicts can be reconciled by discussion. It assumes that some can be reconciled through discussion and that the only way of finding out which ones is through a sincere attempt. Second, there does seem to be evidence within liberal democracies of generally agreed solutions to deep disputes. Most

14. John Rawls, *Political Liberalism* (New York: Columbia University Press, 1993), pp. 3–4.

15. Przeworski, *Democracy and the Market*, p. 17.

16. Ibid., p. 18.

liberal democracies no longer have religious wars; religious toleration is generally accepted as an appropriate solution to this problem. In what sense toleration is a "unique" solution, I am not sure. If history had taken a different turn and led all people to converge on a universal religion, this too might have been a solution, but history did not unfold along these improbable lines. If the solution is perhaps not unique, we have good grounds for claiming that toleration is the right/reasonable solution.

Finally, why must we assume that people will not be persuaded by reasons? Why must we assume that people will act strategically? Why must we assume that changing interests will always be moving toward divergence rather than convergence? Przeworski's answer is telling and reflects a widespread set of assumptions within social science, assumptions that must be seen as false. Arguments defending the possibility of reaching agreement through deliberation are premised on the idea not simply that citizens can change their preferences through deliberation but also that citizens can come to value deliberation as a means of dispute resolution. In other words, convergence depends on fostering the value of agreement and the cooperative search for solutions. If preferences can change, then there is no reason why preferences for one type of dispute resolution might not give way to preferences for another type. Rational-choice theorists such as Przeworski must exclude such changing value orientations from the beginning. Values, he says, "are collectively optimal, individually irrational, and not externally enforced. Game theory claims they do not exist."[17] What he really means is that values and norms are "not necessary to understand the way democracy works." The strategic pursuit of interest is "sufficient" for such a task. He adds, however, in a footnote: "This assertion does not imply that culture does not matter. Culture is what tells people what to want; culture informs them what they must do; culture indicates to them what they must hide from others. I take it as an axiom that people function in a communicative and a moral context."[18] This axiom is admitted but then dismissed as unimportant to an explanation of social choice. If the axiom is true, however, then the question of the likelihood that individuals will or will not pursue cooperative solutions to political disputes must be answered at the level of culture. Rational-choice theory has no defense against the argument that our communicative and moral context might not develop into a more deliberatively

17. Ibid., p. 24.
18. Ibid., p. 24 n. 23.

oriented one. Discourse ethics does not predict that it will but offers some arguments why it is not outrageous to suppose that it might. We cannot predict convergence or divergence, because prediction must be based on stable and fixed preferences. That deliberation can lead to agreement is premised on the idea that preferences are shaped by culture and communication and that certain types of culture and communication are more likely to promote an interest in cooperative dispute resolution. If, for example, we all become convinced that we really are the strategic actors Przeworski says we are, then this self-understanding will reduce the likelihood of cooperative interaction. If, on the other hand, this self-understanding does not become widely shared within our culture, then we may perhaps develop a cultural understanding that is more conducive to discourse. The point is that rational-choice arguments, by self-consciously bracketing out culture, values, and morality from the beginning, do not have strong arguments for dismissing the possibility of convergence. Discourse ethics operates at the level of culture, values, and morality. Indeed, the rational-choice criticism of discourse ethics, that it is unrealistic, can be turned against it. By excluding what appears to be the most important "independent variable," culture, game theory gives us an unrealistic, if perhaps mathematically elegant, picture of social change.

Discourse ethics does not project the ideal of a dispute-free world, nor does it devalue contestation. Not only is such a world unattainable; it is also undesirable. Diversity and difference lead to criticism, and criticism is our avenue to well-founded general norms. Yet whereas discourse ethics does not devalue contestation, indeed points to the critical and productive force of contestation, it does not "valorize" contestation either.[19] Contestation, naysaying, and struggle are not ends in themselves. Practical discourse is not an agonistic but a dialectical forum where the clash of opposing forces can move participants forward in a search for common ground. This common ground might be an agreement on substantive generalizable interests, or it might be an agreement to disagree, or an agreement to settle for a compromise, or an agreement to allow a majority vote to decide the issue, or it might turn out that there simply is no common ground. But even in cases where there is no common ground, especially in such cases, we should

19. For a reading of Foucault which places the valorization of contestation at the center of the French philosopher's thought, see Leslie Paul Thiele, "The Agony of Politics: The Nietzschean Roots of Foucault's Thought," *American Political Science Review* 84 (September 1990): 907–26.

keep our disputes within the bounds of fair communication. If we do not try to persuade and reason with each other, then we are left with the option of forcing and coercing each other.

One response is to say that if we cannot persuade each other, then we have no choice but to force each other. Where there is no common ground something other than discourse must settle the question. The first thing to remember is that in most questions of public policy there will not be consensual agreement. Whether we can agree on a fair procedure for deciding questions of public policy about which there is no consensus is a different question. This is a question that addresses the legitimacy of institutions at a deep level, where a lack of agreement signals a lack of legitimacy. But what if there is no common ground even here? Must the issue be settled by force? The issue might very well be *decided* by force but it is not *settled* by force.[20] Decisions are taken all the time the legitimacy of which remains in dispute. As long as their legitimacy is in dispute, they are not really settled, and the conversation continues.

DISCOURSE AS THOUGHT-EXPERIMENT

If a practical discourse does not project an image of a dispute-free world, can it project an image of just institutions? As a procedure for justifying political principles of justice, could practical discourse be used to generate an ideal conception of the basic political structure which could then be used as a guide in restructuring our own society? At points in his earlier work Habermas seems to think that just such a thought experiment is possible. In *Legitimation Crisis*, for example, he suggests that a "counter-factual reconstruction" could be undertaken

20. I have developed this argument in the context of the Canadian constitutional debate; see Simone Chambers, "Discourse and Democratic Practices," in *Companion to Habermas*, edited by Stephen K. White (Cambridge: Cambridge University Press, 1995). For years and years Canadians had no written constitution of their own—just an act of the British Parliament. Although there was universal agreement that they should have their own constitution, no one could agree on the specific content. In 1982 the prime minister basically said, enough was enough; if there was not going to be any agreement, he would settle the issue without full agreement. He brought in a constitution that was widely but not universally supported, lacking, in particular, the endorsement of the Quebec government. Here something besides discourse (a unilateral decision by the prime minister) settled the issue, except, of course, that it did not "settle" the issue at all. This was just the beginning of the real constitutional debates in Canada. The moral of this story is that many important issues are not settled even when decisions are taken. It is a false dichotomy to say either we come to an agreement at one time and one place or else we settle the issue some other way.

to compare "normative structures existing at a given time with the hypothetical state of a system of norms formed, *ceteris paribus*, discursively."[21]

Habermas never actually undertakes such an ambitious enterprise, nor does he even hint at its possibility in his later work. He introduces the counterfactual reconstruction in *Legitimation Crisis* only as a possible research path, and much of his later work points to the implausibility of such a comprehensive thought experiment. In the first place, it would be virtually impossible to work out what people involved in such a discursive will formation would choose. The conditions of practical discourse are not strong enough to enable us to determine, even hypothetically, how individuals would "have collectively and bindingly interpreted their needs (and which norms would they have accepted as justified) if they could decide on the organization of social intercourse through discursive will formation."[22] The individuals simply have too much information.

But the reason why practical discourse, if properly understood, cannot generate an entire "system of norms" is deeper than the insufficiently stringent knowledge constraints under which it operates. Practical discourse comes into play when a dispute arises over the legitimacy of a norm. When confronted with such an impasse, we place the norm in brackets; that is to say, we suspend the legitimacy of the norm. We do not, however, place our whole social, political, and cultural world in brackets. A practical discourse takes place within an existing social, political, and cultural context. In this sense, it differs from the founding contract in traditional social contract theory. Unlike Locke's or Hobbes's contract, discourse does not serve as a bridge from a state of nature to civil society. Participants are already in civil society. They do not reason and argue in a vacuum. Thus, it is not a device whereby a theorist can postulate how individuals would have set up the basic structure of their society starting from scratch. Nor is it a procedure in which participants themselves can comprehensively rewrite the basic structure.

Discourse is radical in that no aspect of our collective life can claim special immunity from potential devaluation. In a sense, everything is up for grabs. At the same time, discourse is not revolutionary. We reevaluate certain aspects of our collective life only in light of other

21. Jürgen Habermas, *Legitimation Crisis*, translated by Thomas McCarthy (Boston: Beacon Press, 1975), p. 113.
22. Ibid., p. 113.

aspects that we do accept. We cannot rewrite our entire collective life. In reproducing and reinterpreting our social and political world, we can only work with what we have. The traditions that are handed down, the patterns of integration we have inherited, and the identities that have been conceptually opened up to us by our surroundings are our only building blocks in constructing our future. That they are necessarily limits the scope of our discourses such that participants do not have the means to rebuild their whole world from the outside in.

Habermas does sometimes talk as if we can abstract from our given lifeworld context when engaged in a practical discourse.[23] Such abstraction, however, must be understood as a special attitude participants take up toward their context and not as an Archimedean point that participants can achieve outside their context. On the one hand, nothing is taken as given, in the sense that everything can be questioned. On the other hand, the substantive arguments that participants actually use to convince one another must be drawn from within their shared world and language. Furthermore, although participants should try to take a critical attitude toward "givens," it is impossible (and unnecessary) to make each and every background assumption explicit within one conversation.

If practical discourse cannot be employed as a comprehensive thought experiment to project an alternative and complete social structure, the question remains, Can it still be used as a thought experiment in a piecemeal way to validate or invalidate particular normative claims raised within a given social world? The answer is yes, it can be used as a thought experiment; but no, such a thought experiment cannot be the definitive test of justice. It can be used as a yardstick with which an individual can gauge whether or not a norm might be worthy of recognition. Would I have agreed to this norm in free and equal discussion? What kinds of arguments could be brought for and against? Who else is likely to agree to it? What does this issue look like from the other's point of view? Could I possibly imagine everyone agreeing to it and its consequences? The hypothetical answers to these kinds of questions can serve as a partial guide in political deliberation. The outcome of such an inquiry is not authoritative, however, until an actual discourse takes place.

23. In discourses "we must initially abstract from existing traditions, habitual practices, and current motives—in short, from the ethical customs established within society." Habermas, *Autonomy and Solidarity*, p. 257. "Every post-conventional morality demands a distantiation from the unproblematic background of established and taken-for-granted forms of life." Habermas, "Law and Morality," in *The Tanner Lectures on Human Values*, vol. 8 (Salt Lake City: University of Utah Press, 1988), p. 245.

This sort of hypothetical thought experiment is better understood as the private deliberation that can precede a practical discourse or serve to identify the possible subject matter of a practical discourse.

> Subjects capable of moral judgments cannot test each for himself alone whether an established or recommended norm is in the general interest and ought to have social force; this can only be done in common with everyone else involved. The mechanisms of taking the attitude of the other and of internalizing reach their definitive limit here. . . . Ego can, to be sure, anticipate the attitude that Alter will adopt toward him. . . . Ego can even try to *imagine* to himself the course of moral argument in the circle of those involved; but he cannot *predict* its results with any certainty. Thus the projection of an ideal communication community serves as a guiding thread for *setting up* discourses that have to be carried through *in fact* and cannot be replaced by monological mock dialogue.[24]

The ideal speech situation represents the *formal* conditions of discourse. The philosopher reconstructs the conditions that would have to hold if we wanted to say that an agreement was reasonable and authentic. Like Rawls's original position, it is a device through which we represent in an articulated and artificial way the freedom and equality of moral persons. But unlike the original position, the ideal speech situation models freedom and equality in an intersubjective way. As a formal representation, the ideal speech situation is drastically limited. It can tell us what would have to be the case for a political norm to be considered collectively binding, but it cannot, by itself, tell us which norms would or would not pass that test. The ideal speech situation, by itself, has absolutely no content.

The moment we give content to a discourse, we become participants in that discourse. As participants we propose topics of conversation, norms to be assessed and discussed. Our participation can be virtual or actual. As a virtual participant we undertake a thought experiment. We imagine to ourselves what a discourse among all those affected would look like; we project the hypothetical direction this conversation would take under ideal conditions. But this "mock dialogue" has limitations. Simply proposing one particular norm rather than another as the subject of the debate introduces the bias of the imaginer. Furthermore, in

24. Jürgen Habermas, *The Theory of Communicative Action,* translated by Thomas McCarthy, vol. 2 (Boston: Beacon Press, 1987), p. 95; see also Habermas, *Moral Consciousness and Communicative Action,* p. 77.

running through the conversation in my head, *I* must impute lines of reasoning to the interlocutors, *I* must imagine which pieces of knowledge are relevant to them, *I* must imagine the premises from which they will argue, how they understand the basic workings of society, how they rank their goals, and so on. All the blanks are filled in by the single individual performing the thought experiment. This procedure cannot but affect the imagined course of conversation, for even in the optimal case, where the individual is both very knowledgeable and completely sincere in her attempt to visualize a fair discourse, there are likely to be arguments, alternatives, and possibilities that simply did not occur to her. Perhaps she employs "wishful thinking" in imagining what people would agree to.

It is for these reasons that thought experiments should be understood as preliminaries to real talk and rough guides in evaluating maxims. An important correlative is that the limitations of a thought experiment hold just as much for the philosopher as for anyone else. A philosopher has no more privileged access to the course of real conversation than do the rest of us. In the moments when Habermas, for example, suggests possible directions of dialogue or possible outcomes (which is very rarely), he must be understood as a participant in discourse and not as an observer working out the determinate solution to a problem.

The assumption that practical discourse can be employed in the same way as Rawls's original position leads to a misunderstanding of discourse ethics. For example, consider Steven Lukes's criticism of a view of need interpretation which Habermas proposes as an alternative to a liberal theory of "primary goods." Essentially, Habermas says that primary goods are not neutral because not all forms of life are compatible with *this* way of interpreting our basic needs and motives: "The 'pursuit of happiness' might one day mean something different—for example, not accumulating material objects of which one disposes privately, but bringing about social relations in which mutuality predominates and satisfaction does not mean the triumph of one over the repressed needs of the other."[25] Lukes wants to know how we got to this view of happiness through the universalization procedure of discourse ethics. He complains that he "cannot find in Habermas' writings any argument for the thesis that such a form of life (which is, in any case, barely even sketched, except in the most abstract possible manner) is

25. Habermas, *Communication and the Evolution of Society*, p. 199.

either an appropriate interpretation of the principle of universalization or uniquely capable of rational justification."[26] The absence of such an argument is not an oversight on Habermas's part. He is not claiming that such a form of life is the unique and determinate outcome of discourse. He is suggesting a way in which society might develop, not a way he has deduced that it ought to develop. Indeed, he says that "it cannot be known in advance" how participants will answer moral questions.[27] He is pointing out one line of argument which appears preempted by certain liberal assumptions. The rational justification of any conception of justice must be undertaken and carried through in public by all those affected by it.[28] And this necessity moves us from the ideal to the real. Here, we do not imagine what other people might say; rather, we listen to what they have to say. Here, we are dealing not with ideal talk but with real talk. Practical discourse is first and foremost an activity that real social agents, possessing full knowledge of themselves and their social positions, engage in within the context of an already existing social world.

THE LIMITS OF REAL DISCOURSE

But how does this real and presumably imperfect conversation tie in with the ideal conversation? The conditions of an ideally constructed discourse can never be perfectly met in an imperfect world populated by imperfect (not to mention busy) people. Furthermore, we are not likely to come face-to-face with all those affected by a norm.

These limitations lead to certain conclusions. First, universal thought experiments are an important backdrop to the conversation.[29] Thought experiments are not subject to the same limitations of time, space, and social conditions as are real conversations. Not only should the rules of an ideal conversation be a critical yardstick to evaluate the conditions of real conversations, but the hypothetical outcomes of a discursive thought experiment can serve as arguments within the conversation. In a sense, the relationship between thought experiments

26. Lukes, "Of Gods and Demons," pp. 144–45.

27. Jürgen Habermas, *Justification and Application: Remarks on Discourse Ethics*, translated by Ciaran P. Cronin (Cambridge: MIT Press, 1993), p. 24.

28. Michael Walzer makes the same mistake in "A Critique of Philosophical Conversation," p. 194, when he speaks about "Habermasian outcomes" of discourse as analogous to Rawlsian outcomes. There are no outcomes in this sense.

29. Jürgen Habermas, "Justice and Solidarity: On the Discussion Concerning 'Stage 6,'" *Philosophical Forum* 21 (Fall–Winter 1989–90): 41.

and real discourse is optimally one of reflective equilibrium. But unlike Rawls's notion of reflective equilibrium, in which we check our thought experiments against our considered judgments, the discourse version calls for checking our thought experiments against the considered judgments of others as well.[30] Conversely, we may reconsider our considered judgments or challenge and criticize the considered judgments of others from the point of view of our thought experiments. Thus, the process of reaching reflective equilibrium is taken out of the domain of private reflection and brought into the public sphere.

A second conclusion to be drawn from the limitations imposed on conversations by the real world is that discourses must be understood as fallible and open-ended. "Discourse ethics must assert the fallibility in principle of moral insights; nor can it proceed on the basis of the notion that conflicts in the social domain which are in need of regulation can be resolved through consensus within a set period of time."[31] Habermas means that discourse is ongoing and conclusions and agreements reached by means of discourse are always open to revision. Because real agreements can never be perfectly universal, they never settle a question once and for all.[32]

The open-ended nature of discourse suggests that consensual will formation cannot be understood as the outcome of one conversation but must be seen as the cumulative product of many crisscrossing conversations over time. The single conversation, as it is represented in the ideal speech situation, helps explicate the complicated web of conversations which we undertake in the real world. But understood too literally, the model of the single conversation can be misleading. The argumentative dynamic of a web of conversations is somewhat different from that of the single conversation.

Some critics have suggested that the more open and constraint-free our debates, the less likely we are to reach agreement.[33] This is true if we look only at the single conversation. We often require chairpersons, mediators, judges, or time limits to *force* closure. We do not like to admit that we are wrong even in the face of evidence; we are very attached to our own views; we often enter conversations with set opinions and leave with the same set opinions. Furthermore, there are and

30. John Rawls, *A Theory of Justice* (Cambridge: Harvard University Press, 1971), p. 20.

31. Habermas, "Justice and Solidarity," p. 52 n. 16.

32. In "Reply," p. 247, Habermas notes, "The contradiction that is inherent in the idea of complete justice, owing to its in principle irredeemable universalism, cannot be dissolved."

33. Walzer, "Critique of Philosophical Conversation," pp. 182–96.

will always be real differences of opinion, questions upon which agreement is unlikely.

That a single "unconstrained" conversation, especially on a highly charged subject, appears much more likely to end in disagreement than agreement is not strong evidence against the power of rational argumentation. If we step back from the model of the single conversation, we see that people do in fact change their minds; they do find new arguments, positions, and perspectives more convincing than old ones; they are swayed by argumentation. This process goes on over time, however; it does not happen as it happened to Polemarchus in the *Republic*. We often reevaluate our position between conversations, rather than within them. We are sometimes not even aware that our position has subtly shifted in response to and reflection upon a criticism or challenge. Not only is the process gradual but it is fragmentary and partial. We reevaluate fragments of our world view by bringing them into line with cogent argument; we do not reassess our entire view of life, or at least rarely.

Just think of the innumerable arguments one has with family and friends, colleagues and rivals, strangers and countrymen, teachers and pupils, officials and tradesmen. Or think of the internal arguments one has with newspaper articles, books, popular culture, films, public statements, and public acts; it is not uncommon for people to rebuke their television sets or agree with a public billboard. It would be surprising indeed if we did not take some thought from these exchanges of opinion. Becoming convinced of something is often the product of a web of conversational interaction that includes many such exchanges. It is sometimes hard to put one's finger on the exact moment that one gave up an old belief and adopted a new one. Sometimes it is a matter of believing x, then believing $x + n$, then believing $x + n + n$, then realizing that $x + n + n = y$. In any event, that single conversations often do not end in agreement does not mean that people are not swayed by argumentation.

Thinking of the argumentative dynamic of a web of conversations in this way alters what we mean by agreement. Although consensus represents a general agreement, it is not an agreement in the sense that we can point to one particular time or place at which the agreement occurred. A general agreement can emerge as the product of many single conversations even when no single conversation ends in agreement. Consensual agreement, if and when it comes, emerges gradually and is fragmentary and partial. It is also often very hard to put one's finger on.

The point here is simply to highlight the diffuseness a real practical discourse would have to have if its outcome is to be a consensus that underwrites a legitimate social norm. On this reading, then, practical discourse is a long-term consensus-forming process and not a decision procedure. A decision procedure implies a set of rules that govern closure. These rules tell us when the process is over, what counts as a fair decision that can be acted upon. Now, as a decision rule, discourse stipulates that full, rational agreement under the ideal conditions of discourse of all affected by a norm constitutes the point of closure. When it is translated into the real world, however, it turns out that this point can never be definitively reached. Because real agreements can never be perfectly universal, they never settle a question once and for all. Through the idea of an ideal communication community we can imagine the conditions of a perfectly rational consensus, but inasmuch as we can never attain the ideal in the real world, the question becomes the degree of approximation. Discourse is not a contract where there is a privileged moment of promising which is then binding on all parties in perpetuity.

Anyone who has ever participated in a group whose decision rule was consensus knows how difficult and drawn-out such deliberations can be. Discourse is constraint free; therefore no one may force closure. The conversation continues until (ideally) every single participant is in full agreement. The larger and more diverse the group, the more difficult and drawn-out the process. The closer our conversations come to embodying the ideal, the more inefficient they are. The more general the norm under discussion, the more diffuse, fragmented, and complicated will be the web of conversation, and the longer the process is likely to take. With this reality in mind, it becomes difficult even to talk about a decision being taken in discourse; instead, we must visualize discourse as the place where collective interpretations are constructed.

Because discourse is ongoing and fallible, it is best understood as a process of moral and political deliberation which can inform and underpin decisions taken either individually or collectively. Discourse is directed not so much at the decisions taken but at the formation of opinion which precedes decisions. It is the conditions under which individuals and groups initially *form* their opinions and beliefs or *interpret* their needs and interests at which discourse ethics directs its normative gaze. Implementing practical discourse, then, is not so much a question of setting up a constitutionally empowered "body" of some sort as it is of engendering a practice. Discourse as a practice points to a certain type of political culture as a permanent background to political decisions. It involves fostering a political culture in which citizens actively participate in noncoercive, egalitarian debate about the political norms of their community. What discourse lacks in efficiency it makes up, or so I argue in the final chapters of this book, by encouraging a form of rational deliberation which brings together social recognition of a norm with procedures of rational justification.

Practical discourse combines the formal standards of the ideal speech situation with the universalizing potential of hypothetical discourse and the unpredictability and never-ending course of real moral argument. This combination results in a theory of procedural justice which allows for maximum open-endedness without sacrificing normative content. The ideal speech situation by itself tells us nothing about the substance of discourses, but it does give us a standard from which to evaluate real discourses. The thought experiment does not allow for the unpredictability of real talk or for the freedom of participants to interpret their needs in their own way. The thought experiment does allow us to imagine a more universal conversation than we are likely to have in the real world, as well as a strict conformity to the rules. Real discourse counters the inherent selectivity of thought experiments by putting them to the test of real talk.

A practical discourse takes shape when we bring the three moments together—the ideal speech situation, the discursive thought experiment, and *the actual discursive encounter*. There can be no distinction between discourse as criterion of political justice and democratic legitimacy and discourse as a social process; discourse must become a social process to justify and legitimate a norm. That it must means in turn that the justification of concrete norms must be understood not in absolute but in fallible terms.

12 *Justice and the Individual*

Political theorists who deal with questions of justice are often at pains to distance themselves from any claims pertaining to the private moral judgments of individuals. As we saw in Chapter 10, many think that tying a political theory of justice to a general moral philosophy is both unrealistic and a violation of the very values we wish to uphold as being just. It appears unrealistic because of the fact of pluralism. If the public recognition of a conception of justice depends on everyone's holding the same general view of morality, then there does not appear to be much hope that such recognition will emerge. But it is not simply a *fact* that in modern liberal democracies people have developed divergent moral visions; it is also somehow *right* that they should be allowed to do so. Justice itself seems to require that allegiance to just institutions not require conformity to any one moral vision.

The paramount dilemma facing modern political theories of justice can be stated as follows: Somehow a way must be found by which we can all pursue our divergent ways of life while sharing an allegiance to public standards of justice.[1] One possible way is to say that theories of justice do not apply to private moral conceptions but only to public institutions. According to this view, we can make choices for ourselves, our families, our churches, and so on which are biased toward our private visions, but we cannot use public institutions in this way. Public institutions must reflect standards that do not favor one conception of the good over another. The institutions are just and allegiance re-

1. This is, for example, how Rawls frames the problem. John Rawls, *Political Liberalism* (New York: Columbia University Press, 1993), pp. xviii, 4.

mains stable only so long as this separation between private moral vision and public standards is maintained.[2]

I think that this view of the matter is correct up to a point, but only up to a point. For example, it would be wrong to conclude from it that the requirements of fairness and impartiality apply only to governments and not to individuals. This kind of talk makes it easy to forget that when we refer to justice in the state or a fair society, the state and society are not the moral agents. Moral agency is an attribute not of abstract collective entities but of people who make choices and take responsibility for those choices. The distinction between public and private, no matter how essential to our modern understanding of ethics and politics, should not obscure the fact that morality has more to do with questions we ask *ourselves* than with questions we ask about abstract entities such as the state.

Justice as a moral as well as political concept cannot avoid the problem of moral agency. Perhaps as citizens we are called upon to make different types of ethical choices from those we make as private persons, but it is not at all clear how the citizen/person distinction corresponds to the way people understand their moral responsibilities. Do we think, "I believe such and such as a citizen but not as a person"? A political theory concerned with just institutions cannot simply bracket out the private sphere from the beginning. The question for theories of justice is not simply how the state mediates between the private and the public but how *we* mediate between our private and plural ends, values, and interests, and our commitments to public standards of right. The problem of justice is not simply an institutional problem; it is a problem for the individual as well.

This is what Thomas Nagel has called the "division of the self." The tension between public and private, or what he calls the impartial and partial perspective, is a tension within the individual. On the one hand, most individuals are partial toward their own goals, interests, and needs and recognize that these will come into conflict with other people's goals, interests, and needs. From this perspective one's ends and goals must take priority. On the other hand, most individuals also recognize an impartial perspective; that is, they recognize that they are not the only ones with goals, interests, and needs. From this larger view one's ends and goals cannot count for any more than anyone

2. This separation is most clearly seen in Rawls's distinction between a political conception of justice and comprehensive moral views. Rawls, *Political Liberalism*, pp. 12–13.

else's. The problem is not, as rational-choice theorists would have us believe, that individuals do not recognize an impartial perspective. Individuals recognize the legitimacy of an impartial perspective, but they do not agree on how important it is, or when it should trump their partial perspectives, or why they should look at the world impartially when no one else is. Thus, for Nagel, the question of justice is a question of reconciling these two aspects of the individual; the problem, he says, "must be solved within the individual soul if it is to be solved at all." Thus, institutional solutions "will be valid only if they give expression to an adequate response to the division of the self, conceived as a problem for each individual."[3]

I want to investigate Nagel's proposition that impartiality cannot simply be understood as an attribute of institutions and officials. If impartiality is to have efficacy within our political world, it must be understood as a perspective taken up by the individual as well. What concerns me here is primarily a question of allegiance. I want to show that we can maintain a viable political conception of justice only if it is rooted in private conceptions of justice. I mean this in both a weak and a strong sense. The weak sense is that people must be committed to justice in the public sphere as a moral value in itself and not simply as a modus vivendi. This is Rawls's position. I believe that a stronger sense follows, though Rawls does not embrace it. As moral agents, we are not bifurcated into citizens and persons. I do not think we can believe this as a citizen and that as a person. In order for us to be morally committed to fairness and impartiality in the public sphere we must be, to some extent, committed to it in the private sphere. That states should treat people fairly does not make sense in a world where people do not believe that *they* should treat each other fairly. Of course, one of the reasons why we need states is because people do not always treat each other fairly. But the issue of whether citizens live up to ideals of fairness is different from the issue of whether citizens think they ought to treat each other fairly. I am not saying that we must turn ourselves into a Kantian race of angels in order to maintain a just political system. I am saying a race of devils could not do it.

The model of discourse I have so far outlined has a unique contribution to make to this particular debate. Discourse, by collapsing procedures of justification into procedures of recognition (in Rawlsian

3. Thomas Nagel, *Equality and Partiality* (Oxford: Oxford University Press, 1991), pp. 16–17.

terms, collapsing the original position into the public use of reason), is able to solve the problem of the "division of the self."

PERSONS AND CITIZENS

The person/citizen distinction serves to divide our commitments into different categories. As persons we are said to have conceptions of the good, the content of which varies from person to person or group to group. These conceptions can be and often are at odds with one another. As citizens, however, we take on a different attitude than as persons. In this way we are able to transcend, negate, or neutralize our private differences.

The person/citizen distinction has very deep roots within the liberal tradition. It also has many different variations, however. For example, a modus vivendi view of justice is premised on a radical split between person and citizen. According to this view, the plurality of moral visions is too great to expect that each private conception will include the same substantive ideal of justice. Nevertheless, there is something we do agree upon: the need for general rules to govern our interaction. Without such rules, social peace could not be maintained, nor could the space necessary to pursue our private interests be guaranteed. We approach the question of justice as a matter of expediency or as a "means of accommodation."[4] We agree upon general rules not because they reflect our deepest commitments as persons but because they solve the problem at hand. Here the citizen's perspective need have only minimum moral content (e.g., social peace is a moral good) or none at all (e.g., social peace is an instrumental good); indeed, it may be at odds with many of our strongest moral commitments. A modus vivendi view of justice allows for a radical disjunction between what I believe as a person and what I accept as necessary as a citizen. The paradigmatic case of a modus vivendi solution, the acceptance of the principle of toleration in the sixteenth and seventeenth centuries, highlights the potential for disjunction. Here, one could accept the princi-

4. Charles Larmore, *Patterns of Moral Complexity* (Cambridge: Cambridge University Press, 1987), p. 74. Larmore is one of the few contemporary liberal, as opposed to libertarian, theorists who explicitly embraces a modus vivendi view. His is not a pure modus vivendi view, however, in as much as he includes a shared moral commitment to the idea of mutual respect as part of the citizen's perspective. For another example of a modus vivendi view of justice, see Walter Lippmann, *The Phantom Public* (New Brunswick, N.J.: Transaction, 1993), esp., pp. 87–93.

ple of toleration for the sake of social peace, as Jean Bodin did, for example, while believing that in the best of all possible worlds (or perhaps even in a future world) the just state would uphold and protect the true religion.[5]

A pure modus vivendi view of justice, as opposed to temporary modus vivendi solutions to problems of justice, is quite difficult to maintain. Even such libertarians as Robert Nozik, who defends a very minimal type commitment on the part of citizens, relies on some quite strong moral assumptions about what governments may and may not do.[6] Thus, his view of politics will make sense only to persons who share those moral views. Rational-choice theories of justice, which also see justice as a means of accommodation, must stretch the meaning of self-interest in order to arrive at full theory of justice.[7] The closest thing to a pure modus vivendi view of justice is perhaps implied in some radical postmodern theory. The combination of radical skepticism and the ubiquity of power makes it difficult for some postmodern thinkers to answer the question, Why should I obey the laws? The only reason we can have to choose between anarchy and justice must be that systems of justice, although a form of domination and ultimately not justifiable on moral grounds, nevertheless make our life somewhat easier.

The possibility of a radical disjunction between person and citizen, as exemplified in a pure modus vivendi view, has its antinomy in a reconciliarist view. On that view, there is a reconciliation between the person and the citizen such that our identities as persons mirror the norms we uphold in the public sphere. Hegel's *Philosophy of Right* represents the clearest expression of this view: "Particular interests should in fact not be set aside or completely suppressed; instead, they should be

5. Jean Bodin, *Six Books of the Commonwealth*, translated by M. J. Tooley (New York: Barnes and Noble, 1967), 138–44. It should be noted that modus vivendi was not the only argument used to defend toleration; prominent also were moral/religious arguments that torture, incarceration, and mass murder were not very Christian things to do (Menno Simons, "A Rejection of the Use of Force," in *Sources of the Western Tradition*, edited by Marvin Perry, Joseph R. Peden, and Theodore H. von Laue [Boston: Houghton Mifflin, 1991], pp. 332–333), skeptical arguments that we cannot know for sure what the true religion is (Michel de Montaigne, "It Is Folly to Measure the True and False by Our Own Capacity," in *The Complete Essays of Montaigne*, translated by Donald M. Frame [Stanford: Stanford University Press, 1965], pp. 132–35), and freedom-of-conscience arguments that one cannot command faith (John Locke, *A Letter concerning Toleration* [Indianapolis: Hackett, 1983], p. 27).

6. Robert Nozick, *Anarchy, State, and Utopia* (New York: Basic Books, 1974).

7. David Gauthier, *Morals by Agreement* (New York: Oxford University Press, 1987); James Buchanan, *The Limits of Liberty: Between Anarchy and Leviathan* (Chicago: University of Chicago Press, 1975).

put in correspondence with the universal, and thereby both they and the universal are upheld."[8] Some, but not all, communitarians can also be described as reconciliarist. For example, communitarians such as MacIntyre who see individualism as irreconcilable with virtue and the common good are not reconciliarist.[9] Here, the liberal idea of the person is to be set aside. Communitarians such as Bellah and Taylor who believe that modern notions of the person can be harmonized with the pursuit of strong community are reconciliarist.[10]

I understand Rawls, Scanlon, and Habermas as steering a middle course between these two alternatives. Rawls, however, while rejecting a pure modus vivendi view, retains a relatively strong commitment to the distinction between person and citizen, whereas implicit in Scanlon's work as well as discourse ethics is the rejection of the person/citizen distinction as representing two fundamentally different moral points of view. The reason is that we undertake their deliberative procedures fully aware of both the partial and the impartial perspective.

Rawls's rejection of a modus vivendi view of justice rests on the argument that the motivational factors that underpin such a view are too weak to support a public system of justice over time.[11] If accommodation or expediency is the ground for our recognizing public rules as valid, then there is no reason why we will not violate those rules in order to further our preferred goals. Rawls goes on to say that constitutional protections might have arisen initially as a modus vivendi but that they endure only if citizens come to see their value above and beyond their worth as pragmatic compromises. Further, on a pure modus vivendi view, we are unable adequately to explain public allegiance to the full range of constitutional protections provided in a liberal democracy. Why should we respect the rights and freedoms of the powerless if failing to do so would neither threaten social peace nor endanger our freedom to pursue our conception of the good life?

No doubt there will always be individuals and groups in society who accept public institutions as a modus vivendi; and further, conflicts will

8. G. W. F. Hegel, *Philosophy of Right*, translated by T. M. Knox (Oxford: Oxford University Press, 1967), para. 267.

9. Alasdair MacIntyre, *After Virtue* (Notre Dame: University of Notre Dame Press, 1981).

10. Robert Bellah et al., *The Good Society* (New York: Vintage, 1992); Charles Taylor, *Sources of the Self: The Making of the Modern Identity* (Cambridge: Harvard University Press, 1989).

11. John Rawls, "The Idea of an Overlapping Consensus," *Oxford Journal of Legal Studies* 7 (1987): 1–2.

arise which will be eased in the short run through modus vivendi solutions; but such instances do not add up to an account of justice. There must be some kind of commitment to the idea that public institutions represent not simply a workable compromise but just principles. This is Rawls's position. While saying that a stable commitment to just institutions is a moral commitment, however, he retains the idea that it is a commitment we undertake as citizens and not necessarily as persons.

In *Political Liberalism*, for example, Rawls declares that "the ideal of citizenship imposes a moral, not a legal, duty—the duty of civility. . . . This duty involves a willingness to listen to others and a fairmindedness in deciding when accommodations to their views should be reasonably be made." Here we have the idea of dialogic respect, which is also a central component of discourse ethics. Rawls, however, has a narrowly political understanding of when the duty of civility is required of us. So, for example, we are not bound (morally) by civility in our "personal deliberations and reflections about political questions, or to the reasoning about them by members of associations such as churches and universities, all of which is a vital part of the background culture." We are bound by civility when engaged in political campaigns and when we hold political office.[12]

Rawls is primarily concerned with excluding the appeal to comprehensive moral views in the public sphere. To do so he must have a clear line between spheres, but this clear line creates an odd picture. First of all, it represents a narrow view of where political deliberation takes place. It is a view in which primarily officials, candidates, and spokespersons for advocacy groups are bound by the rules of civility and public reason. But ordinary citizens do not form and revise their political views, for the most part, while acting in these capacities. It is much more likely that ordinary citizens will form and revise their political views while participating in their chosen associations or debating within informal public forums. More worrying still is the idea that the background culture that is to underpin a political conception of justice need not be imbued with this idea of civility. Thus, we have the picture of people donning their civility hats when entering the public arena but perhaps hanging them up for the vast majority of their daily interactions.

The clear line Rawls wishes to maintain between the political and the personal undermines his claim that political commitments are

12. Rawls, *Political Liberalism*, pp. 217, 215–216.

moral commitments. There is something odd about the image of a
world where we believe it is morally right that the state and its officials
be bound by standards of respect and civility and yet individuals (persons?) are under no such moral expectation in their daily lives. There
are, no doubt, individuals who believe that not all persons are deserving of their respect, but people who are morally committed to that
view can support an institutional system that confers equal respect
only as a modus vivendi. A *moral* commitment to public standards of
civility and respect is incompatible with a widespread private rejection
of those standards. A moral commitment to public standards of civility
and respect must be embedded in a "background culture" that takes
these values seriously.

LIBERALISM AND MORAL EDUCATION

The issue Rawls raises in his discussion of citizenship has now become a central theme in liberal theory. The debate centers on the inadequacy of a liberal theory that understands the protection of liberal
institutions as guaranteed by the countervailing forces of self-interest
rather than the moral character of citizens.[13] Talk of the moral character
of citizens has often been thought unnecessary for the liberal. Indeed,
one of the great advantages of a liberal system was thought to be that it
could solve the problem of justice even for a "race of devils." For example, against the republican ideals of the antifederalists, James Madison
argued that virtue could not always be relied upon; much sounder and
more dependable was the assumption of self-interest.[14] This view appeals to both a realist/rational-choice strain in liberal thought and a
"neutral" strain. Realists believe self-interest to be the strongest, in the
sense of being the most dependable and predictable, motivating factor
in the public realm, and defenders of the neutral state believe that the
state should not be in the business of moral education and so should
not be in the business of inculcating virtues.

The problem with the realist/rational-choice position, as we saw in
my discussion of Rawls, is that it unrealistically underestimates what is
needed to maintain a stable liberal state. Even Adam Smith acknowl-

13. The following discussion describes a strand of liberal thought that is represented in
the work of such theorists as William Galston, Amy Gutmann, Stephen Macedo, Thomas
Nagel, Nancy Rosenblum, and Dennis Thompson, among others.

14. James Madison, Alexander Hamilton, and John Jay, *The Federalist Papers* (New York:
Penguin, 1987), no. 50.

edged that a certain "fellow feeling" that could act as a moral restraint was also necessary for maintaining a stable system.[15] David Gauthier, although wedded to a rational-choice model of liberalism because he feels it is the only one that can account for a motivation to be just, has voiced misgivings about how just utility maximizers can be expected to be. He has conceded that perhaps Locke was "right to insist that 'a great many plain duties' cannot be accommodated within the secular morality available to Hobbes and those who share Hobbes' outlook." He has also suggested that because "love and patriotism are myths" to the utility maximizer, they will disappear as we come more and more to acknowledge our rational natures, but it is love and patriotism, he adds, and not rational self-interest, which have held society together; the result of their disappearance might be that "the bargaining order will collapse into competitive chaos."[16] Despite the rational plausibility of the self-interest account, it appears to be thin stuff out of which to secure the bonds of society. Human activity, understood primarily as a quest for more rather than less of whatever it is that we want, is ultimately corrosive of sociability. More and more liberal theorists are coming to accept that it is and turn toward ways of promoting sociability without violating individual autonomy.[17]

The neutral argument fares no better because the very idea of neutrality seems less and less plausible. The most obvious objection is that neutrality is not itself neutral. For those who believe that the state should promote a particular conception of the good life, a state that leaves it up to each individual is not being neutral but rather promoting an alternative view of the good life—one based on individual autonomy. The very idea that the state *should* be neutral represents a substantive moral position that citizens can dispute.

In addition to the question of whether the state should be neutral is the question of whether it can be neutral. No matter how much liberals would prefer not to be in the business of moral education, politics is always, partially anyway, a form of paideia. As George Will notes, politics is always a matter of legislating morality because "the enactment of laws and implementation of policies that proscribe, mandate,

15. Adam Smith, *The Theory of Moral Sentiments* (London: Henry G. Bohn, 1853), p. 4.

16. David Gauthier, *Moral Dealing: Contract, Ethics, and Reason* (Ithaca: Cornell University Press, 1990), pp. 27, 353.

17. Amy Gutmann, one of the leading advocates of liberal virtue, notes, "The question is not whether to maximize freedom or to inculcate virtue, but how to combine freedom and virtue." "Undemocratic Education," in *Liberalism and the Moral Life*, edited by Nancy L. Rosenblum (Cambridge: Harvard University Press, 1989), p. 75.

regulate, or subsidize behavior . . . will, over time, have the predictable effect of nurturing, bolstering, or altering habits, dispositions, and values on a broad scale."[18] Liberals turn their back on this aspect of politics at the risk of leaving it to conservatives like Will.

In response to mostly communitarian criticism of the corrosiveness of individual self-interest and the myth of neutrality, liberal theory is staking out new ground.[19] This new ground involves introducing a theory of liberal virtues and a study of preference, interest, and attitude formation. The leading questions are, first, what virtues are necessary to maintain the liberal state and, second, how to inculcate these virtues without violating basic liberal ideas of individual autonomy? These arguments in turn require that liberalism be more open to the idea that it contains a particular conception of the good life. The stability of the liberal system is now seen as requiring that the ideals of liberalism become deeply embedded in the ways of life and general practices of its citizens and not simply in their political commitments.

In distinction to communitarian ideas of the good life, however, the liberal conception is defended as being minimally demanding and maximally impartial.[20] It is minimally demanding in the sense that it does not prescribe a whole way of life complete with a range of pursuits and a list of goods. Instead, a liberal conception of the good life has one primary good, justice, and this is understood as a sine qua non for the pursuit of particular ways of life. It is maximally impartial in the sense that the liberal conception of the good life includes the idea that people should be able to pursue, within the bounds of justice, their own particular conceptions of the good life. Thus, liberalism cannot be said to be impartial to a full range of conceptions of the good life. Conceptions of the good life which involve discrimination, cruelty, or oppression might be tolerated as opinions, but the liberal system, from schools to the courts, cannot be said to give these conceptions equal place to flourish. Indeed, liberalism must actively work against the possibility that too many citizens are illiberal in this sense. The whole idea here is that the stability of the liberal state is jeopardized if there is a large gap between political ideals and private beliefs. The liberal conception does claim to give the maximum room for diversity, however, while maintaining the moral foundation necessary to sustain a liberal state.

---

18. George Will, *Statecraft as Soul Craft: What Government Does* (New York: Simon and Schuster, 1983), pp. 19–20.

19. A good discussion of the moral turn in liberal thought can be found in Nancy Rosenblum's introduction to *Liberalism and the Moral Life*, pp. 1–17.

20. Gutmann, "Undemocratic Education," p. 77.

The concern for the moral character of the liberal citizen has led to a different understanding of the role of institutions in the liberal state. In the past, much of liberal theory has focused on the fairest way to mediate, channel, organize, and aggregate competing and divergent interests and beliefs. Interests and beliefs themselves were taken as given, as in a sense, belonging to the person and not to be questioned. What we are seeing is a shift in focus from the coordination of interests and beliefs that are taken as given, to the generation of interests and beliefs that are understood as malleable. The *formation* of individual interests, beliefs, and values has replaced the *competition* among individual interests, beliefs and values as a central theme in liberal theory. The two most common areas in which the question of formation is addressed are liberal education and democratic theory. Although the question of liberal education is central within this debate, my interest at the moment is with democracy.[21]

There is a long-standing tradition within a strand of democratic theory which says that democracy should be valued not simply because it is a fair system or produces the best outcomes but because democratic participation is an education in citizenship. There are two versions of this view. One is a republican or radical view and the other is a liberal or, as it is increasingly called, a deliberative view.[22] Both views set themselves against the market model of democracy, which understands democratic procedures to be a fair arena in which individual and group interests can compete or be aggregated. Both value democratic participation for the role it plays in interest and belief formation.[23] From a philosophic perspective the difference between the two views is that the republican/radical view usually takes ancient Greece or Rousseau's general will as its model, and the liberal/deliberative view takes deon-

21. For a discussion of education in the liberal state, see Amy Gutmann, *Democratic Education* (Princeton: Princeton University Press, 1987); Benjamin Barber, *An Aristocracy of Everyone: The Politics of Education and the Future of America* (New York: Ballantine, 1992); William Galston, "Civic Education in the Liberal State," in *Liberalism and the Moral Life*, ed. Rosenblum, pp. 89–101; and Anita Mercier, "Civic Education and the Idea of an Overlapping Consensus" (Diss., Columbia University, 1990).

22. Examples of the republican/radical view can be found in the work of Hannah Arendt, Benjamin Barber, Robert Bellah, and Carol Pateman. As this lists suggests, there is a great deal of divergence within this group. Examples of the liberal/deliberative view can be found in the work of Charles Beitz, Joshua Cohen, John Dryzeck, Helmut Dubiel, James Fishkin, Jürgen Habermas, Bernard Manin, and David Miller.

23. Here, I disagree with Jon Elster who characterizes the difference between deliberative models and republican models on the grounds that the first looks at democracy instrumentally, as a means to a fair outcome, and the second views democratic participation as an end in itself. Jon Elster, "The Market and the Forum: Three Varieties of Political Theory," in *Foundations of Social Choice Theory*, edited by Elster and Aanund Hylland (Cambridge: Cambridge University Press, 1986), pp. 103–32.

tological procedures (e.g., Kant's notion of publicity, Habermas's idea of discourse, or Scanlon's idea of reasonable agreement) as its starting point. Another difference is that republican/radical models usually stress the idea that political participation is part of the good life and that through such participation we can collectively construct a shared idea of the good life. On their side, advocates of liberal/deliberative models usually stress the idea of autonomous, yet intersubjectively mediated will formation, the use of public reason, and the search for consensual solutions to political problems of justice. Having said that, I must add that there is a great deal of overlap between the two views. Many theorists do not fall squarely within one or the other category.

Generally speaking, advocates of deliberative democracy find republican models of democracy too demanding; they require a level of civic virtue not likely to be attained in liberal democratic societies, put too much stress on the creation of a community that acts as one, and finally, are not concerned enough with safeguarding the autonomy of the individual within collective procedures. With the exception of the question of autonomy, the difference is really one of degree. As we shall see, deliberative models of democracy are also quite demanding. If they do not require as high a level of civic virtue as republican models, they certainly require a higher level of civic virtue than is presently evident in the practice of democracy. Although the idea of deliberative consensus does not require the creation of strong community ties among members of a polity, it does require a certain amount of solidarity among them. It is really on the issue of autonomy that one can see the most important differences between the two. Models of deliberative democracy have a Kantian component that is not usually found in republican models of democracy. Here, we have the idea that democratic opinion formation is not a matter of getting in touch with the affective ties of community but a is matter of assessing and evaluating one's opinions from the point of view of impartial reason. Impartial reason is understood on a communicative model. We gain an impartial perspective by engaging others in discourse under fair conditions.

DELIBERATIVE OPINION FORMATION

One way to understand the procedures of deliberative democracy is as a democratic reformulation of Kant's principle of publicity. Publicity reconciles the requirements of right (justice/general interest) with the requirements of politics (obedience/stability).[24] The idea of public right finds expression in the following principle: "All actions affecting the rights of other human beings are wrong if their maxim is not compatible with their being made public." The idea is that the sovereign is the guardian of the general interest and therefore should have no reason to fear public debate on the legitimacy of his actions. Indeed, a sovereign who fears public debate is a sovereign who fears that his actions are not in the general interest: "[A maxim] which cannot be publicly acknowledged without thereby inevitably arousing the resistance of everyone to my plans, can only have stirred up this necessary and general (hence *a priori* foreseeable) opposition against me because it is itself unjust and thus constitutes a threat to everyone."[25]

In addition to serving as a negative test for the justness of laws, publicity also serves as a means of gaining obedience while respecting each citizen as an autonomous moral agent capable of making rational judgments: "There must be a *spirit of freedom*, for in all matters concerning universal human rights, each individual requires to be convinced by reason that the coercion which prevails is lawful, otherwise he would be in contradiction with himself." Thus, by making public the grounds for state action and subjecting these grounds to the critical force of "independent and public thought," one can ensure that the state has just reasons for its actions and that citizens believe these reasons are just.[26]

Kant, as we know, was no democrat in our modern sense. The sovereign's mandate to rule could be explained through the idea of a contract and therefore through consent, but the principle of publicity did not require actual, universal, and renewable consent. Furthermore, although citizens should not be discouraged from judging the actions of the sovereign, they should definitely be discouraged from actively opposing the sovereign. Thus, although the principle of publicity sets out the rudiments of a theory of political legitimacy, it is limited by Kant's failure to tie it to a theory of popular sovereignty. Kant was still preoccupied with the problem of who will judge between the people and the sovereign when they make opposing claims to right. The adjudication of such competing claims presupposes that "there would have to be

---

24. Immanuel Kant, "Perpetual Peace," in *Kant's Political Writings*, edited by Hans Reiss (Cambridge: Cambridge University Press, 1970), p. 130.

25. Ibid., p. 126.

26. Immanuel Kant, "On the Common Saying: 'This May Be True in Theory, but It Does Not Apply in Practice,'" in *Kant's Political Writings*, p. 85.

another head above the head of state to mediate between the latter and the people, which is self-contradictory."[27]

When we join Kant's idea of publicity with modern notions of democracy, we arrive at a deliberative theory of democratic legitimacy. Rather than pure consent, this theory stresses the deliberative processes that lead to consent and the reasons that underpin consent. The central idea is that citizens should be "convinced by reason" that the institutions and norms of their community are in the general interest. Conversely, the institutions and norms of the community are not in the public interest when citizens cannot be convinced by reason that they are.

But what does it mean to be "convinced by reason"? In answering this question, Kant appealed to the distinction between the public and the private use of reason.[28] Reason is used privately when it is put into the service of one's private interests or when one thinks in terms of one's particular post or office—as a policeman, as a lawyer, as a businessperson. Reason is used publicly when it is put into the service of the common good or general interest. Here, we must try to rise above our particular place in society and assess public issues and policies from a more general perspective. For Kant, to be "convinced by reason" meant to be convinced by public reason. But how do we know whether citizens are really convinced by public reason or simply acquiesce to the rules that are imposed upon them? Kant does not suggest a test. Furthermore, Kant tended to think that only the highly educated, particularly philosophers, who are accustomed to viewing questions from an impersonal point of view, were capable of using reason publicly.[29] The general public in forming their opinions should take their cue from these "men of learning."

It is at this point, where theories of deliberative democracy must go beyond Kant, that Scanlon's and Habermas's theories of moral deliberation enter. Discourse ethics is particularly useful because it both democratizes this idea of public reason and suggests procedural guidelines to encourage and secure the public use of reason. The structure of discourse sets out what is entailed and presupposed by the idea of being convinced by reason or rational opinion and will formation. When this is tied to the idea of democratic legitimacy, we have a picture of what is entailed in rational *public* opinion and will formation.

27. Ibid., p. 81.
28. Immanuel Kant, "An Answer to the Question: 'What Is Enlightenment,'" in *Kant's Political Writings*, p. 55.
29. Ibid., 55.

To recap the structure of discourse, it will be recalled that it entails a set of rules designed to guarantee discursive equality, freedom, and fair play. No one with the competency to speak and act may be excluded from discourse; everyone is allowed to question or introduce any assertion whatever as well as to express her attitudes, desires, and needs; no one may be prevented, by internal or external coercion, from exercising these rights.[30] These rules lead to reasonable agreement only when participants adopt the attitudes of respect and impartiality.

In Habermas's earlier writings, the discursive solution to practical questions of the type, "What should I/we do?" is tied almost exclusively to practical or moral discourse. He later adds two more types of discourse: pragmatic and ethical.[31] Pragmatic discourse concentrates on means/ends issues, ethical discourse on the self-understanding of individuals and groups, and moral discourse on generally valid moral principles. All are governed by the rules of equality, freedom, and fair play. All aim at mutual understanding through the power of reasoned argument. Only moral discourse, however, sets itself the high standard of rational consensus.

Democratic deliberation entails all three types of discourse.[32] The more the issue under public discussion involves deep foundational issues of justice, the more important rational consensus becomes. We may also try to reach agreement on questions of the best means to achieved a desired end or on who we are and what we want. But these agreements, when reached, are more closely tied to contingent problems or particular ways of life than to the search for just principles. In conversations about just principles we try to achieve the maximum amount of impartiality and universalization. Further, democratic deliberation is valued even in cases where agreement is not reached. A discursively formed public opinion can represent a process of *Bildung* or education in which citizens build better foundations to their opinions through discursive interaction. Through discursive interaction on various issues from who we are to the best means of securing deficit re-

30. Jürgen Habermas, *Moral Consciousness and Communicative Action*, translated by Christian Lenhardt and Shierry Weber Nicholsen (Cambridge: MIT Press, 1990), p. 89. Examples of external coercion are threats and bribes; examples of internal coercion are psychological pressure, rhetorical manipulation, and deception.

31. Jürgen Habermas, *Justification and Application: Remarks on Discourse Ethics*, translated by Ciaran P. Cronin (Cambridge: MIT Press, 1993), pp. 1–18; see also Jürgen Habermas, *Faktizität und Geltung: Beiträge zur Diskurstheorie des Rechts und des demokratischen Rechtsstaats* (Frankfurt: Suhrkamp, 1992), pp. 138–43.

32. Habermas, *Faktizität und Geltung*, pp. 349–98.

duction, citizens become more informed about the issues; they become aware of what others think and feel; they reevaluate their positions in light of criticism and argument. In short, through defense of their opinions with reason, their opinions become more reasoned. The result of such interaction is that public opinion and the exercise of democratic responsibility are embedded in reasoned convictions, although reasoned convictions do not always need to reflect consensus on an issue.[33] There is such a thing as reasonable disagreement. Questions of legitimacy, on the other hand, are also questions of justice, and on these issues consensus is still the goal.

In what follows I concentrate on questions of legitimacy. These present the hardest case because questions of legitimacy require a level of agreement which most questions of public policy do not. In many questions of public policy we are willing to accept the outcome of a fair compromise, or to abide by the decision of the majority. But fair compromises and majority decisions are legitimate to the extent that citizens believe there are good reasons to settle for these decisions rules. Thus, questions of legitimacy usually address deep structural issues and are not raised by every decision a democratic society must face. Also, it is important to remember that any discourse about public issues will naturally alternate among the three types of discourse. Questions of justice will naturally include questions of instrumental feasibility or the best means of achieving a proposed principle. But even more important will be ethical discourse. Habermas divides ethical discourse into ethical-existential and ethical-political.[34] The first refers to a hermeneutical investigation about who we want to be as individuals, and the second refers to conversations about collective identity and the pursuit of collective goods that are part of that identity. If deliberative democracy is able to solve the person/citizen dilemma, then questions of justice will always include an element of the ethical. In practical discourse I want to know what is just. But it is I, complete with my identity and conception of the good, who wants to know what is just. If I really become convinced that something is just, then this conviction must signal a corresponding shift in my understanding of myself. I am now the sort of person who believes that such and such is just.

33. Bernard Manin says that majority rule can be justified only when preceded by such deliberation. He questions whether consensus is a realistic goal of discourse but insists that if sincere and fair deliberation has taken place, then majorities have good or at least not arbitrary reasons for coercing minorities. "On Legitimacy and Political Deliberation," *Political Theory* 15 (August 1987): 357–62.

34. Habermas, *Justification and Application*, p. 4; Habermas, *Faktizität und Geltung*, p. 139.

The idea of deliberative democracy and democratic legitimacy which emerges from discourse theory can be defended from two overlapping perspectives. The first is from the point of view of outcome. Agreements reached under these conditions have the power to legitimate institutions and political principles in a way that the simple aggregation of votes does not. Agreements reached under the egalitarian and fair conditions of discourse ensure that consent is free and reasonable. Under these conditions we can be confident that arguments rather than numbers or inducements sway participants.

The second perspective is from the point of view of process. Here, deliberative democracy is valued because it solves the problem of justice at the level of the individual. That is, it solves Nagel's problem outlined at the beginning of this chapter and transcends the person/ citizen distinction without violating individual autonomy. It does so in two ways. The first is that we enter deliberative procedures as whole people fully aware of who we are and what we want. To be convinced by reason within deliberation means that *I* am convinced: *I* as both person and citizen am convinced. The second way in which deliberative democracy transcends the person/citizen distinction is that the practice of collective deliberation inculcates, in a noncoercive way, the virtues of respect and impartiality.

Deliberative democracy is premised on the idea that preferences and interests are malleable. Taking them as given accords the individual no more autonomy than taking them as malleable. Indeed, deliberative democracy, because it asks participants to examine, justify, and deliberate about their preferences and interests, gives the individual the opportunity to shape her preferences and interests autonomously. Deliberation, the end of which is agreement, is intended to foster the public use of reason. Or to use Nagel's language, it is intended to encourage the participant to look at her preference from both the partial and the impartial perspective. Joshua Cohen describes this feature of deliberative democracy in terms of motivational factors:

> While I may take my preferences as a sufficient reason for advancing a proposal, deliberation under conditions of pluralism requires that I find reasons that make my proposal acceptable to others who cannot be expected to regard my preferences a sufficient reason for agreeing. The motivational thesis is that the need to advance reasons that persuade others will help to shape the motivations that people bring to the deliberative procedure. . . . the discovery that I can offer no per-

suasive reasons on behalf of a proposal of mine may transform the preferences that motivate the proposal. Aims that I recognize to be inconsistent with the requirements of deliberative agreement may tend to lose their force.[35]

The way in which the deliberative process itself shapes preferences is a central feature of theories of deliberative democracy. Citizens themselves come under a publicity requirement in deliberation such that they must offer reasons for their positions and claims. Reason giving initiates a learning process in which participants acquire discursive skills. Participants are asked to defend their preferences in terms that others could find convincing. They are asked to look at their preferences from both the partial and impartial point of view. If Scanlon's and Habermas's arguments about a general interest in being justified are valid, then this procedure would lead most participants to reevaluate or reformulate unjustifiable preferences autonomously. This picture of democracy represents the cooperative as opposed to the adversarial search for solutions to political problems. Solutions, if they are found, will be embedded in the convictions of participants, for they will have been convinced that there are good reasons for one course of action over another.

Will the need to advance reasons actually lead to the inculcation of virtue? The practice of deliberative democracy inculcates the virtues of respect and impartiality in a simple way: Only if we adopt these virtues will it work; only if we are discursive as opposed to strategic actors will deliberation be genuine and agreement authentic. If we are interested in reaching authentic agreements, then this interest should lead us to an interest in civility, for only in treating one another with civility will the process move forward. To put it another way, it is inconsistent to desire to reach a reasoned and authentic agreement and yet be unwilling to listen to reason, to consider the merits of other arguments sincerely, or to reconsider the merits of one's own arguments. Thus, the argument that deliberation will foster respect and impartiality assumes that citizens are interested in genuine deliberation and authentic agreement, that is, that citizens are motivated to find consensual solutions. Once this motivation is in place, then the motivation to listen to

35. Joshua Cohen, "Deliberation and Deliberative Democracy," in *The Good Polity: Normative Analysis of the State*, edited by Alan Hamlin and Philip Petit (Oxford: Basil Blackwell, 1989), p. 24. See also David Miller, "Deliberative Democracy and Social Choice," *Political Studies* 40, special issue (1992): 61; and Robert Goodin, "Laundering Preferences," in *Foundations of Social Choice Theory*, ed. Elster and Hylland, pp. 75–102.

others, to be persuaded by reason, to look at questions from the other's point of view should fall into place.

The next and most obvious question is, Where does an interest in agreement spring from? Sometimes the significance or importance of a disputed principle in coordinating an action can partially explain the motivation to search for a solution on which all can agree. Motivation then is tied to the value to the participants of the action the norm coordinates and to how fundamental the norm is to the continuation of that action.

A somewhat trivial example will illustrate this point. Let us say that you and I go sailing every Sunday and we have done so for quite some time; I am always the skipper and you are always the crew. One day you say that you wish to be in charge and give the commands. I, however, am adamant that I know more about sailing and so should remain in charge. The more value we place on sailing together, even on just sailing, the more motivated we will be to resolve this problem rather than simply walk away from it. The length of time we have been sailing together, the benefits and satisfactions we have each received from the activity, and so on will all be factors in how we approach the problem as well as in how we approach each other to solve the problem.

Another important factor is how fundamental the disputed norm is to the continuation of the activity itself. We cannot go sailing at all unless someone steers the boat and decides when it will come about and so on. There are many other types of disputes we might have, about technique or good seamanship, which need not be resolved *in order* for us to go sailing. Indeed, these disputes may be part of what we like about sailing together. The point here is that the less fundamental a norm is to the continuation of an activity we value or the less the dispute actually threatens the very possibility of the activity, the less we are motivated by the circumstances to find a solution all parties accept.

Thus, the motivation to find a legitimate solution to political problems can often be tied to a hypothetical imperative: "If we wish x to continue, we must resolve dispute y." The hypothetical nature of the imperative is quite important. It implies that there is no necessity that x continue. We need not go sailing together every Sunday. We need not continue a cooperative enterprise with each other. That this risk is there and in some sense real is essential to the process. Although deliberative democracy contains the ideal of a consensually based and discursively coordinated public realm, failure to gain agreement on funda-

mental principles, and the costs of such a failure, always stand in the
background. Secession, civil war, violent protests, the use of force and
coercion are always options. The recognition that any one of these
might be the cost of not finding a legitimate solution can be a strong
motivating factor.

The value of the activity and the importance of the norm in coordinating the activity can explain the motivation to find a solution to a
normative impasse. It cannot by itself explain the motivation to find a
discursive solution. The defense of this position must return to the idea
of legitimacy, that is, to the idea of outcome. The argument must go
something like this: Citizens in liberal democracies generally believe
that legitimacy rests on the consent of the governed; market models of
democracy are an inadequate representation of this idea of consent because they imply winners and losers; a better and more accurate interpretation of this widely shared intuition can be found in deliberative
models of democracy; therefore, citizens, if they are given the opportunity to deliberate cooperatively with one another, will see this as a
more legitimate procedure than the competitive model. This, at any
rate, is the argument I put forward.

13 *Approximating Discourse*

How do we implement a discursive model of deliberative democracy? What is required to operationalize practical discourse? Where is discursive will formation to find institutional expression? We must be very careful here. Terms such as implementation, operationalization, and even institutionalization already introduce a misleading tone to the discussion. They suggest a form of rationalism which is inappropriate to discourse ethics. Blueprints are implemented; plans are operationalized; constitutions are institutionalized. Discourse ethics offers no blueprints, plans, or constitutions. Although discourse ethics points to a general principle of democratic will formation, it does not point to a particular way of organizing that formation. It is not only that we cannot determine a priori what will be said in discourse; we also cannot determine a priori how, when, where, or even whether anything will be said. The institutional form of democratic will formation must itself meet standards of discursive validity.[1]

Apparently we have generated a circle: the institutional arrangements that make practical discourse possible must first be justified by a practical discourse. If the mandate to set up a practical discourse can be conferred only in a practical discourse, we are left with no means of justifying the initial establishment of discourse. The issue of an original mandate to justify the establishment of discourse comes up only if we assume that discourse represents a revolutionary practice that must be established *de novo*. But political discourse is not set up the way a

1. Jürgen Habermas, *Communication and the Evolution of Society*, translated by Thomas McCarthy (Boston: Beacon Press, 1979), pp. 185–86.

constituted assembly is set up. The political ideal contained in discourse ethics centers on a more reflective and widespread undertaking of an activity that already has a place in our lives.

A discursive theory of political legitimacy has two aspects. First, there is the Weberian recognition and analysis of the real-world processes through which a citizen body generates the recognition necessary to sustain a stable system of justice.[2] Culture and communication underpin this process. This analysis brings out the consensual foundation to all stable systems of rules and norms. Overlaid upon this social analysis is the theoretical/ethical analysis, which points to the optimal conditions under which this process ought to take place if the outcomes are to represent what is in the common interest. Thus, rationalism is introduced not as a rational plan for society but as a process of rationalizing the consensual foundations to society. By rationalization I mean the critical evaluation of the reasons we might have to support or not support a system of rules and norms. Like Kant's publicity requirement, discourse ethics joins the requirements of stability (that people actually consider institutional arrangements to be in their interest) with the requirements of justice (that institutional arrangements actually are in everyone's interest). This is what Habermas means by bringing together the moment of facticity (*Faktizität*) with that of validity (*Geltung*).[3] Thus, discourse ethics calls for a radicalization, rationalization, and democratization of preestablished practices of social integration.

All this points to the conclusion that there is no need for a special mandate to set up discourse. As a rationalized version of the processes through which culture and social integration are reproduced, discourse can take place at all levels of society—from one-on-one debates in informal settings to debates in the national parliament.[4] What this means is that the defining characteristic of discourse cannot be found in any one set of institutional rules. The radicalization, rationalization, and democratization of public opinion formation is not simply a matter of setting up the right institutions. It is also a matter of the right motivations. Certain institutional rules can be *necessary* conditions for discourse but not sufficient conditions. For example, at the most general level, institutionalized rights are part of the context that can enable us

2. Max Weber, *The Theory of Social and Economic Organization* (New York: Free Press, 1964), pp. 324–28.

3. Jürgen Habermas, *Faktizität und Geltung: Beiträge zur Diskurstheorie des Rechts und des demokratischen Rechtsstaats* (Frankfurt: Suhrkamp, 1992).

4. Ibid., pp. 361–66.

to pursue discursive solutions. The legal protection of free speech is part of such an enabling context. But the First Amendment does not enforce the reciprocal requirements of practical discourse. It does not require us to *listen* to what others have to say; it does not require us to attempt to *understand* the other's point of view; it does not require us to *engage* others in a cooperative search for agreement.

Other types of institutions, for example, some town-meeting formats, might go farther in encouraging and fostering the attitudes necessary for productive discourse. But in the final analysis, people must be convinced that there are good reasons to work through disputes cooperatively as opposed to strategically or even coercively. Here is the real circularity of a discourse model of democracy, but it is not a damaging circularity. It implies that many existing institutions are well suited to discourse if we choose to engage in discourse. Engaging in discourse often involves arguing why the cooperative search for mutual understanding is both a more stable and a more just approach to dispute resolution than win/lose approaches.

In distinguishing discursive democracy from republican or communitarian ideals of democracy, Habermas points out that discourse does not depend on a shared community ethos, a high level of civic virtue, or the creation of a collective subject that acts as one. These are unrealistic ideals in a modern pluralist context. Instead, discursive democracy depends, on the one hand, on institutionalizing the necessary procedures and conditions of communication and, on the other, on the interplay between institutionalized decision making and informally, yet rationally shaped public opinion.[5] In avoiding the pitfalls of communitarianism and the need for a high level of civic virtue, however, Habermas overstresses the purely procedural requirements of discursive democracy.

Discourse does depend on institutionalizing the necessary procedures and conditions of communication, but it also depends on citizens' participating in institutionalized as well as informal discourse as discursive actors. If citizens do not possess this willingness, then no matter how well designed institutional arrangements are for the purposes of discourse, discourse will not take place. Everyone might have the opportunity to speak, but if no one is listening, we have the equivalent of a tower of Babel.

Habermas does not deny that discourse requires an interest in mu-

5. Ibid., p. 362.

tual understanding, but he never deals fully with the possibility that citizens might generally lack such an interest or not possess the competencies to pursue it. In a world where negotiation, instrumental trade-offs, and strategic bargaining are the most common routes to reaching collective "agreement" and resolving disputes, it is plausible that the most serious barrier to discourse can be found in the conversational habits to which citizens have become used. This does not mean that strategic bargaining has no role to play in the political arena or that on all political issues we must work cooperatively. It does mean that we need to think very carefully about when and where bargaining is appropriate and when and where it is not. Citizens' rights, for example, are not the sorts of things that should be subject to horse trading.

Discourse ethics sets out to expand the public sphere in cooperative directions and not to replace all political interaction with discourse. To the elite marketplace of ideas in which interests and understandings compete for domination, is added the idea of public debate as a democratized forum, in which we cooperatively construct common understandings and work through our differences. The more the issue is an issue of justice that affects all, the more the forum should replace the market. Part of this expansion can take place by opening up opportunities to participate, by including excluded voices, by democratizing media access, by setting up "town meetings" and "deliberative public opinion polls,"[6] by politicizing the depoliticized, by empowering the powerless, by decentralizing decision making, by funding public commissions to canvass public opinion, and so on. But all such initiatives will fail to produce a discursively formed public opinion if citizens are uninterested in acting discursively or unwilling to do so.

There is a final reason why we should be cautious about relying too heavily on the role of institutions, as opposed to the role of argumentation itself, in approximating the conditions of discourse. If we understand institutions simply to mean established practices, then it is correct to say that advocates of discursive or deliberative democracy are interested in institutionalizing discourse. That is, they are interested in wide acceptance of the practice of discourse and deliberation. But if we understand institutions in a more formal and strictly political sense, then I think overreliance on them unduly narrows the role of discourse. Practical discourse, understood as a process that generates a societywide consensus on legitimate political principles, is really a set of

6. James Fishkin, *Democracy and Deliberation* (New Haven: Yale University Press, 1991).

interconnected discourses, some of which will take place in formal settings but many of which will not. As I have noted, the complex web of conversations that make up a practical discourse can range from one-on-one discussions in private settings to debates in the parliament.

The argument I want to make is that on questions of legitimacy, as opposed to public policy, discourse must be understood as a cultural as well as a strictly political phenomenon. It must, of course, have political expression to have any efficacy. That is, deliberation must inform and underpin decisions taken in the political arena. But the formation of reasonable public opinion requires the creation of a discursive political culture in which citizens do not don their deliberative hats only when they take up political positions of power or are members of formal deliberative bodies. A discursive political culture means that citizens are for the most part interested in public issues that affect them, are willing to reevaluate their political opinions in the light of argument, and make an effort to look at public questions from an impartial point of view. These attitudes must be present whenever citizens contemplate deep public issues and ask themselves questions about their political preferences and interests.

The more the social, political, and *cultural* processes that come into play in overcoming deep normative impasses can be understood as conforming to a model of practical discourse, the more just and stable will be the solution of the impasse. The rules of discourse, it will be recalled, stipulate that no one may be excluded; anything may be said, questioned, or challenged; and no force may be used. These rules break down into conditions of universality, rationality, noncoercion, and reciprocity. The more these conditions are met, the more confident we can be that the emerging consensus represents a genuine shared interest backed by reasonable convictions.

APPROXIMATING THE CONDITION OF UNIVERSALITY

Approximating the condition of universality means, first of all, that there should be no barriers excluding certain people or groups from the debate. The absence of exclusionary barriers is not enough to guarantee the condition of universality. If the emerging consensus is to represent a general interest, then it is essential that as many voices as possible are heard in the debate. A practical discourse is made up of a web of talk. The more people caught in that web, the better the guarantee that all possible objections to the proposed claims have been given a hearing. Thus, universality also requires that a high level of participation be maintained, not necessarily a high level of political activism but a high level of political interest. In other words, citizens may "participate" in a collective discourse in many different ways including in the comfort of their homes by, for example, reading and weighing the merits of editorial opinions, discussing political issues with friends and family, or undertaking impartial thought experiments.

To ascertain whether an actual discourse comes close to fulfilling this condition, we look first to see whether any groups have been systematically excluded from the process. If we have reason to believe, for example, that the concerns of a minority were not addressed, that the objections of the disempowered were not taken seriously, that peripheral groups are not part of the emerging consensus, then the status of that consensus as representing a generalizable interest is put into question. Next we must ask whether the debate reaches out beyond the negotiations of elites, whether there are organizations and movements through which the public can voice opinions, whether there is a high level of interest and involvement on the part of all those affected. This last condition is very important. The major barrier to discursive resolution in liberal democracies usually comes in the form of political apathy, not conscious suppression. People have little interest in the decisions that affect them and are willing to allow others to debate the issues and find solutions.

If citizens at all levels are not part of the process, then we would be in a position to question the universality of an emerging consensus. Indeed, we would be able to question whether it was a consensus in any real sense, as opposed to a negotiated settlement between elites. This is not to say that negotiated settlements necessarily run counter to the interests and needs of citizens. It is to say, that we cannot be sure whether negotiated settlements run counter to citizens' self-interpretation of needs without involving citizens in the process.

The question of participation brings up a difficult problem with regard to the initiation of discursive will formation, which concerns the role of established political tradition in opening up discursive potential. The development of the discursive potential we all possess is in no way inevitable. Whether or not discursive solutions are sought will depend on contingent factors. As Seyla Benhabib notes, "The *interest* in rational discourse is itself one which *precedes* rational discourse, and is *embedded* in the contingency of individual life histories and in collective patterns of memory, learning and experience. This interest can be enabled or frustrated in the life of the individual; just as available patterns of political culture and traditions in society may encourage or hinder the development of discursive rationality."[7]

It seems clear that successful discourse is dependent on the willingness and conviction of the participants, and willingness and conviction develop within a cultural context. At a very general level, modern liberal democracies have opened up the potential for discourse and criticism, but particular communities within that broad category can be seen to have exploited that potential to a greater or a lesser degree. Thus, the task of initiating discourses will be more difficult or require different sorts of activity in communities with, for example, a low level of political participation and interest.

Habermas, as I have already noted, tends to downplay how dependent discursive democracy is on the development of an ethos of participation on the part of citizens. His position is understandable. He thinks that republican ideals are too demanding in our complex pluralist world. One common criticism of strong theories of democracy is that they often presuppose that the active life of participation is part of the good life.[8] What if I have chosen the life of contemplation instead? What if I have better things to do than engage in endless talk? What if I prefer to spend my time on Boston Common counting blades of grass?[9]

Among the responses to this criticism is one put forward by Joshua Cohen, which makes a distinction between justification and necessary conditions for stability. He maintains that theories of democracy which appeal to a particular conception of the good life as a justification are objectionable. In contrast, theories of democracy which are "organized around a view of political justification—that justification proceeds through free deliberation among equal citizens—and not a conception of the proper conduct of life" are not similarly objectionable even though the stability of this conception might depend "on encouraging the ideal of active citizenship."[10] Thus, participation is not defended as

7. Seyla Benhabib, *Critique, Norm, and Utopia: A Study of the Foundations of Critical Theory* (New York: Columbia University Press, 1986), p. 319.

8. This is, for example, Jon Elster's criticism of Hannah Arendt in "The Market and the Forum: Three Varieties of Political Theory," in *Foundations of Social Choice Theory*, edited by Elster and Aanund Hylland (Cambridge: Cambridge University Press, 1986), pp. 125–28.

9. John Rawls, *A Theory of Justice* (Cambridge: Harvard University Press, 1971), p. 432.

10. Joshua Cohen, "Deliberation and Deliberative Democracy," in *The Good Polity: Normative Analysis of the State*, edited by Alan Hamlin and Philip Petit (Oxford: Basil Blackwell, 1989), p. 27.

a good in and of itself. It is defended as a means of gaining the type of justification required by standards of democratic legitimacy.

But in the end, this argument simply shifts the dispute to a different level; it does not do away with it. The nonparticipant can still ask, Why should I be interested in justification? And the answer will not be able to avoid the question of what the good life is. The idea that participation is required to maintain the stability of a system, invites the question, Why should I be interested in stabilizing the system; what's so *good* about it?" Here, the argument must appeal to the idea that the liberal conception of justice is a good and that the only way to maintain this good is to involve citizens in the pursuit of it. This is not a neutral argument, but nor is it highly sectarian.

There is another way to approach the question of participation. We might contend that a deliberative democracy, although requiring a higher level of public interest and participation than market models, is not so demanding as people think. This is true particularly if we see discourse as a long-term process of collective interpretation, rather than a decision procedure. Groups that adopt consensus formation as their decision rule usually understand and have consciously accepted the time, commitment, and energy this procedure will require of them.[11] The reaching of a hard-and-fast consensus, at one time and in one place, among even a relatively small group of people will often involve marathon sessions in which participants must put aside all other concerns. If this procedure were what was required by deliberative democracy, then we would all have to become political activists of a sort, and this is clearly an unlikely development within pluralist liberal democracies.

Fortunately, deliberative democracy, or making our democratic system more deliberative than it is now (that is, *approximating* the ideal) does not require such a high level of commitment. Deliberation as a process of public opinion formation does not involve giving up the life of contemplation or engaging in endless talk or forgoing one's most important and valued pastimes. It does involve finding some time within one's life to think about and talk about public issues. This type of participation does not have to be a priority in one's life, but there must be some recognition that politics, because it shapes the legal, social, and even cultural framework within which one pursues one's

11. For a discussion of discourse as a small-scale decision procedure, see Simone Chambers, "Practical Discourse/Feminist Discourse," in *Habermas and Feminism: Autonomy, Morality, and the Gendered Subject*, edited by Johanna Meehan (London: Routledge, 1995).

chosen pastime is important. Its importance rests not on an argument that participation is a good in and of itself but on the idea that participation has some efficacy and power to shape politics.[12]

If citizens believe that their opinions are irrelevant to the political process, they are not going to have much interest in taking the time to form their opinions deliberatively. Market models of democracy and the social science research that goes along with those models tell citizens pretty much just that. The message we get from these studies is not only that the aggregation of votes leads to "suboptimal" outcomes but that individual votes make no difference and it might even be irrational to cast them.[13] These arguments, if true, seem to represent very strong reasons why market-type participation must be supplemented by some other forms of participation.[14] But can public opinion have efficacy other than through the aggregation of votes? In the next chapter I take up a "case study" that illustrates the role that public opinion has other than through votes to show that having the votes, that is, having a majority, does not necessarily resolve questions of legitimacy. Having persuasive arguments resolves questions of legitimacy. Political elites, even when they have the votes, are often forced to justify their positions in terms that "losers" can accept. The requirement to justify controversial political positions in terms other than the power that majorities have to coerce minorities points to a relationship between public opinion and political decisions which market models of democracy cannot account for. It also indicates why it is important that we think and talk about our opinions on public issues. Our opinions can shape political decisions and political policies in powerful but not always directly observable ways.[15]

It is perhaps unrealistic to think that we will ever achieve a perfectly discursive political culture in which all citizens take an active interest in

12. Seyla Benhabib, for example, makes this argument in defense of discursive participation. Instead of creating a sense of belonging (what communitarians think is lacking in the modern world), discourse can create a sense of "political agency and efficacy" (what Benhabib thinks is lacking in the modern world). Seyla Benhabib, *Situating the Self: Gender, Community, and Postmodernism in Contemporary Ethics* (New York: Routledge, 1992), p. 77.

13. William Ricker, *Liberalism against Democracy: A Confrontation between the Theory of Democracy and the Theory of Social Choice* (San Francisco: W. H. Freeman Press, 1982); Anthony Downs, *An Economic Theory of Democracy* (New York: Harper, 1957).

14. David Miller believes, for example, that deliberative democracy avoids many of the problems that social-choice theory has identified as endemic to the model of simple aggregation of votes. See "Deliberative Democracy and Social Choice," *Political Studies* 40, special issue (1992): 54–67.

15. Stephen K. White, *The Recent Work of Jürgen Habermas: Reason, Justice, and Modernity* (Cambridge: Cambridge University Press, 1988), p. 141.

the public issues that affect them. It is not unrealistic to hope that our political culture could become more discursive than it is now. A reason why it might, as Seyla Benhabib says, is that discourse is one way to regain a sense of political efficacy—"the sense that we have a say in the economic, political and civic arrangements which define our lives together, and that what one does makes a difference."[16] Models of democracy that offer this sense give citizens a reason to participate.

Approximating Rationality and Noncoercion

The conditions of rationality and noncoercion are intended to ensure that discourse reaches the highest level of reflectiveness possible, that persuasion is rational in the sense that only the "force of the better argument" should sway participants, and that agreement is autonomous and authentic in the sense that only what all sincerely want should be the object of agreement. The first requirement is that overt coercion, bribery, and threat not force agreement. Indeed, participants cannot be said to have really agreed if they acquiesce under pressure, which is to say, if we have good grounds to believe that they would not have agreed had force not been applied. But external influences that might put the autonomy of the consent into question are often not overt but hidden and implicit. For this reason, the conditions of autonomy and authenticity also require that participants critically evaluate arguments and radicalize discourse to bring hidden premises to light and also that they critically reflect on their own interests and needs. These conditions are designed to ensure that consensus is brought about without deception or undue influence, that it is rooted in the sincere convictions of the participants, that discourse has exhaustively examined the possible objections to a proposed norm.

But how can we determine that only the force of the better argument has swayed participants? One possibility is that we attempt to measure the extent to which material pressure, such as that of money and power, is brought to bear within the process of consensus formation. This path raises a number of difficulties, however. Only in ideal theory can we imagine the total exclusion of these considerations. Furthermore, it is not clear that all material considerations ought to be illegitimate within discourse. Which considerations represent undue influence and which represent legitimate concerns on the part of participants?

16. Benhabib, *Situating the Self*, p. 81.

The best we can do in our real-world analysis is to become aware of the distortions in communication and discourse which could be produced by these influences.

In addition, the exclusion of distorting influences can be achieved only when participants themselves come to the conclusion that these factors are derailing discourse. Within a constituted body, say a legislature, one can have an enforced code of ethics intended to exclude the distorting influences of money, power, and self-interest. But talk within a legislature is only one small part of the public and largely informal process of consensus formation. There is no authority, other than the objections of participants, which can prohibit interlocutors in discourse from backing their arguments with rewards or sanctions or from introducing misleading or false information. Even when individuals do not consciously employ such tactics, economic and political constraints inevitably influence the sorts of arguments we are likely to use or find convincing. People are naturally and legitimately interested in their economic security and swayed by arguments that appeal to their economic interests. It is also the case that even when nothing is actually said (or done), everyone knows, for example, that majorities have the political power to make dissenters' lives difficult. Money and power talk even when no one is consciously using them to gain ends.

We can all see, at an intuitive level, the difference between consenting with a gun to our head or as the result of a direct bribe and freely consenting to something because we believe it to be true or right. The problem is to translate this intuition into real political terms. What constitutes the discursive equivalent of a gun to one's head? More important, who decides whether the consent is autonomous or not? We must be careful not to fall into a problematic theory of false consciousness which denies that participants are able to discern when or if they are acting autonomously. Such a theory would run counter to the basic tenet of discourse ethics, that individuals themselves are the best interpreters of their needs and interests.

Discourse ethics is clearly incompatible with a simplistic version of false consciousness, that is, one assumes that there is a true consciousness that can be ascertained independently of the subject's own understanding. Generalizable interests do not exist prior to or independent of their construction and formation within a discourse.[17] But what of more subtle ideas of false consciousness, for example, the view that can

17. For a discussion of needs and interests and criteria of authentic self-expression, see White, *Recent Work of Habermas*; pp. 69–73, 147.

be found in some applications of psychoanalytic theory? Here, the argument is that the patient must come to see the true causes of her, say, neurotic behavior in order to overcome the neurosis. This truth cannot be brought to the patient from the outside (by a "vanguard" analyst) but must be discovered by the patient all by herself. But of course she is not all by herself. She has the help of the analyst.

Habermas once thought that this model of emancipation could be applied in social theory.[18] The idea then would be that the social scientist could play the role of social analyst, could facilitate the honest self-examination of citizens. This self-examination might then reveal the true historical or social causes of interests, which in turn might emancipate us from certain pathologies, for example, desires to dominate.

Although the idea of an awareness of the genesis of one's interests does play a role in the achievement of deliberative autonomy, the psychoanalytic model is inadequate for two reasons. The first is that it rests on an essentialist view of human consciousness. It too, like the simplistic version of false consciousness, assumes that there is a true consciousness whose truth is independent of our grasping it. The only difference is that the psychoanalytic model introduces the patient's voyage of self-discovery as an essential component to emancipation. That is, the patient must be rationally convinced of the truth if there is to be a cure.

The second problem is that the relationship between the analyst and patient is asymmetrical. Although the analyst is not supposed to make any definitive statements about the truth of consciousness but is only supposed to ask questions (this is why psychoanalysis takes so long), there is a definite inequality of power in this relationship. One need only think of the role transference plays in a successful analysis to see that this is not a discursive relationship. Habermas now maintains that social theorists have no privileged access to the unfolding of discursive understandings; they are participants like everyone else. As such, they must respect the requirements of equality and reciprocity, which preclude any analyst-patient relationship.

Despite a rejection of simplistic accounts of false consciousness and psychoanalytic accounts of emancipation, discourse ethics must admit that individuals can be mistaken in their interests. It is not simply that interests and preferences are fluid but that they are corrigible. This recognition is not, however, equivalent to a theory of false conscious-

18. Jürgen Habermas, *Knowledge and Human Interests*, translated by Jeremy Shapiro (Boston: Beacon Press, 1971), p. 214.

ness, although it does reject the rational-choice assumption that preferences are not open to rational evaluation. Rather than a theory of false consciousness, discourse theory assumes a theory of mistaken consciousness. In other words, people can come to see that they were mistaken in thinking that such and such was in their interest or that they had good reason for preferring this over that or that *x* is really good for everybody. Thus, consciousness is not true or false; rather, conscious beliefs can become more or less compelling through critical examination. The question of whether they are or are not compelling, however, cannot be answered from the observer's point of view.

If discourse is our only means of ascertaining what is in the general interest, if philosophers and social scientists have no privileged access to the outcomes of these conversations, then the question of autonomy must be left open to the scrutiny of the discursive process. Participants themselves must question their motives, look at the genealogy of their beliefs, ask what interests their arguments serve. Participants are the last court of appeal on whether arguments are legitimate or interlocutors are employing undue force. Participants themselves must judge whether money and power are being used as a coercive force or as a legitimate consideration in formulating a generalizable interest. This requirement in turn means that arguments within discourse must be made as transparent as possible, that is, that the place of money and power within argumentation must become explicit, so that participants can evaluate the potential for distortion. The truly illegitimate move in discourse is not necessarily to introduce money and power into discourse but to *mask* the introduction of money and power, to dress threats up in rationalizations, or to use rhetoric to cloud whose interests are being served by a particular proposal.

In order to bring about agreement without deception citizens must know what they are agreeing to. They must themselves decide on the legitimacy of arguments, and such decision calls for an unmasking of interest, hidden agendas, and power plays. Participants must themselves question the background of each other's claims and bring all relevant material to light. A theorist evaluating the autonomy or authenticity of a consensus does not have direct access to these things. She cannot look into the hearts and the minds of the participants and say whether they agreed freely and sincerely. Instead, she must rely on secondary indicators that can put into doubt the autonomy or authenticity of a discourse. This type of evaluation would center on the extent to which public debate dealt with issues at a substantive level and how deeply arguments penetrated the background assumptions and interests of the parties. Another indicator might be whether or not information was readily available to the public and how reliable such information was. Evaluation would also involve a content analysis of public debate, public statements, and public information.

The role of demagoguery and "slogan-politics," for example, would be an indicator of a possible lack of reflectiveness. As discourse spreads to a wider circle of participants and reaches out to include people from all walks of life, there is a natural tendency to simplify the issues under discussion. This simplification can easily descend into a war of slogans and catchphrases such as "Make my day!" or "Read my lips!" intended to sway large numbers of people often by camouflaging the real interests and issues behind the words. Public involvement of this sort falls short of the conditions of discourse because participation becomes largely passive for the majority. The moment of reflection is missing in this situation. Again, however, the theorist must be careful. Although one can question the autonomy and authenticity of a consensus brought about by superficial slogans and clever orators, one is not in a position to say that this consensus does not represent the real interests of the participants. One is in a position to say only that the conditions under which this consensus was brought about do not contribute in any way to our confidence that the consensus is autonomous and authentic. In other words, the consensus has yet to be tested by the critical force of real discourse.

There is a final question regarding the creation of a coercion-free zone within discourse. Is it possible to have equal participation in a world full of inequalities? Nancy Fraser suggests that it is not possible.[19] In her view Habermas's model of discourse, in asking participants to "bracket" inequalities, does not take this problem seriously enough. Communicating "as if" we were all equal, when in fact we are not, simply will not be enough to immunize discourse from the distorting effects of economic inequality. I agree that bracketing inequalities and pretending they do not exist will not be enough. The alternative that she proposes is also problematic, however: "A necessary condition for participatory parity is that systemic social inequalities be eliminated."[20] Although she is not specific about what such an elimination would

19. Nancy Fraser, "Rethinking the Public Sphere: A Contribution to the Critique of Actually Existing Democracy," in *Habermas and the Public Sphere*, edited by Craig Calhoun (Cambridge: MIT Press, 1993), pp. 109–42.

20. Ibid., p. 121

entail, it is clear that it would involve a radical restructuring of the economy. The problem with this argument is that it does not really solve the difficulty.

Distribution questions are questions of justice. These are properly the subject matter of discourse. In calling for a redistribution of wealth, Fraser must be understood as a participant in discourse offering a proposal for general consideration. The argument or reason for such a proposal is that it will enhance democracy and equal citizenship. If she is sincerely committed to democracy, then Fraser must be committed to persuading citizens to reevaluate the relationship between the economy and politics along the lines put forward by Marx in "On the Jewish Question." But such a reevaluation must start from within the existing system, in which systemic inequalities have not yet been eliminated. In other words, we must find a way of talking with each other as equals about the elimination of systemic inequality before we can eliminate it. Fraser does suggest a discursive alternative to direct economic restructuring when she says that "in most cases it would be more appropriate to *unbracket* inequalities in the sense of explicitly thematizing them."[21] Such thematizing could involve, for example, challenging unfair advantage in the public sphere due to social and economic position; introducing the effects of privately owned and profit-driven media on the circulation of information in discussion; and in general investigating the way social and economic subordination filters into and distorts the public sphere.

APPROXIMATING RECIPROCITY

With regard to reciprocity we are interested in the question of how close discourse comes to maintaining respect and impartiality. To put it another way, the question is to what extent participants approach disputes discursively as opposed to strategically. Discursive actors allow the other to speak her mind, listening to what she has to say and responding to her questions and claims. Discursive actors will also be open to persuasion, willing to meet people halfway, and sincere in their search for agreement.

Amy Gutmann and Dennis Thompson have asserted that the character and depth of moral conflict in liberal democracies point to the ne-

21. Ibid., p. 120.

cessity of cultivating the virtue of mutual respect within our debates. Mutual respect

> requires a favorable attitude towards, and a constructive interaction with, the persons with whom one disagrees. It consists in a reciprocal positive regard of citizens who manifest . . . a distinctly democratic kind of character—the character of individuals who are morally committed, self-reflective in their commitments, discerning of the difference between respectable and merely tolerable differences of opinion, and open to the possibility of changing their minds or modifying their positions at some time in the future if they confront unanswerable objections to their present point of view.[22]

Their defense of respect relies on the assumption that we should value reaching conclusions through moral deliberation rather than self-interested bargaining or force, and that respect is an unavoidable presupposition of moral deliberation. I will not outline their full argument here. In many respects it parallels the discourse ethics account of respect. What I find interesting about their discussion is that they suggest a number of indicators that might be helpful in assessing whether or not citizens and officials live up to this ideal.[23] For example, they say that a discursive as opposed to strategic actor must approach moral debate sincerely, that is, defend positions that she believes are right. Three possible indicators that a speaker is acting sincerely are consistency in speech, consistency in speech and action, and coherence.

Consistency in speech is intended to indicate when people hold moral positions out of conviction rather than for reasons of political advantage or instrumental benefit. If, for example, someone defends one position in one situation with one set of interlocutors and then defends another in another situation with another set of interlocutors, we would have grounds for doubting his sincerity. Consistency in speech and action implies that speakers should act in ways consistent with their professed beliefs. For example, public statements condemning sexual harassment should be accompanied by behavior that does not sexually harass. We cannot always live up to our principles, and action often falls short of our ideals; nevertheless, we can doubt the sincerity of those whose behavior consistently or repeatedly violates their professed moral principles. Coherence refers to a broader sense of

22. Amy Gutmann and Dennis Thompson, "Moral Conflict and Political Consensus," *Ethics* 101 (October 1990): 76.

23. The next three paragraphs follow the argument put forward on pp. 76–88, ibid.

consistency. We might question the sincerity of a speaker who, although consistent in speech and action, refuses to see the broader implications of her views for other issues or debates.

The question of sincerity refers to how a speaker presents his moral position within the debate. Also important is how a speaker regards the moral positions of others within the debate. Here Gutmann and Thompson also single out three indicators that can give us confidence that speakers are approaching their interlocutors with respect and impartiality. The first is that speakers must acknowledge the moral status of opposing views. In other words, it is a violation of respect to enter debate assuming that you are the only one with a moral position to defend and that everyone else must be instrumentally motivated. This criterion involves acknowledging that other people do have reasonable grounds to disagree and addressing those reasonable grounds. The second requirement is that citizens cultivate a disposition to openness. That is, although citizens and officials should be morally committed to the positions they defend in debate, they should be willing to modify their positions if they encounter unanswerable objections. The most obvious indicator that this disposition is present is, of course, when people do change their position in response to argument. An indicator that this disposition might not be present can be seen in statements intended to discourage argument, that is, statements that add up to "Nothing you can say or do will change my mind."

Finally, speakers must approach the debate from the point of view of possible agreement. The arguments they use should appeal to their opponents as opposed to being designed to augment or exacerbate conflict. That is not to say that we should seek neutral arguments. Often there are no neutral arguments, or neutral arguments would misrepresent one's position. But the use of, say, inflammatory rhetoric is an indicator that interlocutors are not very interested in finding agreement, persuading their opponents, or easing conflict. Sometimes there are good reasons to heighten conflict or refuse to cooperate—as, for example, in situations where nobody is listening—but these tactics do not make sense as ends in themselves. They make sense as means to get one's concerns and claims on the discursive agenda.

Gutmann and Thompson's discussion of respect and moral deliberation should not be understood as banning all political conflict. Approximating the conditions of discourse sometimes involves "forcing" people to enter discourse. What, for example, is the point of protest? It can be seen either as a threat or as a way of bringing attention to a cause that has been excluded from public debate. As a threat, protest says, "You had better change your policy or else!" This is not a discursive move but a coercive move. It is not intended to persuade people that there are good reasons, other than the fear of civil unrest, to adopt the policy. Alternatively, protest can be used as a means to dramatize the urgency of an issue, to focus attention on a problem, or to place a claim on the discursive agenda. Actual protest movements often exhibit both characteristics, but movements that are clearly uninterested in dialogue do not contribute to the possibility of a long-term and stable solution to a moral conflict. Bombing abortion centers will not persuade prochoice advocates that there are good reasons to restrict access to abortions. Conversely, public statements implying that all prolife advocates are unreasonable religious fanatics will serve only to inflame opponents, not to convince them.

The abortion issue brings up another problem. What if there simply is no possibility of ever convincing one's opponent? What if the positions are so far apart, as perhaps they are on the abortion issue, as to offer no rational solution? In these types of disputes what is the point of approximating the conditions of discourse if such an approximation will not yield an agreement? There are two answers. The first is to say that from the point of view of public policy, the abortion issue (and indeed many apparently irreconcilable disputes) breaks down into a complicated set of questions running from sex education in public schools to the rights of biological fathers in cases of pregnancy termination. Although there may not be any hope of agreement on the fundamental question, there may be room for agreement or compromise on subissues. Such agreement or compromise requires that the parties actually talk to each other, and talk to each other in reasonable ways.

The second answer to the question of irreconcilable differences is to point out that preserving levels of discursive civility is especially important when the disagreement is deep and not likely to be resolved in any foreseeable future. Because we disagree so much, it is important that we respect each other within these disagreements and maintain a civility that allows us to continue in peaceful political association. This civility might not lead to agreement, but it might create a certain amount of trust that allows us pursue productive discourse in other areas. A lack of civility and respect within a particular public dispute can contribute to a general atmosphere of distrust and bad feeling about moral controversies. This spillover effect can influence our general motivation and willingness to seek discursive solutions.

Ironically, a lack of civility within public debate can also serve as a learning catalyst through which the need for civility is brought to an explicit level. Arguments about issues that are deeply felt produce a great deal of acrimony, bad feeling, and resentment toward others who do not share one's point of view. Discussions of this sort often descend into name-calling. Prejudices and biases that block understanding will rise to the surface. Talk will break off as participants feel that they are getting nowhere, that no one is listening to what they say or taking them seriously. Public debates can at times appear very uncivil, full of partiality and bias and lacking consideration and respect for the other. At these times the discourse goes nowhere. These very breakdowns of the discursive process, however, can often bring participants closer to an understanding of the requirements of reciprocity. That is, when people break the rules, they often become aware of the rules for the first time.

We often withdraw from discussions in which we are not treated as full dialogue partners because we realize that a condition of productive and cooperative search for a point of mutual understanding no longer holds. It is precisely in situations where participants are aware of the precariousness of the process, where breakdowns are an imminent threat, that the presuppositions of discourse often come to the surface. The implicit rules of the debate surface when they are broken. When people say and do things that are unfair or show a lack of respect, the process is brought to an impasse. It is at this point that individuals begin to realize the terms and implied rules of continued search for common ground. They begin to realize that a shared rejection of violent conflict has its source in a much richer notion of deliberation.

14 *An Illustration*

Theories of discursive democracy have normative and social scientific components—normative in that theorists of discursive democracy are also usually advocates of discursive democracy and social scientific in that models of discursive democracy are used as interpretive frameworks to understand, organize, and describe political events. These two aspects are not independent of each other. The normative claim is supported by plausible interpretations of events, and the social theory includes a critical evaluation of events.

In this chapter I offer such a normative interpretation. Using a model of discourse as an interpretive/critical tool, I describe a political dispute that has been ongoing in Quebec politics since 1977. My intention is not to offer a comprehensive analysis of political events. Instead, I want to look at the political dispute from the point of view of the argumentative content. In other words, I outline the arguments that were put forward by the interlocutors and assess the shifts of opinion and interest formation that took place as a result of public debate. It is my hope that this "case study" will do three things: give the reader a more concrete picture of what is involved in discursive dispute resolution; show that although discourse is more demanding than voting, it is through discourse and not through votes that laws gain their legitimacy and efficacy; and show that the possibility of preference convergence, or the construction of generalizable interests on highly controversial issues, is not an unrealistic hope in liberal democracies. Of necessity, I have employed a great deal of simplification and a certain amount of idealization. The events and issues under investigation here deserve a

book-length study. Nevertheless, I believe my discussion can give sufficient illustration of how discourse ethics can prove helpful in understanding the process through which fundamental political principles
become legitimated.

INDIVIDUAL RIGHTS VS. COLLECTIVE IDENTITY

The dispute between the French and the English over language
rights in Quebec is a good example for my purposes because the questions being raised are questions about the basic structure of society. In
dispute are the fundamental terms of social and political cooperation.
The dispute has been deeply divisive and the cause of much conflict
and hostility among the interlocutors. In this sense, it might be considered a hard case, for the differences to be overcome through consensual
will formation are not superficial and the problems to be solved are not
easy ones. For many years the French and the English were thought of
as "two solitudes," isolated from each other by insurmountable cultural
barriers.[1] The clash between individual rights of expression and the
protection of a collective way of life is anchored deep in the self-understandings of the participants, and yet, I believe, discourse has offered a
way of overcoming some of these differences. The dispute in Quebec
can also be seen as an example of a new and pressing type of conflict
facing modern societies. As Habermas comments, "In the past decade
or two, conflicts have developed in advanced Western societies that de-
viate in various ways from the welfare-state pattern of institutionalized
conflict over distribution. . . . the issue is not primarily one of compen-
sations that the welfare-state can provide, but of defending and restor-
ing endangered ways of life. In short, the new conflicts are not ignited
by distribution problems but by questions having to do with the grammar of forms of life."[2]

When the separatist party, the Parti Québecois, came to power in
the 1976 provincial election, a crisis that had been brewing for many
years broke to the surface. It became necessary for Quebecers to deal
with the deep divisions between the English and the French communities with far more explicitness than hitherto. The crisis was of a different order from the crisis of law and order which had rocked the

---

1. Hugh McLennan, *Two Solitudes* (Toronto: Collins, 1945).
2. Jürgen Habermas, *The Theory of Communicative Action*, translated by Thomas McCarthy, vol. 2 (Boston: Beacon Press, 1987), p. 392. The dispute in Quebec is literally about the
grammar of a form of life.

province (and the nation) six years earlier. In the "October crisis" a
radical separatist group, the Front de Libération du Québec (FLQ),
launched a terror campaign that included bombing, kidnapping, and
assassination. This crisis did not signal a widespread loss of support for
the rules of the game the way the landslide victory of the Parti Québecois did. Although many French Canadians sympathized with the
separatist cause in 1970 and thus were ready to challenge the status
quo, the tactics employed by the FLQ served to point out a deeper
commitment to nonviolent democratic forms of challenge. This commitment was, and remains, stronger than the particular goals and aspirations of the French community. The experiences of 1970 played an
instrumental role in shaping the subsequent political developments by
underscoring this commitment. Having the premises of democratic
politics challenged in such a radical way brought those premises to a
reflective level. No matter how sympathetic many people were to the
separatist cause, or how outraged they were at the oppressive way in
which the central government imposed martial law, the general consensus against nondemocratic political action was strong and explicit.
By 1976 Quebecers were very much aware of what they had to lose by
allowing the situation to move in destructive and nondemocratic directions. Thus, one aspect of the situation which can partially explain the
motivation to find a discursive solution was the visible cost of failure.

In 1977 the Parti Québecois passed language legislation known as
Bill 101, or the Charter of the French Language, which was intended
to protect the French language and culture from internal and external
factors that threatened to erode them. The external threats came from
Quebec's encirclement by a sea of English speakers in North America.
There has been a steady infiltration, backed by money and power, of
U.S. cultural influences into Quebec. Further, the birthrate is now so
low that population growth in Quebec has and will continue to come
from immigration. Many immigrants see themselves as coming to
"America" and wish to learn and teach their children the language of
success and opportunity, that is, English. This trend seemed likely to
lead to the rapid attrition of French as the predominant language of the
work force in Quebec.

The internal economic and social history of Quebec, until recently,
created a situation in which English was the language of social and
economic advancement. The economic power of the English minority
created a state of affairs in which members of the French majority were
constrained to learn a "foreign" language in order to get ahead,

whereas the English minority was under no such economic constraint. Thus we can see internal and external threats, underwritten by economic and social power, to the reproduction of culture, forms of social integration, and socialization. The phrase "colonization of the life-world" aptly captures the loss of power over cultural reproduction which French Canadians perceived.

Bill 101 was an attempt to stem the tide of colonization through legal protections. Very briefly, it established French as the official language of Quebec. It stated, for example, that all business must be conducted in French; that all commercial signs must be written in French; that children whose parents had not gone to primary school in English in Quebec must receive a French education. It was at the time of its enactment and remains today a popular piece of legislation within French Canada. It has also taken on a symbolic significance beyond the content of its particular clauses. Bill 101 represents French Quebec's assertion of its right to cultural self-determination and attacks on the content of the bill are often seen as attacks on French culture itself.

For the past eighteen years this piece of legislation has been the focus of a debate about principles of justice. The law challenged a long-standing assumption about the conditions of political cooperation. This old understanding was based on the idea that Quebec was a *bilingual* province and that linguistic collectives did not have any special rights or status within the basic structure of society. With regard to rights and justice, the relevant political unit was the individual, not the group. The popular support for the new legislation clearly showed that the old understanding was no longer backed by a consensus. A new understanding of the rules of interaction put forward the claim that cultural self-preservation outweighed other considerations, in particular considerations of individual rights of expression, and should dictate the patterns of communication within the community. But one interpretation of basic principles is not replaced with another simply by passing legislation. Enactment of the law put the new interpretation of what was "right" on the discursive agenda in an immediate and explicit way; it did not automatically legitimate this new understanding. The justification and legitimation of the principles, beliefs, and interests that stand behind Bill 101 could be achieved only by redeeming the validity claims involved, which is to say, by bringing about a reasoned consensus among all those affected that this was indeed a justified interpretation of a generalizable interest. In tracing the search for a reasonable solution, I think we will see the learning process involved in discursive public opinion formation. Both sides have come to new self-understandings in their move toward a consensual resolution to the conflict.

One aspect should be pointed out from the start. Old understandings are dismantled and new ones are forged over time. The course of consensually oriented public opinion formation is neither straight nor narrow but full of regression, breakdowns, and sidetracking. My discussion focuses on the steps toward consensus, not to gloss over the real setbacks suffered in the past eighteen years but to stress that *despite* setbacks there has been real progress.

THE ENGLISH COMMUNITY

When the Parti Québecois came to power and passed Bill 101, I do not think it is an exaggeration to say that the English community was put into a state of panic. Most condemned the legislation out of hand. Subtle and not so subtle comparisons were made between the French nationalist feeling and German nationalism of the 1930s. Many English-speaking Quebecers resorted to threats and bribes, saying that they would leave the province, pull out all their money, move their factories and businesses, and so on. And in fact, many did pull up stakes and move to other parts of the country. At this fundamental impasse in normative regulation, they chose to disengage themselves from the normative context altogether. But a great many English speakers, indeed the majority, chose to stay.[3] For some, no doubt, there was little choice; not all were in economic or work situations that allowed them just to get up and go. But most did have a real choice.[4]

The important question whether to go or to stay was hotly debated in the English community by everyone, at every level of society—in the press, on the floor of the legislature, on every radio talk show or television public affairs show, in the home, at the workplace, in the

3. Between the census years 1976 and 1986 the number of Quebecers claiming English as their mother tongue declined from 800,680 to 580,030. Some, of course, left for reasons other than the new language policy. The total population of Quebec in 1986 was 6,532,461. *Statistics Canada Census Summary* (Ottawa: Statistics Canada, 1976 and 1986).

4. From an economic point of view this choice did not necessarily represent a trade-off, in the sense that English Quebecers stayed only because of economic advantage; Quebec is one of the poorer provinces, considerably outstripped in economic opportunities by the English-speaking West, especially in the seventies. Thus economics, although a factor, cannot explain why so many choose to stay.

local tavern, in the classroom. Wherever English speakers met it was a topic of conversation, and talking about it had an interesting consequence. It made the English community aware for the first time, in a widespread and explicit way, that they *were* a community. To be sure, it was a forced and defensive coming together. There was and still is, to some extent, a siege mentality within the English community, brought about by the perceived threat to its members' identity. But before the threat it would have been difficult to say that English speakers reflectively realized that they had an identity that could be threatened. In analyzing the threat they had to make explicit the identity, way of life, values, and principles they wished to protect. And one of the most telling developments in the early stages of the discourse was the realization on the part of many English-speaking Quebecers that they belonged in Quebec. Quebec was their home, and they did not want to leave. The economic opportunities of Toronto, Calgary, or Vancouver, not to mention the unconstrained opportunity to speak and interact in English, were not enough to outweigh their attachment to Quebec. And part of what it meant to be a Quebecer was that one lived in a place that was predominantly French.

Ironically, it was the "French threat" that brought home to many English speakers that it was the "French flavor" that distinguished Quebec and made it the place they called home. The Francophone culture was also a part, although in a different way, of who they were. The self-examination forced on the English community by Bill 101 produced a new self-awareness for many English speakers that they shared an interest in protecting the cultural elements that made Quebec different from the rest of Canada. As one English-language Quebec journalist has put it, "The Frenchness of Quebec is a part of the English community's personality, making its members different from other Canadians; they are proud of that fact."[5]

As this "ethical" discourse was taking place among the English speakers, a practical discourse was developing between the two communities. The English community first had to become more organized in its opposition to Bill 101. Many organizations, movements, and initiatives sprang up, and quite a few coalesced under the umbrella group Alliance Quebec, which has become the most prominent actor in defending English-language rights. But a great deal of independent activ-

---

5. Gretta Chambers, "Ici, ensemble," in *Liberté: Seize intellectuels anglophones s'expriment* 31 (June 1989): 56.

ity (rallies, marches, conferences, letter writing to the press and legislators, public awareness and publicity campaigns, civil disobedience in
the form of positing English signs, and so on) continued.

The English community had to put forward a coherent and compelling set of arguments against the conception of justice contained in Bill
101, and in order to make strong arguments, one must know what one
is arguing against. Thus a learning process was initiated in which the
English community had to listen carefully to the arguments and justifications brought in support of Bill 101. They had to become familiar
with the feelings and aspirations that made Bill 101 such a highly
charged symbol for French Canadians. As the English set out to make
their case stronger, they acquired a better understanding of how deeply
important the issue of cultural self-determination was to the French.
The discursive process required participants to take up the other's
point of view in order to understand it. And although the English
community cannot be said to have adopted the other's point of view,
this discursive role taking has contributed to a shift of opinion within
the English community over the last eighteen years.

By the mid-eighties there was widespread agreement that the French
had a legitimate interest in trying to protect the French language and
culture, indeed, an interest that English Quebecers *shared*.[6] For the
most part the spirit and intent of Bill 101 were accepted. Under dispute were the spirit and intent, not to mention the justice, of certain of
its clauses, in particular the ban on English signs.

The English community contested the sign ban on three fronts.
First, they claimed that it infringed on their right of free expression.
Second, they appealed to an idea of reciprocity, asking, in essence,
"How would you feel if your language were banned by a majority."
And third, they maintained that the ban was not integral to the stated
ends of the bill.

The issue of freedom of expression, unlike most free-speech disputes
in the United States, revolved not around content but around form. No

6. For example, a 1988 poll showed that 78 percent of English respondents agreed with
the statement that "The French language should be promoted and protected without limiting
the rights of minorities and individuals." "Poll Results Show That Quebecers Opt for Mod-
eration," *Alliance Quebec Report* (Montreal), May 28, 1988, p. 4. Another indicator that
Aglophones share an interest in maintaining French culture is that in the 1992 referendum a
vast majority of them (85 percent) supported the Charlottetown Accord on the constitution,
which included a clause in the preamble recognizing Quebec as a distinct society. See James
Tully, "Diversity's Gambit Declined," in *Constitutional Predicament: Canada after the Referendum
of 1992*, edited by Curtis Cook (Montreal: McGill-Queen's Press, 1994), pp. 184–88.

one was arguing that commercial and public signs contain important speech in the way that political pamphlets do. People were fighting not for the freedom to say certain things but for the freedom to use a certain language. The freedom to express oneself in one's own language was considered important because one's native language, whether it be English, French, Japanese, Hebrew, or Swahili, is the seat of one's cultural identity. To ban the use of it is to infringe on one's freedom to choose one's own identity, to be who one wants to be. This issue became as symbolic to the English community as Bill 101 was to the French. Banning all English signs in Quebec effectively removed the visible evidence of the English presence in the province. In a sense, it denies that English speakers are an important part of the community. And many English speakers believed that the real reason behind the ban was not to protect French but to retaliate against the English. The French wished to wipe out offensive reminders of the existence of an English minority. And this was thought to be an illegitimate reason. Thus part of the English community's argument involved an effort to "unmask" the real interest behind the ban and show that it was not part of the stated interest—the generalizable interest.

The reciprocity argument appealed to French Canadians' own strong feelings. Language is the medium of culture and to suppress a language is to suppress that culture. Why should English Quebecers not feel just as strongly about their language as the French feel about theirs? If the French believed that protecting their language was their right, how could they deny that right to other language communities?

The third argument maintained that the banning of English signs did not further the shared interest in protecting a way of life. The English community was complaining not about having to display French signs but about being forbidden to display English signs as well. English speakers held that guaranteeing a place for French was enough to protect the French "face" of Quebec. Banning English signs did not make Quebec more French; it made it less English. This argument represented a concerted effort to come up with a solution that served to perpetuate a strong and healthy French culture without infringing on minority and individual rights. The English community's acknowledgment that it also had an interest in protecting the French culture represented a transformation in the way English speakers interpreted their needs and interests. And it was a transformation that was brought about in large part through the critical force of discourse.

A more cynical interpretation is possible of course. We could see the shifting terms of the debate in Quebec as representing not a fundamental transformation of belief within the English community but rather strategies adopted to maximize political gain. For example, we might interpret the concentration on one aspect of Bill 101 instead of the whole as a strategic maneuver: the English really wanted to see the whole bill go, but they realized that their only real hope given the political atmosphere was to argue against certain aspects of it. The argument that the ban on English signs did not further the shared interests in protecting a way of life could then be seen as a rhetorical move and not a sincere and reasoned conviction that protecting a collective way of life was in the English community's interest as well. On this interpretation, political arguments were employed as expedient devices and do not necessarily signal a real transformation on the part of English speakers regarding how they interpreted their needs and interests.

Of course, a great deal of strategic maneuvering and old-fashioned politics have been part of the process. Advantages are gained or lost; positions are evaluated from a strategic perspective; and so on. But this is not all that is going on. I suggest that evidence against a cynical interpretation can be found in a corresponding shift in the terms of day-to-day interactions. In order to defend the view that discourse has led to a deep transformation of understandings, one has to show that along with public pronouncements by English community spokespersons, press, and organizations, individuals also treat and regard each other in a new way. There is some evidence that they do.

In 1987 the major French-language newspaper in Montreal, *La Presse*, commissioned a CROP (Centre de Recherches sur l'Opinion Publique) poll on Anglophone attitudes toward the language issue. It published the findings under a headline that translates as "A discrete revolution." The analysis began: "Anglophones say they approve of what has been done over the past ten years to improve the position of the French language." Along with a new openness to the "French fact" in Quebec, there remained a strong disapproval of the ban on English signs. But the most interesting finding was that only 17 percent of English-speaking respondents believed in complete freedom of choice on that question. A full 81 percent thought that one should be allowed to post signs in the language of one's choice while accepting the requirement that French appear on every sign.[7]

7. Forty-three percent thought that French and another language should be allowed equal place, and 38 percent said French should predominate on bilingual signs. *La Presse*, April 11, 1987, pp. A1, B2.

Moreover, even as the English community continued to protest the banning of English signs, it was adopting bilingual habits of interaction. It is true, of course, that the new legislation imposed a handicap on anyone who could not function in French in the business, commercial, and bureaucratic sectors of society. It was also true, however, that there was no protest about having to learn and speak French. Rather, there has been a certain amount of public and private embarrassment within the English community about the deficiency of its communicative skills in comparison to those of the French. English Quebecers, for the most part, want to learn French and want to interact in French.[8] Many made this conscious choice when they decided they wanted to stay in the province. It was not simply that those already fluent in French decided to stay. Many unilingual English speakers were made aware of the habits of communication their social position had made possible. They were made aware of their habit of initiating conversations in English with the expectation of being understood and responded to in the same language. The discourse in Quebec made it clear that French Canadians perceived that kind of behavior as expressing a general lack of respect for their language and culture, indeed, for their persons. And such behavior is slowly disappearing at the grass roots.[9] The willingness to initiate a conversation in French, even when one knows that one's interlocutor probably speaks English better than one speaks French, is a growing and evident social phenomenon in Quebec. It suggests a recognition that to do otherwise is a sign of disrespect.

Coercive legislation cannot account for the rate and extent to which English unilingualism is disappearing in Quebec.[10] These can be explained only by a new understanding of why it is important that French remain the hegemonic language in Quebec. Thus, behind the public arguments employed by the English community to further its cause, there has been a real change of heart and attitude which can be

8. A recent task force on the English school system in Quebec, made up of prominent members of the English community, reported that it should be a number-one priority that young English-speaking Quebecers leave school functionally bilingual. *Task Force on English Education: Report to the Minister of Education of Quebec.* (Quebec: Government of Quebec, April 1992), p. 3.

9. Whereas in 1971 only 37 percent of Anglophones were bilingual, in 1986 the number jumped to 60 percent. *Statistics Canada Census Summary* (Ottawa: Statistics Canada, 1971 and 1986).

10. In 1990, 80 percent of Anglophones reported speaking French most or some of the time in "across the counter" interactions (e.g., in stores, supermarkets, and financial transactions) and only 5 percent reported never speaking French in these situations. "Analysis of Sorecom Poll Results," *Alliance Quebec Report* (Montreal), May 1990, p. 4.

seen in the way individuals treat and interact with each other in every-day, nonpolitical settings.

THE FRENCH COMMUNITY

What about the French community?[11] Can we see new understand-ings of self and other emerging from the discursive procedure? In some sense, the French community has had less ground to cover than the English in moving toward understanding, although it has had a great deal more resentment to overcome. The obstacles to understanding have been different. French Canadians are very aware of their self-iden-tity. They have made conscious efforts through culture and art, litera-ture and film, mass media and education, social movements and politi-cal aspirations to give concrete expression to that identity. Thus, the discourse about language rights did not initiate the same process of self-discovery evident in the English community. Self-discovery was the product of the "quiet revolution" of the sixties, which saw the Catholic church replaced by nationalism as the center of collective identity. Social and economic conditions had been such that ambitious, upwardly mobile French Canadians had had a strong incentive to learn how to move in English circles. Whereas the discursive learning pro-cess through which the English have become familiar with the French has engendered a certain amount of respect, the forced learning im-posed on the French by social circumstances engendered a great deal of resentment. In 1976 while certain elements within the English commu-nity were alluding to Nazi Germany, the French were making refer-ences to South Africa. Some felt that they had been treated as *nègres blancs*. They were second-class citizens in their own country. And when the Parti Québecois came to power, many felt they had finally won control over their world and could do with it what they wanted.

The learning process the debate brought about within the French community led to the realization that power does not allow the major-ity simply to do what it wants. To put it another way, it became clear that behind the particular aspirations of their collective identity stood principles of liberal democracy which also, upon consideration, had a hold on the French. Whereas the learning process within the English community focused on coming to see a shared interest in protecting a

11. I thank Alain Noël from the Université de Montréal for his helpful comments and suggestions about how the Francophones understood the language controversy.

collective way of life, the learning process within the French community has moved toward recognizing a shared interest in maintaining certain liberal democratic standards of political interaction.

It became evident that it was not enough for French Canadian leaders simply to say, We are in the majority; we will do what we want. Unquestionably some said precisely that, but even within the French community this argument rang false. It contradicted intuitively held notions about what is just. Simple numerical advantage did not make Bill 101 a just piece of legislation; rather, the particular reasons for the bill made it just. That majorities can do what they want proved to be a weak and counterproductive argument because French Canadians did not believe that in principle majorities have the right to dictate to minorities. Rather, they believed that in this case the reasons for the bill outweighed the interests of the minority in question. Thus the legitimacy and efficacy of the legislation depended on the ability of the French to defend it rationally and not on their having the political power to enact it.

The presuppositions of liberal democratic legitimation came to the surface and forced French Canadians to respond to publicly raised objections to the bill. They too found it necessary to listen to what their opponents were saying in order to come up with strong counterarguments. The legitimacy of Bill 101, even in the eyes of the French community itself, depended on how successful and convincing were those counterarguments.

In the end, the supporters of Bill 101 could not persuasively demonstrate that banning English signs strengthened French culture in any clear way and could not refute the argument that banning English signs denied the English community the means to preserve its culture. The road taken to this reconsideration was a long one, however. One step on the journey was the Supreme Court of Canada ruling in December 1988 that the ban on English signs was a violation of individual rights of expression. This did not, however, have the immediate effect of repealing the legislation. Instead, the government, headed at the time by a Liberal majority, introduced a "notwithstanding" clause to the legislation (Bill 178), which in effect exempted Quebec's Charter of the French Language from a requirement to conform to the Federal Charter of Rights. This was a serious setback for the English community, and there was an upsurge of resentment, bad feeling, and mistrust between the interlocutors.

The arguments put forward to defend Bill 178 and the "notwith-

standing" clause were first, that Quebec is sovereign in matters of linguistic policy; second, that despite the court ruling, commercial signs
do not represent a fundamental question of individual rights; and
third, in areas of cultural reproduction the question is not about rights
but about survival. The dispute centered on a situation definition. The
question was not whether survival of the French culture was desirable.
Almost everyone agreed that it was. The debate was about whether the
threat to cultural survival was great enough to justify the suppression
of non-Francophone linguistic communities. The situation, some maintained, required exceptional measures to protect the erosion of French
culture.

These arguments also proved weak under scrutiny and criticism.
The United Nations Human Rights Commission, like the Canadian
Supreme Court, found them unpersuasive, and its decision was, in
many ways, more significant than the court judgment in turning the
tide. The wider constitutional controversies between Quebec and the
rest of Canada have generated a certain amount of distrust with regard
to federal institutions such as the Canadian Supreme Court.[12] Thus,
the court decision did not automatically carry moral authority for
French Quebecers. But, when an international judicial body, standing
above the fray of Canadian politics, also found that the language legislation violated human rights, French Quebecers took note. The UN
finding put Quebec into some very bad company and prompted a serious reevaluation at the legislation. Everywhere the government
turned, from academic articles to editorials in the press, it was confronted with strong arguments against its claims, to which it felt
obliged to respond. These arguments included demographic studies in-
dicating that the erosion of French culture was not as imminent as
feared, that in any case the ban on English signs did not contribute to
the protection of French culture, that the English community was an
integral part of Quebec culture, and that the Francophone public was
becoming more and more open to the cogency and persuasiveness of
these arguments.

By 1992 the government felt that it had to reopen the language issue.
By then, many Francophones questioned the fairness of the French-
only sign policy. For example, while the reopened debate was taking
place in the National Assembly, a group of prominent nationalist Fran-

12. See Simone Shambers, "Discourse and Democratic Practices," in *Companion to Habermas*, edited by Stephen K. White (Cambridge: Cambridge University Press, 1995), for a
discursive interpretation of the Canadian constitutional debate.

cophone intellectuals circulated a proposal in the French press.[13] They called for a new language accord to underpin future linguistic policy. Although the statement strongly endorsed Quebec's right to cultural self-determination, it also acknowledged that banning English signs was not necessary to achieve that self-determination. The English community should be recognized as an important part of Quebec: "It is time for Quebecers to state officially that which they have always known instinctively: English is part of the Quebec 'difference' in North America. . . . French must continue to be the official language, but if we want that Quebec be recognized as a nation and not as a society, we must admit that English is part of our national heritage. Such recognition does not subtract from the status of French as the only official language and the only language of citizenship."[14]

Such a statement from nationalists with strong feelings about Quebec's cultural, if not political, autonomy represents a significant move away from the distrust and resentment of the seventies and eighties. Although it fell short of agreeing that the ban on English signs infringed on a fundamental individual right, this statement did acknowledge a responsibility to find a solution to the language question which respects the differences between the communities. Furthermore, the signers also understood that solutions cannot be mandated by courts or by legislatures: "What Quebec needs is a genuine language accord, an accord which all Quebecers will recognize as legitimate, and of which they will be genuine masters. Without such agreement, no serious and lasting language policy can be constructed."[15] Thus, not only did the document call for repealing the ban on English signs, it also challenged the government to find a solution that was legitimate, that is, able to withstand criticism and generate agreement. In response to this challenge and many other criticisms, in 1992 the government once again amended the Charter of the French Language; Bill 86 repealed the ban on English signs and brought the legislation into conformity with the Canadian Charter of Rights.

Over the last eighteen years, the English and French communities in Quebec have been slowly constructing a new consensus on the funda-

13. An English version of this statement was reprinted in 1994 under the title "The Case for a New Language Accord in Quebec," *Inroads* 3 (Summer 1994): 9–17. The signatories were Claude Bariteau, Gary Caldwell, Yolande Cohen, Alain G. Gagnon, Guy Laforest, Daniel Latouche, Alain Noël, Pierre-Paul Proulx, François Rocher, Daniel Salée, Daniel Turp, some of whom had strong affiliations with the Parti Québecois.

14. Bariteau et al., "The Case for a New Language Accord in Quebec," p. 16.

15. Ibid., p. 10.

mental terms of their continued political association. The process is not yet completed; there are other issues to address. Nevertheless, there has been a discernible reinterpretation of each community's respective needs and interests in light of the needs and interests of the other. Each side has recognized a generalizable interest embedded in the other's position. The English community has come to see the value of strong cultural protection; the French community has come to recognize that one must respect the rights of others in the pursuit of collective goals.

The English and the French communities will always remain distinct. Discursive public opinion formation should not be equated with collective identity formation. What is emerging is perhaps best described as an overlapping consensus in which the participants retain their separate self-understandings, goals, aspirations, and ways of life but are able to converge on an understanding of the terms and side constraints within which they can each legitimately pursue their chosen ways of life. Although the communities retain their separate self-understanding, there is a new mutual understanding between them.

What was really at issue in this debate was not public signs but public recognition and respect between communities. From the early eighties on, some of the most common questions asked in public opinion polls dealing with the language issue were "Do you think that the English-speaking community has a legitimate place in Quebec society?" "Do you think that Anglophones living in Quebec should be encouraged to stay in Quebec?" "Do you think that the French language should be promoted and protected?" The data show a progressive convergence between the French and English on these questions.[16] But the very questions themselves point to the underlying issue in the debate. At issue was the construction of mutual respect and through mutual respect the cooperative search for a solution to the dispute. Of course, the debate did not always look cooperative on the surface. But the fact that the interlocutors continued to argue and to respond to each other's criticisms and challenges indicates that there was a logic of fair discourse at work here. It indicates that the participants felt obliged to justify their positions and claims with reasons, and that the question of legitimacy came down to the cogency and persuasiveness of these reasons.

The obligation to justify controversial policies publicly creates a counterweight to coercion. It allows us to draw the distinction between

16. *Alliance Quebec Annual Reports* (Montreal, 1985–91).

power understood as coercion and power understood as argumentation. French Quebecers possessed the power (election mandate, legislative votes, popular support) to impose language legislation on the minority. They, in fact, exercised that power. The question, then, is why they repealed the offending clauses. I say that they repealed it, partly anyway, because they were *persuaded* that it was indeed unfair and unnecessary. If this is a plausible reading of the debate, then it indicates that persuasion can be an effective weapon against coercive power. Public opinion and critical debate have a power within liberal democracies, if we choose to exercise it, which goes beyond the power of the vote. Coercive power is acquired through majority votes, but legitimacy is not equivalent to this type of power.

The building of communicative ties between the two communities has taken place despite the disintegration of such ties between Quebec Francophones and the rest of Canada (ROC). The growing popularity of the sovereignty option has been due, in part, to a feeling that, unlike Anglophone Quebecers, ROC has made little effort to understand or recognize Quebec aspirations.[17] Anglophone Quebecers have been equally frustrated by the lack of movement on the part of ROC and have fielded such eloquent emissaries as Charles Taylor and Jeremy Webber to try to sell Quebec's constitutional vision to Canadians.[18] The larger constitutional impasse now threatens the progress made by the English and the French in Quebec. It would be sad indeed if, after having come so far, "external" factors forced the interlocutors to choose between Quebec or Canada. Not only is the question of separation a very different one from that of language policy, but by being posed in the form of a stark choice it works against and indeed undermines mutual understanding.

17. This can be seen in the October 1995 referendum on sovereignty which the No side won by the slimmest of majorities: 50.6 percent, No; 49.4 percent, Yes.

18. Charles Taylor, *Reconciling the Solitudes: Essays on Canadian Federalism and Nationalism* (Montreal: McGill-Queen's University Press, 1993); Jeremy Webber, *Reimagining Canada: Language, Culture, Community, and the Canadian Constitution* (Montreal: McGill-Queen's University Press, 1994).

15   *Culture and Politics*

The English and the French communities of Quebec resolved their dispute largely through the power of reasoned argument, but the settlement took a long time. Indeed, fifteen years of argument preceded the resolution of one small issue of language legislation. What sort of dispute resolution model takes fifteen years? Not a very efficient one, but one that offers a stable resolution to disputes because they are anchored in the convictions and public culture of citizens. Fifteen years might seem a long time to resolve one small, if highly symbolic, issue of language legislation, but it does not seem that long if we think of the result as a transformation of public culture. The participants in the debate were engaged in building a common understanding of the rules of their particular political game. This common understanding required modification of deeply held beliefs and convictions. Such transformations cannot happen overnight; yet they are essential if solutions to deep disputes are to be long lasting.

Few deny that the underlying beliefs and convictions of citizens are important elements in political stability. A great deal of social science research on political culture has attempted to prove this point. For the most part, however, the study of political culture involves aggregating individual beliefs, for example, through public opinion surveys, or pinpointing external variables that can account for changing beliefs, for example, changing material conditions.[1] The communicative and cogni-

---

1. Herbert McClosky and John Zaller, *The American Ethos: Public Attitudes toward Capitalism and Democracy* (Cambridge: Harvard University Press, 1984); John Zaller, *The Nature and Origins of Mass Opinion* (Cambridge: Cambridge University Press, 1992); Ronald Inglehart, *Culture Shift in Advanced Industrial Society* (Princeton: Princeton University Press, 1990).

tive processes of opinion and belief formation are not usually the focus of political culture studies. But if opinions and beliefs underpin stable systems, then we should be interested in *how* opinions are formed and not simply what variables can be correlated to their formation. We should be interested in how beliefs become weakened or strengthened, how they change or mutate. In short, we should be interested in the communicative processes through which political culture is reproduced or modified.

My discussion of discourse ethics and deliberative democracy has focused on this level of analysis and this level of politics. I have described some of the features and benefits of a discursive or deliberative political culture. The Quebec example brings to light a type of communicative politics that goes on, or can go on, behind the scenes, so to speak, of day-to-day decision making, voting and electioneering, crisis management, bargaining and negotiation, and so on. This is the politics of public opinion formation. What happens at the level of culture—that is, how the attitudes, beliefs, and convictions that determine the interests we will pursue in the political arena shift and alter as a result of discourse—is an important dimension of politics. It is, however, only one dimension. Also important to politics is the study of day-to-day decision making, voting and electioneering, crisis management, bargaining and negotiation, and so on. My point is not that the discursive politics I have been describing can replace these other dimensions but that discursive politics can inform and create a context in which these other political practices take place.

In fact, the claim I have been making is quite a bit stronger than this. It is not simply that theories of communicative action, social evolution, and discourse give us a framework for understanding how culture is reproduced and modified; it is also that these theories give us insight into how we may gain more control over the processes of cultural reproduction. The claim here is that in becoming conscious of the ways in which we reproduce our beliefs we can direct that reproduction in a rational manner.

This might appear to be an overly rationalistic not to mention utopian approach to cultural reproduction. How much control can we really have over culture? Romantic conservatives such as Burke insisted that citizens could have no reflective control at all. It is a natural process and must be left to develop much as a tree might be left to grow. A certain amount of pruning and cultivating may be in order, but ultimately, nonrational nature as opposed to rational man governs the process. Discourse ethics puts forward a very different claim: through a rationalization of the process through which culture and tradition are reproduced, citizens can reflectively reproduce shared values for which they think there are good reasons.

Michael Walzer also doubts that changing cultural values and understandings can be rationalized in the sense of being the product of rational conversations and underpinned by rational convictions. For him, the process through which we reach new shared understandings is nothing like a conversation:

> The understandings that come to be shared will never have been rationally defended by a single speaker who managed to see the whole. Nor do they arise in the course of a debate among many speakers who contribute different pieces to the whole, and who argue until a conclusion is reached incorporating all the pieces. Nothing like that: for no conclusion is imaginable without authority, conflict, and coercion (socialization, for example, is always coercive). And yet the conclusions have some sort of binding force, which derives from the common life that is sustained on the basis they provide.[2]

What Walzer says might be true at a very general level. One cannot imagine social interaction that is completely free from authority, conflict, and coercion. Furthermore, authority, conflict, and coercion no doubt play a role in social transformation. But Walzer allows us to make no distinctions, of either a normative or a descriptive sort. We can make no normative distinctions between shared understandings because as long as they sustain a common life they are binding. But perhaps Walzer is simply uninterested in the question of whether shared understandings *ought* to be binding. That is, he is interested not in why we should recognize certain values as binding but in how we actually come to see certain values as binding. And this process, he says, has little to do with good or bad arguments and much to do with authority, coercion, and conflict. The question he seems to preclude is, How little and how much?[3]

Understanding is a cognitive process. It involves grasping the world

2. Michael Walzer, "A Critique of Philosophical Conversation," *Philosophical Forum* 21 (Fall–Winter 1989–90): 33.

3. This question is also precluded by Foucault's analysis of power. Stephen White, for example, asks Foucault a similar question: "There comes a point where the question of *weighing degrees of constraint against degrees of enablement* must be faced." Stephen K. White, *The Recent Work of Jürgen Habermas: Reason, Justice, and Modernity* (Cambridge: Cambridge University Press, 1988), p. 145.

in a certain way. We can distinguish, in principle anyway, between complying with someone else's understanding of the world and actually coming to share the same understanding. How compliance might come about is usually quite straightforward. This, for example, is what Galileo was forced to accept in 1633 when he recanted his heliocentrist views in front of the Holy Roman and Universal Inquisition. It is not likely that Galileo actually came to believe that the sun revolves around the earth. But how do we come to see the world in a new way? Locke believed that coercion could play no role in this process. One cannot force someone to believe *x* when he believes *y*. Unlike outward behavior, true belief and conviction can be swayed only by argument and persuasion.[4]

We live in a much more psychologically sophisticated world than did Locke. We are no longer confident that belief and conviction are completely immune to coercion. What is terrifying about George Orwell's *1984* is not the external regimentation of Ociania but that Winston Smith actually comes to love Big Brother and to believe that two plus two equals five. Does this conversion undermine Locke's argument? It certainly undermines it as a psychological fact but not as a compelling account of the processes of understanding.

Winston Smith's transformation chills us in a way that Galileo's recantation does not. We can still believe that in his heart of hearts Galileo retained his conviction that the earth moved around the sun. The authorities could not touch Galileo's heart of hearts, but they could transform Smith's. Must we conclude that the modern techniques of internalizing discipline have done away with any meaningful distinction between persuasion and coercion? No. What we must understand is that the distinction between persuasion and coercion is much more important and critical in our world than in Galileo's. That modern forms of coercion are more insidious is not a reason to conclude that we can no longer recognize coercion or that everything is coercive. It is a reason to become more familiar with the ways in which coercion works and to develop clearer ideas of how persuasion differs from coercion.

The crucial component of the Winston Smith story is not that the authorities were able to make him believe that two plus two equals five; the crucial component is that this story horrifies us, that we think there is something terribly wrong here. With numberless other accounts of the internalization of discipline, *1984* gives us knowledge of how au-

---

4. John Locke, *A Letter concerning Toleration* (Indianapolis: Hackett, 1983), p. 27.

thority and coercion can work on us, and this knowledge is a type of power. It is a power to unmask the ways in which authority and coercion distort cognitive processes of understanding. This unmasking is the point of *1984*, just as the point of Foucault's *Madness and Civilization* is to unmask the disciplinary side of clinical "advances" in the treatment of the insane.

A theory of communication can give us the power to unmask, because it presents an ideal account of the cognitive processes involved in coming to understand something in a certain way or coming to an understanding with someone. In asking myself, how did I come to believe such and such to be true, or what arguments or reasons do I really have to support this conviction, or in what ways has this belief been disciplined into me, I can gain some control over the formation of my own beliefs. I might never be able to see the whole picture, that is, all the influences and factors that shape my beliefs, but I can see more rather than less. I can take a more rather than less reflective attitude toward my own belief formation. A rational reflection on the genealogy of my own beliefs can be empowering, but it is very difficult to achieve alone. Clarification of what I believe and why I believe it often requires the critical distance that only a dialogue partner can offer. And here it is very important that my dialogue partner be not the voice of Big Brother but the voice of an equal.

The argument I have put forward so far implies that we can create a coercion-free discursive zone in which I can clarify what I believe and why I believe it. Some postmodern critics have suggested that no such zone is possible within discourse.[5] Discourse, they say, might eliminate hierarchy and asymmetry from conversations, but it does not eliminate subtler forms of domination and repression. Indeed, discourse is dependent on these, for it depends on the self-surveillance of the "communicatively rational agent (who has internalized the hegemic conception of what constitutes 'the better argument')."[6] Discourse is an example of normalization and we should resist normalization. The meaning of normalization is often (sometimes intentionally) ambiguous, however, slipping back and forth between two understandings. The first understanding appeals to the distinction between normal and abnormal. Here we see a socially constituted and often internalized category that divides the "ins" from the "outs," "us" from "them." What is normal and what is abnormal are thought to be a matter of science, or

5. One of the clearest statements can be found in Danna Villa, "Postmodernism and the Public Sphere," *American Political Science Review* 86 (September 1992): 712–21.

6. Ibid., p. 715.

self-evidence, or nature. But this, the postmodernist points out, is an essentialist fallacy. *We* draw the line between the normal and the abnormal, and we often draw it for arbitrary reasons. Thus we must resist and contest definitions of normal/abnormal, to keep aware of how these definitions push the "other" out into the cold simply because the other is "not like us."[7] This view of normalization and what is wrong with it is not incompatible with discourse ethics. Discourse offers a forum where this type of resistance and challenge can take place.

But normalization is sometimes used in a slightly different way that is not compatible with discourse theory. Normalization also implies the introduction of and adherence to norms. To act according to a norm is to be normalized in some sense. Under this reading, the norms of discourse are a form of normalized discipline. If it is objected that in discourse these norms are self-imposed—that is, a form of self-discipline and therefore not coercive—the postmodernist often responds by asking how this self, the one imposing the norms, came to be. This self is the product of a modern world in which ideals of rationality, autonomy, and agreement have been disciplined into our identities. There is, in each one of us, a little of Winston Smith.

This argument, however, leads to several problems. If the conclusion is that we must resist all normalization, then we must resist all norms, no matter what their particular content, because they are by definition confining, constraining, and disciplining. This reasoning leads to "affirmative nihilism . . . a politics engaged in the endless subversion of codes."[8] Discourse, in contrast, offers a politics engaged in the endless *questioning* of codes. But the very possibility that we might be able to subvert codes, to free ourselves from internalized domination, to lead "undisciplined lives," undermines the claim that discourse itself is a form of (illegitimate?) discipline. Theorists such as Jean-François Lyotard and Danna Villa attempt to unmask the hidden disciplines in discourse theory. They do so through argument. They try to persuade their interlocutor that discourse and the search for consensus repress spontaneity, initiation, and difference.[9] This attempt assumes that their

7. This argument is a large part of William Connolly's version of postmodernism. *Identity/Difference: Democratic Negotiations of Political Paradox* (Ithaca: Cornell University Press, 1991), esp. pp. 81–87, 171–81.

8. Villa, "Postmodernism and the Public Sphere," p. 719.

9. Jean-François Lyotard, *The Postmodern Condition: A Report on Knowledge*, translated by Geoff Bennington and Brian Massumi (Minneapolis: University of Minnesota Press, 1988), pp. 10, 65–66; Villa, "Postmodernism and the Public Sphere," p. 716. It is interesting that Foucault, near the end of his life, seemed to think that a deliberative consensus could be a critical and perhaps liberating force in politics: "The idea of consensual politics may indeed at a given moment serve either as a regulative principle, or better yet as a critical principle with

interlocutor is persuadable. It assumes that she can evaluate the argument, come to see the disciplinary nature of discourse, and understand
that it is embedded in Enlightenment modes of thinking. It assumes
that such critical reevaluation empowers the interlocutor against the
domination of rationality. It assumes, that is, the norms of rationality
and discourse. Postmodernism endorses a reflective attitude toward belief formation. It implies that arguments, criticism, and dialogue can
be liberating, that we can come to grasp and therefore, to some extent,
control (perhaps through resistance) the subtle factors that shape us.
By engaging in argumentative criticism, postmodernism presupposes
that there is a difference between persuasion and coercion.

Political culture is transmitted, reproduced, or altered through symbolic interaction of *individuals*. If we can make a distinction between
persuasion and coercion at the individual level, then we can make the
same distinction at the macrolevel of political culture. If we can distinguish between a Stockholm syndrome and autonomous value formation
at the individual level, then we can distinguish between distorted cultural reproduction and discursive cultural reproduction.[10] While it is
true that at the level of political culture we often cannot point to one
conclusive argument, one moment when a shared understanding becomes settled, we can trace the patterns of public debate (or lack
thereof) to discover how little or how much authority, coercion, and
conflict are involved in shaping understandings. It is simply false to
assume that authority played the same role in the creation of a shared
set of beliefs in Calvin's Geneva as it did in Quebec in the 1980s. Socialization might always be coercive to some extent, but even Walzer
must admit that some forms of socialization are more coercive than
others. If the process of socialization is backed by strong (implied or
explicit) threats, such as ostracism, anonymous denunciations, public
reprimands, even burning at the stake, we can say that socialization is
more coercive than in situations where individuals do not live under
these threats. William Connolly finds an unbroken line between the
demonization of the other in the early Christian church and the demonization of the other in contemporary society. He claims that we
have simply replaced such terms as heretic, infidel, and sinner with
other terms: insane, sexually deviant, and abnormal. For example, he
notes a continuum "of original sin at one end and mental illness at the

---

respect to other political forms." See "Politics and Ethics: An Interview," *The Foucault Reader*,
edited by Paul Rabinow (New York: Pantheon, 1984), p. 378.

10. The Stockholm syndrome refers to the phenomenon whereby hostages begin to identify and sympathize with their captors.

other. A variety of individuals and groups have been nailed to this cross whenever the problem of evil has become too intense to bear." What he does not acknowledge, and this omission is characteristic of much postmodern discussion of coercion and repression, is that there is an enormous difference between being literally nailed to a cross (or burned at the stake) and being figuratively nailed to a cross. That we do not literally nail people to crosses anymore is not an insignificant advance in dealing with "evil."[11]

Can discourse theory show us how to control cultural reproduction? It does not mean that we can plot the future course of cultural value systems. Such rationalized planning of culture is neither possible nor desirable. What it does mean is that we can become more rather than less reflective not only about our individual beliefs but about our shared beliefs as well. Just as individuals are not born with a set of beliefs but develop them over the course of a lifetime, so too public opinion and political culture do not fall from heaven. They develop over time, mediated through the patterns of symbolic interaction. Being aware of how some patterns, say, strategic and competitive or hierarchical and coercive patterns, affect the production of meaning can give us insight into whether shared understandings ought to be binding. It is impossible to separate the question of whether a shared value ought to be binding from the question of whether it does actually bind people into a common life. For a value to be binding within a common life enough people must think that it ought to be binding. How then, the question arises, did people come to think that such and such value ought to be binding? Some ways of coming to shared values are more rational than others. Shared values cannot be the product of one rational conversation, but they can be underpinned by rational convictions, which are the product of many crisscrossing conversations over time. And why should we care if our convictions are rational or not? One reason to care is that underpinning our shared beliefs with rational convictions is one way to create strong and stable foundations for those beliefs.

CULTURE AND JUSTICE

If the Quebec government had been "forced" by a more powerful Supreme Court to repeal the language law this would not have represented a legitimate solution in the eyes of Francophones. As Claude

11. Connolly, *Identity/Difference*, p. 113.

Bariteau and his colleagues write, "It is in Quebec—among citizens of Quebec—that we must arrive at an equitable just agreement. Whatever its merits, a language policy, if imposed by the federal government or by the Supreme Court of Canada, cannot guarantee the true recognition of Quebec's linguisitic communities and their rights."[12] A lack of legitimacy at the grass-roots level undermines stability. But perhaps we want to say that the issue here is right and wrong and not stability. If it was wrong for the Quebec legislature to ban the use of English signs, then this conclusion should be enforced despite the opinions of the public. This argument, after all, corresponds to our intuitive understanding of the priority of justice. Justice means that there are certain rules (usually understood as rights) which we should not violate while pursuing our collective goals. Furthermore, these rules should not be affected by the vagaries of public opinion. But separating justice from public opinion formation is a very risky strategy in the long run. If we are interested in justice, then we should also be interested in maintaining justice over a long period of time, and it is not clear that justice can be maintained by "enforcing" just solutions to moral dilemmas in the public sphere.

A supreme court cannot by itself sustain a stable system of justice over time. If citizens are not in some way attached to that system, if they do not respect it, revere it, or believe in it, then no number of court orders will sustain its viability. One need only think of the highly juridified system of the Weimar Republic to see the limits of a system of justice which is not mirrored in the political culture of citizens. Rawls refers to this requirement as the need for what he calls an overlapping consensus on fundamental principles of justice.[13] The consensus serves to anchor a system of rights and liberties in the political culture and thus to produce the public allegiance necessary to maintain that system over time. The consensus is overlapping because it does not represent a homogeneity of moral or philosophical outlooks but rather a convergent agreement on principles of justice which is compatible with a plurality of moral and philosophical outlooks. So, for example, I might endorse a system of rights and liberties because it represents a political embodiment of the Christian ideals of equality,

12. Claude Bariteau et. al., "The Case of a New Language Accord in Quebec," *Inroads* 3 (Summer 1994): 9.

13. John Rawls, *Political Liberalism* (New York: Columbia University Press, 1993), pp. 131–72; idem, "The Idea of an Overlapping Consensus," *Oxford Journal of Legal Studies* 7 (1987): 1–25.

whereas you might endorse the very same system because it embodies the idea of Kantian autonomy.[14]

So far, I am in full agreement with Rawls that a stabilizing consensus under the conditions of modern pluralism will have to be an overlapping consensus. But the issue here is not really whether we do or do not need a consensus of some sort to maintain our political institutions. As I have already noted, few would disagree with this general conclusion. The real issues are what sort of consensus we need and how we maintain it or bring it about. Sometimes Rawls describes this consensus in very abstract terms. For example, he says that "an overlapping consensus exists in a society when the political conception of justice that regulates its basic institutions is endorsed by each of the main religious, philosophical, and moral doctrines likely to endure in that society from one generation to the next."[15] This is a matter of common sense. If the main religious, philosophical, and moral doctrines of a given society were incompatible with a particular political conception of justice, then it is unlikely that that political conception would remain viable. But Rawls has not said enough. That our fund of cultural knowledge is compatible with, indeed endorses, a particular conception of justice is not enough if the principles and content of that conception are not made explicit in an actual consensus. The overlapping consensus able to maintain a system of justice cannot merely reflect a consensus of *available* doctrines; it must reflect actual attitudes, convictions, and practices of citizens.

For example, in the United States there could plausibly be said to be an overlapping consensus on something like Rawls's first principle of justice.[16] Despite pluralism, there is a general and shared belief that people have rights, that the protection of these rights has priority, and that these rights should be equally distributed. This view is endorsed by the main religious, philosophical, and moral doctrines. Furthermore, people at all levels of society talk in terms of rights. There is a pervasive awareness of rights within American culture. Does this mean that we have a strong and binding consensus on rights? Not neces-

14. Rawls, *Political Liberalism*, p. 145; Rawls, "The Idea of an Overlapping Consensus," p. 9.

15. John Rawls, "The Domain of the Political and Overlapping Consensus," *New York University Law Review* 64 (May 1989): 233n. See also Rawls, *Political Liberalism*, p. 134.

16. "Each person has an equal claim to a fully adequate scheme of equal basic rights and liberties, which scheme is compatible with the same scheme for all; and in this scheme the equal political liberties, and only those liberties, are to be guaranteed their fair value." Rawls, *Political Liberalism*, p. 6.

sarily. For example, some survey research indicates that there is also a great deal of misunderstanding, distortion, and ignorance on the part of the general public as to the content, meaning, and significance of the American rights tradition.[17] How much of our rights talk is really rights rhetoric? How often is the appeal to liberty and equality an appeal to "dead dogma"? How unusual is it for citizens to claim a right to something when actually they are claiming a privilege? How can we reconcile our rights tradition with persistent racism, anti-Semitism, or sexism? If our rights talk has become rhetoric, if ideas of equality and liberty are "dead dogma," if we confuse things that we want with things we have right to, if we claim to believe in rights and yet practice racism, anti-Semitism, or sexism, then we do not have a strong and binding consensus on rights. We have only the appearance of a consensus. Our culture appears to embody a strong tradition of individual and equal rights, but does this tradition have feet of clay? A shared tradition begins to crumble when ordinary citizens no longer understand the content of that tradition and no longer engage in the practices that embody that tradition. Thus, to maintain a stable system of rights we must make our rights tradition explicit in a public consensus that reflects actual attitudes, beliefs, convictions, and practices of citizens. This procedure, in turn, calls for a theory of consensus *formation*.

Rawls has little to say on the subject of consensus formation, particularly at the grass roots. Because he understands public reason to be limited to an autonomous and narrowly defined political sphere, he does not have a theory of how ordinary citizens within civil society more broadly understood might come to share a conception of justice. Sometimes he implies that they do not really have to. The overlapping consensus needed to stabilize a system of justice is a consensus only among "politically active citizens."[18] At other times he has implied that consensus formation is somewhat like a trickle-down theory of socialization. Citizens who live under just institutions will see that they are just and will internalize the values represented in those institutions.[19] One such institution—and with regard to rights and liberties I think Rawls would say the major institution—is the Supreme Court.[20] I

17. Gabriel Almond and Sidney Verba, *The Civic Culture* (Boston: Little, Brown, 1963); Herbert McClosky, "Consensus and Ideology," *American Political Science Review* 58.1 (1964): 361–82.

18. Rawls, *Political Liberalism*, p. 134.

19. Rawls, "Idea of an Overlapping Consensus," pp. 21–22.

20. Rawls believes that the "supreme court is the branch of government that serves as the exemplar of public reason." *Political Liberalism*, p. 231.

agree that judicial decisions are part of the process through which a consensus is reproduced or changed, but they are only one voice among many in this process. How much weight judicial interpretation carries is a matter of tradition and context. In the United States, for example, the courts have a much larger role to play in consensus formation than in any other Western nation, including Canada.[21] Although courts lend force to interpretations that make up a consensus, their decisions do not automatically produce the recognition of principles and values needed to maintain a system of justice.[22]

In the long run what counts is how convincing these interpretations are to the citizens. Threats to rights come in the form of changing attitudes and beliefs. The danger facing any system of rights arises when citizens no longer believe in any immediate sense in the values that sustain and underpin that system. This, for example, was the fear of many English speakers when the Quebec legislature first passed the language legislation. The widespread popularity of the language legislation among French Canadians, when it seemed obvious to the English that it infringed on a right of free expression, inspired the fear that French speakers simply did not take rights seriously. What was called for in this situation was not the enforcement of rights so much as a public discourse that could remind French Canadians why it is important to safeguard rights while pursuing collective goals—that is, a conversation that could reestablish public trust. Anglophones were not afraid that the Supreme Court would not uphold their rights; they were afraid that Francophones would not find the court's arguments persuasive.

21. The Supreme Court of Canada is a very young institution (1982), which is one more reason why its decision on Bill 101 did not carry very much moral weight in Quebec.

22. Gerald Rosenberg, in a detailed study of the social consequences of Supreme Court decisions, concludes that the Court has been ineffectual in bringing about change. His findings relate to direct causal influence, for example, "whether the change required by the courts was made" (p. 7), as well as indirect influence, for example, by "inspiring individuals to act or persuade them to examine and change opinions" (p. 7). Particularly startling is the evidence (public opinion data, media coverage, elite and public political action) that *Brown v. The Board of Education of Topeka, Kansas* not only had little positive impact in promoting liberal goals but actually hardened resistance to civil rights among elites and the white public. "By stiffening resistance and raising fears before the activist phase of the civil rights movement was in place, *Brown* may actually have delayed the achievement of civil rights" (p. 156). As a background to these findings, Rosenberg cites public opinion data to the effect that only a small percentage of the American public actually knows what the Supreme Court is doing and "the more knowledgeable a person is about the Supreme Court, the more likely he or she is to disagree with it," therefore showing that "there is little evidence that court decisions legitimate action" (p. 126). Gerald Rosenberg, *The Hollow Hope: Can Courts Bring about Social Change?* (Chicago: University of Chicago Press, 1991).

A supreme court has a limited ability to stem the erosion of rights at the cultural level. It is not enough for the courts to compel people to desegregate their schools, to pay an equal wage for equal work, to stop polluting their environment, to respect one another's privacy, or to allow freedom of expression. This kind of legal activism sets external constraints, but such constraints cannot durably sustain a system of justice. It is *also* necessary to convince people that there are good reasons to desegregate their schools, pay an equal wage for equal work, preserve the environment, respect one another's privacy, or allow freedom of expression. In the process of consensus formation, as opposed to rule compliance, court opinions, like all other utterances in discourse, must be put forward as arguments and not inducements. For example, respect for the authority and good judgment of the Supreme Court is perhaps one such argument. But perhaps more important are the arguments that convince people that these are norms worth recognizing on their own merit. Convincing takes dialogue and discourse. Convincing citizens takes democratic rather than elite discourse.

Attitudes, beliefs, and shared understandings are fluid and change over time. They have a tendency to erode, subtly shift, and mutate. Why shouldn't a commitment to individual rights erode, as, for example, the commitment to religious intolerance did in the sixteenth century? The answer cannot be simply that respecting the autonomy of individuals is right and religious intolerance is wrong. The continuity of an understanding over time does not depend on the *existence* of good grounds for such an understanding but on the reproduction of those good grounds and that understanding within a culture. Assuming we reject any claims regarding the necessary course of history, there is no reason why historically specific understandings must continue. That historically specific understandings can be justified on noncontingent ahistorical grounds (natural rights theory, neo-Kantianism, and so on) is not a reason why they *will* continue; it is only a reason why they perhaps *ought* to continue. And if these understandings are to continue, the reasons why they ought to must be kept alive within the cultural belief system of the community. A discursive rationalization of the process through which modern values are reproduced is one way to do so.

The constitutional scholar Cass Sunstein says, "Reliance on the courts diverts political energies and resources from democratic channels. The substitution of litigation for politics has large costs. Citizen mobilization is a public good, inculcating political commitments, broader understanding, and the practice of citizenship."[23] Placing rights on the discursive agenda might create a broader understanding of why rights are worth protecting; this, at any rate, is what happened in Quebec. It may also change our understanding of the content and scope of those freedoms; this too happened in Quebec.

The consensus that emerged in Quebec has two components, representing the two sides to the dispute. On one side, English speakers recognized that protecting French culture is also in their interest. There followed a slow process whereby their own understanding of individual rights was brought into coherence with this new recognition. On its side, the French community recognized that the power of numbers is not enough to establish the legitimacy of a policy that affects the fundamental terms of political and social interaction as Bill 101 did. Majorities simply cannot abolish rights of minorities without very good reasons. And as the debate moved on, more and more French Canadians came to doubt that there were good enough reasons.

The agreement on language legislation represents a new understanding of rights which has become incorporated into the prevailing conception of justice. Thus, Quebecers have been involved in democratically defining the interpretation of rights which is to govern their political association. This idea might appear troubling to some, and understandably so. Public opinion has not always been the strongest protection against the abuse of rights. Indeed, the Quebec example also highlights the dangers involved in making rights open to the democratic process. For a long time French Canadian public opinion was in favor of suspending individual rights of expression for the sake of cultural survival.

Thus, in response to Sunstein we might also want to say that the substitution of politics for litigation also has some costs. Do we really want to appeal to the public on such important questions as rights? What about rights individuals have *against* the public? What if public debates about rights turn into bargaining sessions? The first step in answering these questions is to point out that if the initial conditions of discourse are met, none of these fears is warranted.

The conditions of discourse include individual freedom, equality,

23. Cass R. Sunstein, "Constitutional Politics and the Conservative Court," *American Prospect* 1 (Spring 1990): 60. In questioning the power of the Supreme Court to bring about lasting social change, Sunstein adds, "The fate of civil rights and civil liberties in a democracy depends far more fundamentally on the character of our political and social life than on the nine justices" (p. 60).

and mutual respect. All individuals must have the freedoms necessary to participate in discourse; all must be treated as equal partners in the process of will formation; no one may be coerced, pressured, manipulated, or deceived into accepting an argument. If these conditions are respected, then we can be confident that agreements are not forced through against the will of some parties. It is unlikely that bigoted, racist, or intolerant arguments will sway those against whom they are directed. In addition, these conditions ensure that democratic deliberation about rights does not descend into a form of political bargaining which simply reflects shifts in the balance of power within society.

But it will surely be asked who enforces these rules? The answer will not be very comforting for those who want hard-and-fast guarantees. Yet I am convinced that it is the right answer. In the final analysis, we enforce these rules, we as citizens and private persons, as members of the public. Sunstein's argument, as well as my own, proceeds with inevitable circularity. The values of liberty, equality, and mutual respect are maintained through the practice of liberty, equality, and mutual respect. This argument does not mean that we should do away with courts or that citizens should never be coerced but only persuaded. It does mean that every time we do coerce we must not only have arguments that *could* persuade but also make an attempt to persuade. It means that the rights individuals have against the public are enforced when the public understands why it is important that these rights be respected. Take, for example, the now-infamous *Bowers v. Harwick* decision, in which the Supreme Court upheld a Georgia law criminalizing homosexual sodomy. If the Supreme Court had decided the other way, would it have done away with a public morality that views homosexuality as a crime? Would it have made homosexuals more accepted, tolerated, respected by the community at large, a community that did not see the need to revise its criminal code? The injustice of this case, if there is one, resides in the public culture not in the Supreme Court decision.

The values of liberty, equality, and mutual respect are sustained and upheld within a culture. As Hanna Pitkin says, we are both the creatures and the creators of culture.[24] As creatures, we are the product of our cultural environment. But culture is not some independent external force. We create and reproduce culture through our actions and beliefs; we make culture. Politics takes place within culture and is bounded by

24. Hanna Fenichel Pitkin, "Justice: On Relating Private and Public," *Political Theory* 9 (August 1981): 343.

the limits and understandings of culture. As we are the carriers and creators of culture, our understandings and practices set the broad limits for politics within our world. Because we are creatures of culture, we have a responsibility as creators of culture. We have a responsibility to ensure that we do not drift down paths that lead to an erosion of shared beliefs that underpin and sustain justice. To avoid these paths, we must talk about and think about our collective future. "Only in public life," writes Pitkin, "can we jointly, as a community, exercise the human capacity 'to think what we are doing,' and take charge of the history in which we are all constantly engaged by drift and inadvertence."[25] Noncoercive public debate, in which we talk about our deepest differences as well as our shared commitments, is one way of taking charge of our history and of avoiding an inadvertent erosion of those shared commitments.

JUSTICE AND SOLIDARITY

Habermas has often said that discourse ethics offers the opportunity to unite two values that have hitherto been separated by a gulf between philosophical traditions. These are the values of justice and solidarity.[26] The practical activity of constructing cultural foundations to a conception of justice through discourse requires that we interact with one another, thus creating communicative bonds between citizens. This process makes us aware of the interdependence involved in political association. Discourse can produce a solidarity among individuals who do not share communal ties. But the solidarity that can emerge through discursive procedures is different from that found in a communitarian understanding of political association.

To explain why, I draw on a useful distinction introduced by Charles Taylor between common meanings and intersubjective meanings.[27] Intersubjective meanings give us a language with which to talk about our social reality, and although we rely on intersubjective meanings to make sense of our world, we do not necessarily consciously

25. Ibid., p. 344. "To think what we are doing" is a phrase Hannah Arendt uses in *The Human Condition* (Chicago: University of Chicago Press, 1958), p. 5.

26. Jurgen Habermas, "Justice and Solidarity: On the Discussion Concerning 'Stage 6,'" *Philosophical Forum* 21 (Fall–Winter 1989–90): 32–52.

27. Charles Taylor, "Interpretation and the Sciences of Man," in *Philosophical Papers* (Cambridge: Cambridge University Press, 1985), pp. 38–40. I employ these distinctions in a way that Taylor himself might find objectionable.

identify with them. These meanings are usually deeply embedded and come to our awareness only in times of change and dissatisfaction, when social and political premises are called into question. They are held in common in the broadest sense and are constitutive of historical eras or stages, civilizations, and societies, as in classical, feudal, advanced capitalist, liberal democratic, patriarchal, modern, and so on. Further, particular cultures give different, nuanced interpretations to these meanings. One element that might shape the particular interpretation of intersubjective meanings is the constellation of *common meanings* to which they form a backdrop.

Common meanings, unlike intersubjective meanings, are specific points of identification. They are "notions of what is significant" and they hold our allegiances in ways that intersubjective meanings cannot. Common meanings can be associated with such identifications as African American, Quebecoise, Catholic or Jewish, German, working class, gay or lesbian. They are tied up with conscious identity in a way that intersubjective meanings usually are not. They may be strong or weak; an individual may possess a number of such identifications, or only one, or perhaps none. Common meanings can be related to intersubjective meanings in an infinite number of ways, from total rejection to almost perfect reflection.

Communitarian political theories rely on the idea of common meanings as the binding force in meaningful political association. In contrast, the idea of a discursive political culture employs the weaker notion of intersubjective meanings to describe a commonality that is not so much *felt* as *practiced* in patterns of symbolic interaction. Thus, the solidarity of a discursive political culture is a mediated solidarity. It is mediated through a common recognition of the terms of fair discourse. It is not the immediate solidarity of a shared identity. What this means is that we do not have to possess affective ties to one another, an unrealistic ideal in the modern world, in order to pursue consensual will formation and communicative solidarity. Instead, we have to realize that when we stop talking to one another, or start talking in coercive, strategic, and disrespectful ways, we have stepped outside an understanding of fairness.

Quebec again serves as an interesting illustration of what I am talking about. There exists and will continue to exist a gulf between the common meanings that are constitutive of each community. Despite this gulf there is a discernible set of intersubjective meanings that not only keep the parties talking to each other but, in a sense, unite them in a common enterprise and create a mediated solidarity. The parties in the dispute are working within a set of meanings that constitute the terms of the debate. They could not be talking at all if they did not share some premises about how the debate should continue. As the debate does continue, as various impasses get resolved, as participants inevitably return to the discussion after a breakdown, the realization is brought closer to the surface that the process itself represents a common commitment. The process itself, by throwing the English and French together, makes them less alien to each other. It is no longer true that the French and the English communities of Quebec represent "two solitudes," nor would it be true to say that the French and the English communities are bound to each other by substantive communal ties. Yet they are tied to each other in a common recognition of their interdependence and through the new understandings being forged in discourse. Discursive solidarity rests not on identification with the other but on understanding the other's point of view.

Although the 1995 referendum on sovereignty has once again divided Quebec along linguistic lines, it has not altered the fact that the English and French in Quebec have, over the years, achieved a deeper and more authentic understanding of each other. Engaging in such prolonged talk creates communicative ties that bind participants, not to each other, but to ways of dealing with and treating each other. What is remarkable about the identity politics in Quebec is not that the players are *still* arguing, but that they are still *arguing* and not bashing each other over the head. Whatever happens in Canadian politics or with the future of Quebec, there is today a strong shared and common commitment to talk which stands above and takes priority over the differences that divide the citizens. Quebecers talk to each other; Bosnians negotiate with each other. This not a trivial difference.

INDEX